D1568198

Theory and Interpretation of Narrative

James Phelan and Peter J. Rabinowitz, Series Editors

CARICATURE OF CONRAD BY DAVID LOW

Joseph Conrad

Voice, Sequence, History, Genre

Edited by

**JAKOB LOTHE,
JEREMY HAWTHORN,
and JAMES PHELAN**

THE OHIO STATE UNIVERSITY PRESS • COLUMBUS

Joseph Conrad : voice, sequence, history, genre / edited by Jakob Lothe, Jeremy Hawthorn, and James Phelan.
  p. cm. — (Theory and interpretation of narrative)
  Includes bibliographical references and index.
  ISBN-13: 978-0-8142-1076-5 (alk. paper)
  ISBN-10: 0-8142-1076-7 (alk. paper)
  ISBN-13: 978-0-8142-5165-2 (pbk. : alk. paper)
  ISBN-10: 0-8142-5165-X (pbk. : alk. paper)
  [etc.]
  1. Conrad, Joseph, 1857–1924—Criticism and interpretation. I. Lothe, Jakob. II. Hawthorn, Jeremy. III. Phelan, James, 1951–
  PR6005.O4Z7535 2007
  823'.912—dc22
                          2007027286

This book is available in the following editions:
Cloth (ISBN 978-0-8142-1076-5)
Paper (ISBN 978-0-8142-5165-2)
CD-ROM (ISBN 978-0-8142-9154-2)

Cover design by James A. Baumann
Type set in Adobe Minion
Text design and typesetting by Juliet Williams
Printed by Sheridan Books, Inc.

The paper used in this publication meets the minimum requirements of the American National Standard for Information Sciences—Permanence of Paper for Printed Library Materials. ANSI Z39.48-1992.

9 8 7 6 5 4 3 2 1

FOR ZDZISŁAW NAJDER

Efficiency of a practically flawless kind may be reached naturally in the struggle for bread. But there is something beyond—a higher point, a subtle and unmistakable touch of love and pride beyond mere skill; almost an inspiration which gives to all work that finish which is almost art—which *is* art.

—Joseph Conrad, *The Mirror of the Sea*

contents

Part I: Voice

Part II: Sequence

Part III: History

Part IV: Genre

works of Joseph Conrad discussed in this book

acknowledgments

One might expect that coediting a collection of twelve essays by scholars who hail from seven different countries (England, France, Israel, Norway, Poland, South Africa, and the United States) would add considerably to the logistical complexity of the task. It is a tribute to the professionalism and cooperative spirit of our contributors that the task of editing this book has been not just logistically smooth but thoroughly enjoyable. We are, therefore, deeply grateful to have had the opportunity to work with each of our contributors.

We owe our own collaboration on the volume to the good offices of the Centre for Advanced Study in Oslo, Norway, directed by Willy Østreng. CAS provided funding for the three of us to participate in a research project proposed by Jakob entitled "Narrative Theory and Analysis" during the 2005–2006 academic year. CAS supported not only that project but also a colloquium on Joseph Conrad in September 2005 that served as the genesis of this book. In addition, CAS generously contributed funding to offset the publication costs of this volume. We have also benefited from the collegial intellectual atmosphere fostered at CAS by the other members of the research team, Daphna Erdinast-Vulcan, Anniken Greve, J. Hillis Miller, Beatrice Sandberg, Anette Storeide, Susan Suleiman, and Anne Thelle.

We are very grateful to Sandy Crooms, acquisitions editor extraordinaire at

The Ohio State University Press, for her careful shepherding of the manuscript through the review process. We thank Peter J. Rabinowitz and the anonymous Press reader for their excellent advice about revising our Introduction, improving the individual essays, and adding the Afterword.

Finally, each of us wants to thank the other two for helping to construct a better book than any of us could have constructed on his own. But each of us is happy to blame the other two for any remaining flaws in this one.

introduction

Joseph Conrad and Narrative Theory

JAKOB LOTHE,
JEREMY HAWTHORN,
and JAMES PHELAN

A collection of essays on Joseph Conrad and narrative theory could take many forms, each of which would involve trade-offs in the volume's contributions to Conrad studies and to narrative theory. The collection could focus on one of Conrad's narratives and treat it from multiple theoretical perspectives, giving us something like "Thirteen Ways of Looking at *Heart of Darkness*." The trade-offs here of course would be between depth and breadth. *Heart of Darkness* studies would be well served but Conrad studies less so. Students of narrative theory would benefit from the survey of its possibilities in relation to a single text, but that benefit would come at the expense of demonstrating the full explanatory power of any one theory. Alternatively, the collection could focus on a single theoretical perspective and apply it to a range of Conrad's narratives—something along the lines of *What Feminist Narratology Can Do for Conrad Studies and Vice Versa*. Here the trade-offs would be flipped. The collection would offer a broader contribution to Conrad studies and a narrower, though deeper, contribution to narrative theory.

A third alternative would be for the collection to analyze a range of Conrad's texts by means of a range of theories, and, in one respect, that is the route taken by *Joseph Conrad: Voice, Sequence, History, Genre*. This collection offers commentary on the following Conrad texts, with many appearing in

1

more than one essay: *An Outcast of the Islands,* "Amy Foster," "Karain," "Falk," *The Nigger of the "Narcissus", Heart of Darkness, Lord Jim, Nostromo, Under Western Eyes,* and *A Personal Record.* And the collection draws on a broad range of narrative and critical theorists: Jacques Derrida, Michel Foucault, Hayden White, Paul Ricoeur, Alan Palmer, Dorrit Cohn, Peter J. Rabinowitz, and Gérard Genette are all cited here. But this description of the collection stops too soon because it does not do justice to Conrad's role in the enterprise. Conrad is not just the subject of theoretical analysis but also the major narrative theorist. In other words, the guiding assumptions of this collection are that Conrad's practice as narrative artist consistently implies an engagement with issues identified by narrative theory, and that bringing out those engagements will offer substantial contributions to both Conrad studies and narrative theory.

Joseph Conrad: Voice, Sequence, History, Genre traces its origins to a symposium on Conrad and narrative theory at the Centre for Advanced Study in Oslo in September 2005. The symposium was organized by Jakob Lothe, who directed the CAS 2005–2006 research project "Narrative Theory and Analysis." The authors of this volume's essays all attended the symposium, and all of the essays (except Gail Fincham's) had their first incarnations as papers delivered at the symposium. The authors revised those papers, first, in light of the spirited discussions they provoked, and then twice more, first, in response to a review by the co-editors, and, then again, in response to the review by the two readers for the OSU Press.

As these essays demonstrate, Conrad's writing practice implies an engagement with issues of narrative theory in two ways. First, Conrad peppers his tales with comments on their status as narratives—on their mode of delivery, the situation of the telling, the response of listeners and readers, and other issues. Second, Conrad's execution of his various narrative projects is remarkably detailed, insistent, and original. He often employs sharp disjunctions between fabula (the chronological sequence of events) and sjužet (the order of appearance of those events in the narrative text), disjunctions that go hand in hand with his use of innovative temporalities and plots. He often involves multiple agents in the narrative transmission. Such transmissions involve experiments with narrative frames and embedding as well as with audiences. Conrad also draws on the discourses of multiple levels of society that create the kind of heteroglossia that Mikhail Bakhtin regards as essential to the power of the novel as a genre. In addition, Conrad deploys the conventions of multiple genres, including such broad ones as fiction and history and such slightly narrower ones as sketch and tragedy. These inventive syntheses of genre as well as his experiments with temporality influence his use of different kinds and degrees of narrative closure. And as any reader of Conrad knows, this list could be greatly extended.

In light of these considerations, the contributors to this volume look as much to Conrad's practice as they do to narrative theory as they conduct their various analyses. Conrad's practice as a writer provides a site both to apply and to test existing theory, to see what kind of mutual illumination the two subjects can generate. The specific issues that the contributors take up fall readily into the four groups named in our subtitle: voice, sequence, history, and genre. But before we introduce the specific projects of the individual essays, we would like to contextualize them by providing a short history of work on Conrad and narrative theory. Our goal is not to offer a comprehensive account of previous scholarship but rather to indicate the major trends, some especially influential studies, and the way our collection fits into this history.

For heuristic purposes, we distinguish between two main variants among previous studies of Conrad and narrative theory. First, there is a large body of Conrad criticism that, while not explicitly engaged with narrative theory, nevertheless incorporates observations about Conradian narrative—whether tied to the analyses of individual texts or generalizing about a range of texts—that are theoretically productive. Second, there is a smaller portion of Conrad studies that engages actively and explicitly with the findings of narrative theory and through that engagement seeks illumination of both Conrad and those findings. Broadly speaking, there are more examples of the second variant after about 1980, but the first is still predominant.

This distribution is not surprising, since narrative theory as a distinct and systematic area of inquiry is a relatively recent phenomenon, and one that has become much more prominent after 1980. Had narrative theory existed as a well-known body of criticism at the turn of the twentieth century, many reviewers of Conrad's fictions might have been a little less frustrated and dismissive. Here is a representative comment by an early reviewer of *Nostromo:* "The sequence of events has to be sought painfully through the mazes of irrelevancy with which the author tries to mislead us. . . . It shows signs of haste both in style and construction" (John Buchan, unsigned review in *Spectator,* November 19, 1904). In this context, one cannot but admire the critical insight of the reviewer who in the autumn of 1900 observed in the *New York Tribune* that in *Lord Jim* "what the author has to say is absorbing, but even more so is the way in which he says it" (Norton critical ed. 1996, 393).

One can draw a line from this observation to a passage in Dorothy Van Ghent's 1953 discussion of *Lord Jim* in *The English Novel: Form and Function.* Considering Jim's actions, including his desertion from the *Patna,* Van Ghent asks:

What, then, *is* the act? The question defines Conrad's method in this book, his use of reflector within reflector, point of view within point of view, cross-chronological juxtapositions of events and impressions. Conrad's technical "devices," in this case, represent much more than the word "device" suggests: they represent extreme ethical scrupulosity, even anxiety; for the truth about a man is at once too immense and too delicate to sustain any failure of carefulness in the examiner. ([1953] 1961, 237; original emphasis)

Van Ghent goes on to stress Conrad's need for Marlow as the main narrator in the novel: "*Marlow has to exist.* For Jim's 'case' is not an absolute but a relative; it has a being only in relation to what men's minds can make of it. And Marlow provides the necessary medium of an intelligent consciousness" (237; original emphasis).

These comments remain critically perceptive and persuasive—about Jim's case, about Marlow's importance, and about the interaction of technique and theme. Furthermore, they anticipate such recent developments in narrative theory as the interest in the relation between technique ("devices") and ethics. In this respect, Van Ghent is an especially compelling example of what we called the first variant of studies of Conrad and narrative theory.

Albert Guerard, writing five years after Van Ghent, provides an example of a different kind. In *Conrad the Novelist* (1958), he identifies a series of paradoxes that can be abstracted from Conrad's works and that establish some of the most original and important thematic tensions of his fiction. One such tension is "[a] declared fear of the corrosive and faith-destroying intellect—doubled by a profound and ironic skepticism" (57). Guerard considers "Conradian technique" as extremely important for the revelation of the thematic tensions, and he introduces the concept of a "Conradian voice." Nevertheless, he is primarily concerned with Conrad's thematics, and he offers no systematic discussion of Conrad's narrative methods.

A third major example of the first variant is Ian Watt's *Conrad in the Nineteenth Century* (1980), which not only offers a wide-ranging thematic and contextual discussion of the early Conrad but also presents thought-provoking close readings of *The Nigger of the "Narcissus", Heart of Darkness,* and *Lord Jim.* These analyses all rely on Watt's paying closer attention to Conrad's narrative methods than had been customary in earlier Conrad criticism. For example, Watt coins the term "delayed decoding" (175) by which he means Conrad's technique of giving information whose specific import is not revealed until later in the narrative. He may, for example, describe an effect but withhold its cause, or describe an action but withhold a significant element of its context.

A simple example, one in which the delay between initial information and the information necessary to complete the decoding is minimal, is Marlow's exclamation in *Heart of Darkness,* "Arrows, by Jove! We were being shot at!" (149). Some of the points elaborated by Watt can be found in an earlier form in two important studies of the late 1970s: Cedric Watts's *Conrad's "Heart of Darkness": A Critical and Contextual Discussion* (1977) and Jacques Berthoud, *Joseph Conrad: The Major Phase* (1978). Part of the value of Ian Watts's study resides in the way he synthesizes earlier Conrad criticism and then draws upon that synthesis in his own readings of the three key Conrad texts. *Conrad in the Nineteenth Century* remains a valuable study for scholars working in both of the critical variants we have discussed.

J. Hillis Miller and Edward Said both started writing about Conrad in the 1960s, and not surprisingly their early work falls into the first variant. When they returned to Conrad later in their careers, after the theory revolution (to which of course they were both significant contributors), their work falls into the second variant. Furthermore, their different theoretical commitments—to deconstruction and postcolonial studies respectively—demonstrate the more general point that constitutes one of the underlying assumptions of this book: Conrad's narratives provide fertile ground for theorists with widely divergent interests. Miller's *Poets of Reality* (1966) includes an influential thematic discussion of Conrad's pervasive nihilism, one that regards Conrad's narrative methods as an especially apt means of dramatizing this *Weltanschauung.* In this respect, the relation between theme and technique in Miller's book is similar to their relation in Guerard's. Miller does not return to Conrad until 1982, by which point he has become a committed deconstructionist. Unsurprisingly, his analysis of *Lord Jim* in *Fiction and Repetition* gives more attention to Conrad's language and his technique than to his themes: "the textuality of a text, a 'yarn' spun by Conrad, is the meaning of its filaments as they are interwoven in ways hidden from an objectifying eye" (1982, 23). The novel does not unequivocally explain the *why* of Jim's actions, because such textuality makes any determinate explanation impossible. In 1985, Miller wrote a similarly brilliant analysis of *Heart of Darkness* entitled "*Heart of Darkness* Revisited." This analysis deconstructs the tropes in the frame narrator's comment that for Marlow the meaning of a tale "was not inside like a kernel but outside, enveloping the tale which brought it out only as a glow brings out a haze, in the likeness of one of these misty halos that sometimes are made visible by the spectral illumination of moonshine" (105). In recent years, however, Miller has toned down his claims about the indeterminacy of narrative texts. In a 2002 essay on *Heart of Darkness* published in *Conrad in Africa* (ed. Gail Fincham and Attie de Lange), Miller sharply disagrees with those who contend that Conrad's novel is racist and imperialist. He characteristically analyzes a variety of major tropes in the novel as a way of emphasizing its literariness and of arguing that such literariness is part and parcel of *Heart of Darkness*'s "powerful exemplary revelation of the ideology of capitalist imperialism, including its racism and sexism" (39). Miller's essay on *Nostromo* in this collection continues in much the same vein. Resisting the idea that literary language and literary texts have univocal meanings, Miller nevertheless proposes that Conrad's novel has sufficient determinacy to serve as an uncanny commentary on global capitalism and U.S. imperialism in the early twenty-first century.

Edward Said's first book, *Joseph Conrad and the Fiction of Autobiography* (1966), is primarily a biographical study, but the long section on *Nostromo* in *Beginnings: Intention and Method* (1975) and the chapter titled "Conrad: The Presentation of Narrative" in *The World, The Text, and the Critic* (1984) are thought-provoking, critically innovative explorations of Conradian techniques. Aided by his discussion of Conrad's novel, *Beginnings* is also a significant contribution to narrative theory, specifically the problem of narrative beginnings. Similarly, Said's 1984 essay considers the complicated relation of Conrad's narrative technique to narrative issues and to historical and literary developments, noting that his fiction is "great for its presentation, not only for what it was representing" (90).

Peter Brooks is a third influential theorist of the 1980s who was drawn to Conrad's fiction. His discussion of *Heart of Darkness* in *Reading for the Plot* (1984) is indebted both to the French narratologists and to Brooks's own psychoanalytically based concept of plot. Referring to Todorov's notion (in *Les Genres du discours* 1978, 169) that Conrad's novella assumes the form of a journey toward an empty center, Brooks also focuses on the narrative's own desire to reach its end as well as the many repetitions, delays, and deferrals that postpone that end.

Less obviously indebted to structuralist narrative theory and more illustrative of further work within the first variant are two 1980 studies. Werner Senn's *Conrad's Narrative Voice: Stylistic Aspects of His Fiction* demonstrates how closely matters of style are related to other elements of narrative in Conrad's fiction. For example, Senn's observation that Conrad's "free indirect style forms an extraordinarily flexible instrument of narration which Conrad handles with increasing competence for a variety of purposes and effects" (173) shows that Senn is aware of the ways in which a single technique can have multiple effects depending upon its interaction with other components of a narrative. In this respect, Senn's work echoes one of the critical premises underlying many of the essays in this book. William Bonney in *Thorns and Arabesques: Contexts for Conrad's Fiction* elaborates on Mark Schorer's point in his classic 1948 essay "Technique as Discovery": that "technique [not only] *contains* intellectual and moral implications, but that it *discovers* them" ([1948] 1967, 72; original emphases). Bonney argues that we need to investigate by the use of "contemporary theoretical criticism . . . Conrad's serious manipulation of traditional generic and characterological models" (ix). Bonney's call for such investigations is, in a sense, answered by Jakob Lothe's essay on *Lord Jim* in this volume.

Later in the 1980s, Lothe undertook the first systematic study of Conrad and narrative theory in *Conrad's Narrative Method* (1989). Using Gérard Genette's *Narrative Discourse* as a primary theoretical basis but supplementing this structuralist narrative theory with elements of deconstruction (with Hillis Miller as the main examplar) and rhetorical narrative theory (with Wayne C. Booth as the main exemplar), Lothe explores various modes of Conradian narrative. In a study which complements and parallels Lothe's work, Jeremy Hawthorn in *Joseph Conrad: Narrative Technique and Ideological Commitment* (1990) analyzes significant aspects of Conrad's narrative technique (free indirect discourse in particular), concluding that, for Conrad, narrative craftsmanship is never enough: only when a moral and ideological anchorage informs his narrative strategies does he produce great fiction.

Since the 1980s, academic Conrad studies have become more diversified. There is a steady flow of new books and articles, many of which deal with issues of interest to narrative theory. For example, *The Cambridge Companion to Joseph Conrad* (ed. J. H. Stape 1996) features a chapter titled "Conradian Narrative," and several of the *Companion*'s other essays also comment on the narrative intricacies of Conrad's short fiction and novels. This last point also applies to many contributions to Conrad journals such as *Conradiana, The Conradian,* and *L'Époque Conradienne,* and to several recent book-length studies of Conrad. Characteristically, these studies tend to link the issue of Conradian narrative to other critical concerns. Although it is impossible to give a full picture, we briefly mention four examples of such studies, stressing the following key words: modernism, imperialism, impressionism, and space.

In *Joseph Conrad and the Modern Temper* (1990), Daphna Erdinast-Vulcan relates Conrad's work to the cultural crisis of the late nineteenth century. Her discussion of Conrad as "a modernist at war with modernity" (5) leads Erdinast-Vulcan to consider the thematic tensions of Conrad's fiction. Highlighting the narrative dimension of these tensions such as that between the virtues of heroic societies and modern ones, she draws on Alasdair MacIntyre's definition of man as "a story-telling animal" (1997, 216), noting that "we all construe our sense of identity in terms of our role in the narrative we are part of" (38). Thus, Erdinast-Vulcan's study exemplifies the critical practice, apparent from the mid-1980s and inspired not least by MacIntyre's *After Virtue,* of considering narrative not just as a set of technical tools (as some applications of French structuralism tended to do), but also as a means of communication and as a mode of being. There is a link between such an understanding of narrative and Erdinast-Vulcan's discussion, in the present volume, of Conrad's sophisticated literary treatment of historiographical issues in *Nostromo*.

In *Joseph Conrad and the Adventure Tradition* (1993), Andrea White draws on the work of Michel Foucault in her concern with how Conrad's narratives respond to British travel writing and adventure tales of the nineteenth century. Where most of those narratives support the ideology of imperialism, Conrad provides a different, more sophisticated way of engaging with the imperialist project. White notes, for example, that "in suggesting that 'civilization' is exactly the term that needs redefinition, Marlow [in *Heart of Darkness*] challenges the very assumption of the discourse that other first-person narrators of adventure fiction had sought to stabilize; his narration unfolds its failure" (183).

White's book exemplifies an approach to Conrad which, though mainly thematic and ideological in its critical orientation, incorporates a number of perceptive observations on narrative issues. In common with Christopher GoGwilt's *The Invention of the West* (1995), it is thus illustrative of the first variant we have identified, but it also signals that the points of transition between the two variants become increasingly blurred. Subtitled *Joseph Conrad and the Double-Mapping of Europe and Empire,* GoGwilt's study argues that the crisis of modernity observable in European culture toward the end of the nineteenth century is closely related to, and actually a catalyst for, the formation of the idea of the West (or Western culture). For GoGwilt, Conrad's complex fictional representations, engendered and shaped by his innovative narrative methods, provide a particularly illustrative example of this transition: a late-Victorian ideological remapping whose effects or "aftertrimmings" are observable even today. There are interesting connections between GoGwilt's sophisticated discussion and some of the key points which Christophe Robin and Hillis Miller make about *Nostromo* in their contributions to this volume.

Inspired by GoGwilt, John Peters argues that "Conrad particularly seems to question a certain popularized and monolithic view of western civilization that saw its methods and practices as originating from absolute truth" (2001, x). In *Conrad and Impressionism*, Peters uses the concept of impressionism to explore the interrelations among Conrad's narrative techniques, his philosophical beliefs, and his politics. His analysis of the connection between impressionism and technique is notable for its attention to Conrad's reader. Whereas "the ordered narration of pre-impressionist novels presents the world of a universal observer . . . the impressionist novel tries to represent the immediate epistemological experience, so the reader almost becomes the one encountering phenomena, just as the characters do, but not in the after-the-fact reflection of traditional narrators" (24).

Activating elements of narrative theory in their critical investigations of Conrad, these studies by Erdinast-Vulcan, White, GoGwilt, and Peters illustrate the close connection between narrative theory and interpretation on the one hand, and between narrative theory and other critical concerns on the other. Several other studies do something similar. Notable among them is Zdzisław Najder's *Conrad in Perspective* (1997), which uses the term "perspective" in ways that both connect with and diverge from its standard uses in narrative theory. A variation on this approach that gives an especially prominent place to narrative theory can be found in Brian Richardson's analysis of what he calls the "posthumanist" dimension in *The Nigger of the "Narcissus"* in the important collection *Conrad in the Twenty-First Century* (2005). Richardson insightfully shows how Conrad effectively and innovatively employs "we" narration in the novella to create "an original—in fact, virtually unprecedented—form for presenting a collective consciousness" (213).

In sum, over the past fifty years Conrad and narrative theory have been very good for each other, and over the past fifteen or so the boundaries between our two heuristic variants have become more permeable. Many of the essays in this book exhibit a similar permeability, one that leads us to forgo such categorization of them in favor of a succinct presentation of their projects. We find it noteworthy that the eventual essays resulting from the Conrad symposium at the Centre for Advanced Study in Oslo have fallen into recognizable groups even as the collection as a whole considers a wide sweep of narrative issues and Conradian narratives.

Voice

Despite the misgivings of many of his early reviewers, as Zdzisław Najder points out in the opening essay in this volume, "for an artistically innovative and challenging writer [Conrad] has been over the years exceptionally popular" (23). We open this volume with three essays that address in different ways Conrad's tantalizingly complex development of the resources of voice in his fiction. Conrad's innovatory manipulation of voice is arguably at the heart of his seemingly paradoxical ability to engage and enthrall the common reader while challenging the theorist with the complexity of his narrative technique.

Najder calls for more attention to the ways in which "the personal voice in Conrad's fiction" engages the reader, and his essay offers some insights that may surprise even those of us who have lived with Conrad's fiction for a long time. It is unlikely that anyone will be taken aback by Najder's assertion that "one of the great strengths of *Heart of Darkness* lies in Marlow's convincing role as a narrator," but many will be brought up short by his additional point that "if we try to recapitulate what we know about him, we find that it does not amount to much" (28). For Najder, Marlow "comes to life through the story he tells and the way he tells it," and is, in fact, "mainly his voice." Turning his attention to *Lord Jim*, Najder returns to the much-discussed contrast between the authorial narrative of the first four chapters and the "personalized knowledge" of Marlow and his interlocutors that the reader encounters subsequently in the novel. His analysis invites further theoretical reflection on the dual roles of homodiegetic narrators (as tellers and as characters), even as it leads him to propose that Conrad's use of personal narrators, his "impulse to be in contact, to activate, to consort with the reader as a person," is "an (if not the most) important organizing principle of Conrad's style and narrative techniques" (38). Najder's suggestion that Conrad's use of the device of personalized narrative is "analogous to Conrad's use, notably in *Lord Jim*, of components belonging to various literary genres" (25) makes interesting contact with Jakob Lothe's exploration, in the final essay in this volume, of Conrad's ability to mine the resources of a range of different genres and subgenres in the creation of the same novel. Taken together, these hints open up the possibility of further work tracing links between Conrad's sophisticated development of the resources of fictional voice, and his indebtedness to a range of generic models.

James Phelan's essay starts with a different but nonetheless related Conradian paradox, one that again involves the challenging nature of Conrad's fiction—"the relation between the novel's artistic achievement and its difficulty" (42). Phelan, like Najder, is very much concerned with how Conrad's texts work on the reader, and for him *Lord Jim* is a paradigm case of the stubborn text. For Phelan a stubborn text is one whose recalcitrance to interpretation is not designed fully to be overcome. His essay offers insights into both the productive potential of such stubbornness, and into the tantalizing appeal of Conrad's novel. Phelan's approach focuses on "narrative as a rhetorical action: somebody telling somebody else on some occasion and for some purpose—or purposes—that something happened" (44). He directs attention to the double progression of *Lord Jim*, a progression that involves on the one hand "Jim as character" and on the other "Marlow as narrator who seeks to come to terms with Jim's story" (45). For Phelan, these textual dynamics relate to a progression experienced by the reader, who is forced to "puzzle through Marlow's puzzling over Jim." Marlow's refusal to "affirm" anything about Jim at the end of his account thus passes the puzzling baton to the reader who, like Marlow's listeners, must grapple on an individual basis with Jim's (and *Lord Jim*'s) recalcitrance. If Najder concludes that it is the reader "who has to contribute the essential component of evaluative order" (35), Phelan's essay suggests rather that the reader's task is, like that of Tantalus, never fully over, and that narrative stability is never finally and definitively established. There are novels that most readers feel they are done with at some point or another. *Lord Jim* is not one of them: it goes on working in and on us whether we read it once or many times.

If Marlow's telling has always been recognized as crucial to the narrative achievement of *Lord Jim*, the telling of the unnamed "teacher of languages" in the later *Under Western Eyes* has met with far more carping responses from readers and critics. For Gail Fincham this negative assessment of the English language teacher bespeaks a failure fully to recognize his crucial role in the novel. For Fincham, "the narrator's mediation is essential to the reader's understanding of this novel of ideas" (60–61), and she focuses in particular on the way in which this mediation allows Conrad to explore "the Enlightenment triad rationality-sympathy-vision" through the telling of a character-narrator who is "torn between logophilia and logophobia, Westernizing rationality and Slavophile emotionality, between the irrational fervor of a lover and the control of a writer" (61). By enlisting Dorrit Cohn's distinctions between psychonarration, narrated monologue, and quoted monologue, Fincham argues that modulations between these techniques focus the reader's attention on to the pressure points between our reason, our sympathy, and our clear-sightedness as these engage with the narrator's account of Razumov's troubled history. She is thus able to present a convincing case for the indispensability of the teacher of languages to the novel, and for the extreme sophistication of the interlocking narrative functions that he performs for Conrad.

It will be noted that if these three initial essays are grouped under the rubric of "Voice," they all share an alert and fascinated concern with Conrad's *reader(s)*. To this extent they all testify, albeit in very different ways, to what one might dub "the rhetorical turn" in narrative theory in recent years. In his "Author's Note" to *Typhoon and Other Stories,* Conrad insisted: "in everything I have written there is always one invariable intention, and that is to capture the reader's attention, by securing his interest and enlisting his sympathies." A more rhetorical, less exclusively textual narratology is well placed to trace the course of this invariable intention.

Sequence

The bemused responses of early reviewers of many of Conrad's novels (but perhaps most of all *Nostromo*) were generally related to their failure to map a straightforward chronological progression from event to event. Why would Conrad run the risk of having readers regard his fractured chronologies as (to cite one early reviewer of *Nostromo*) "mazes of irrelevancy"? What positive benefits does Conrad gain from his frequent use of interrupted, incomplete, repeated, or reversed chronologies?

Jeremy Hawthorn suggests that a good place to begin seeking an answer is Conrad's second novel, *An Outcast of the Islands*. This novel, Hawthorn contends, exposes the varied limitations of conventional metaphors that invite us to see a life as a road, a journey, a sentence, or a straightforward narrative. The novel conducts this exposure, in part, by showing how differently these familiar metaphors transpose the temporal progression of a life into spatial progression. If the opening paragraph of the novel displays the character Willems's self-deceiving sense of "the flowing tale of his life" as fatally flawed, the novel's presentation of Willems's life as anything but a flowing tale implicitly criticizes those "flowing tales" that depict human life in terms of a straightforward unilinear progression. The vantage point of a culture well versed in the nonlinear complexities of surfing the web makes modern readers perhaps more aware of the contrasting linearity of the traditional novel. What is striking about Conrad's fiction is the way in which it regularly highlights and exploits a tension between this textual linearity and the nonlinear lives and experiences his sequentially numbered pages trace. Hawthorn's attention to Conrad's early meditation on narrative sequence provides a nice complement to Phelan's rhetorical approach to progression. In a sense, Hawthorn's essay shows how Conrad's narrative discourse and his plotting of Willems's life come together to offer another theoretical perspective on narrative progressions.

Susan Jones shifts our attention from narrative sequence to character movement, though her analysis is also rich in insights about the overall trajectory of *Heart of Darkness*. Indeed, her discussion nicely complements other important recent essays on the novel such as Daphna Erdinast-Vulcan's "Some Millennial Footnotes on *Heart of Darkness*" and Paul Armstrong's "Reading, Race, and Representing Others." Jones notes that while the "literal and metaphorical resonances of Conrad's focus on travel throughout his fiction" have become a critical commonplace, the way in which the author focuses attention on more local movements that complement "the geographical movements of the narrative with a sense of the physicality of characters' intimate actions (and non-actions)" (100) has been neglected. Jones takes *Heart of Darkness*, Conrad's "most famous exposition of the journey metaphor" (101), as a test case, and she suggests ways in which descriptions of such local and individual movements and stillnesses function as "part of a complex relationship between physical and narrative movement that contributes in significant ways to the author's predominantly skeptical mediation of the story" (101). By focusing on a number of "image schemata" that help us to understand how prelinguistic experience is given metaphorical expression in language, Jones relates "the frequency of references to looking toward, stepping back, or giving in," in *Heart of Darkness* to the way in which physical action is used by both the frame narrator and Marlow to "metaphorize the metaphysical or philosophical register of their narration in terms of physical action" (103).

Jones's discussion of the way in which "[a]gainst an ongoing rhythm of passages accompanying Marlow's slow perceptual dawning, Conrad posits a series of sudden interruptions, freeze-frame images, gestures that catch the reader by surprise" (109) connects both to the concern with the reader manifested by the first three essays in this volume, and also to Josiane Paccaud-Huguet's concern with the "Conradian flash of insight." Asked to name modernist novelists for whom such "flashes of insight" play a crucial and innovative role, many would choose either James Joyce ("the epiphany") or Virginia Woolf ("the moment of being"). But as Paccaud-Huguet demonstrates, Conrad's concern with those "rare moments of awakening when we see, hear, understand ever so much—everything—in a flash" (*Lord Jim,* 87–88) precedes both Joyce's and Woolf's interest in such events. As Paccaud-Huguet reminds us, Virginia Woolf acknowledged this fact, drawing attention to the ability that Conrad's Marlow possessed to open his eyes suddenly, look at an object, and "flash bright" for the reader the thing observed against its mysterious background. These interruptions to narrative progression, Paccaud-Huguet argues, suspend both sense and chronology, and are essential to Conrad's unceasing attempts to make the reader *see.*

Both Jones's and Paccaud-Huguet's essays prompt further reflections, albeit from different angles, along the lines suggested by Phelan and Hawthorn. More specifically Jones and Paccaud-Huguet emphasize the way in which narrative sequence and progression in Conrad's texts are continually threatened, complemented, and qualified by the nonchronological, the nonsequential, the out-of-time. If the essays that follow under the rubric of "History" insist, correctly, on the ways in which Conradian narrative is of its time, this insistence must be set against the frequent occasions when both Conrad's characters and his readers are taken out of time in and through moments of vision that suspend, however temporarily, sequence, chronology, and linearity.

History

In the next essay in the volume, Allan Simmons is also concerned with what Conrad, in his "Preface" to *The Nigger of the "Narcissus",* calls the "moment of vision." For Simmons, however, this moment of vision is not out-of-time (or history), but "has a direct bearing upon the theme of community in the novella" (147). It is, moreover "formulated in terms of a progression in which sensory perception leads, by way of affective conviction, to mental insight" (147). Here progression and vision are not so much in total opposition but more locked in dialectical tension. Similarly, Simmons fastens on the creative tension between the linear progression of the "Narcissus" toward home and the cyclical nature of seaboard life. The additional move Simmons makes is to link this tension to Conrad's political engagements.

If "the personal is political," as the feminist movement has taught us, then the fiction of Joyce, Woolf, and Lawrence can now be conceded to be political. But Conrad has never been thought of as anything other than a political writer, one concerned with the fields of international and domestic politics more conventionally understood in his fictional and his nonfictional writings alike. For Simmons, Conrad's *The Nigger of the "Narcissus"* "offers a maritime myth of national identity" that relies upon particular narrative techniques—especially those involving symmetrical patterning—to construct "a sense of national self-fashioning, focused on the sea" (147). Tracing the voyage of the *Narcissus* as it sails "home" to an England that is not, actually, where many of its characters were born and raised, allows Conrad both to celebrate the British Merchant Marine and also to define the nature of the national identity that unites its crew in spite of their differences, while refusing to efface these differences (of generation, class, nation, and race).

Conrad's interest in linearity and its discontents underlies the three essays on Conrad's longest—and many would argue his finest—novel, *Nostromo,* Unsurprisingly, these three essays, like Simmons's, also address the relationships among narrative, history, and politics. For J. Hillis Miller, *Nostromo*'s "narrative complications . . . oppose what it suggests is false linear historical narration to another much more complex way to recover through narration 'things as they really were'" (161). But not just "were": as Miller reminds us, "certain works of English literature from the beginning of the twentieth century have an uncanny resonance with the global situation today" (161), and he detects such prophetic qualities in Conrad's depiction of the collaboration between Charles Gould and the American financier Holroyd. More importantly, Miller's essay traces the manner in which Conrad's novel uses an alternative way of narrating history to explore "the relation of the individual to the community, or lack of it, in this novel, in the context of an intervention by one stage of global capitalism" (162). Miller concludes his analysis by meditating on the ways in which such generic designations as "parable" and "allegory" do and do not capture the essence of Conrad's alternative mode of narrating history.

Daphna Erdinast-Vulcan agrees with Miller that "[t]here is no 'us' in Sulaco," and her essay urges her readers to consider ways in which this lack is mirrored in the blindness of historians of various shades and hues. Her essay argues that *Nostromo*'s series of historian figures displays Conrad's concern with the relation of historiography and history, a concern that is "triangulated" through the introduction of another set of terms: "fiction, myth, legend, story." If the arguments of Hayden White have forced modern readers to ponder the implications of the fact that both the historian and the novelist produce narratives, Erdinast-Vulcan confirms that these implications were already being pondered and worked through by Conrad in *Nostromo*, which is regarded as both a great achievement and a failure. For Erdinast-Vulcan the result of this working through is the insight that far from being their opposite, myth is, rather, "the suppressed underbelly of historiography and of history itself" (186). Erdinast-Vulcan too hits a note sounded in different ways by Phelan, Hawthorn, Jones, Paccaud-Huguet, and Simmons by arguing that "[a]gainst the supposed linearity of historical progression and its underlying teleology, the regime of legend and myth seems to engender a cyclical conception of human life" (185). For her, though, it is not just circularity but also stasis and sameness that challenge linearity in *Nostromo*: "mythicity—the desire of sameness, self-identity, and totality—is the real curse, or the nightmare of history" (187).

Christophe Robin agrees that the beginning of *Nostromo* "is organized around a shift from the mythic time of the incipit to the historical temporality of the following chapters," but in a claim that chimes in with Erdinast-Vulcan's comments he suggests that "the historical discourses of the characters aim at turning history into a myth" (201). Like Erdinast-Vulcan, Robin sees *Nostromo* as a novel that questions the ways in which we represent and understand the past and the passage of time. More specifically, Robin takes us back once again to the reader to argue that Conrad uses the reader's sense of "a confusing and at times confused narrative temporality" to "question our own relation to time" (197). Thus, what for contemporary reviewers was seen as a defect ("it is often difficult to say when or where we are," a contemporary reviewer of this novel petulantly complained) is recognized by Robin as a crucial and deliberate aspect of Conrad's narrative technique. If Erdinast-Vulcan declares that *Nostromo* is not a postmodernist novel, Robin argues that "in Derridean fashion, it deconstructs time and temporality and seems to disrupt narrative frames and identities" (196). He suggests, further, that "by blurring the epistemological frontier between fictional and historical narratives," Conrad implicitly casts "doubt on the validity of historical discourse" (199). But after the deconstruction there is the reconstruction: in *Nostromo*, Robin argues, "Conrad reinstates through narrativity a truly human and humanized temporality that harbors the other, an other which ultimately resists the totalizing pretension of imperial time to open onto ethical time" (211). A child of structuralism, early narratology was far from immune from the antihumanism of the 1970s and 1980s, but Robin's essay demonstrates that narrative analysis can avail itself of many of the tools of structuralist narratology without committing itself to a thoroughgoing antihumanism. His essay, like Phelan's, productively links narratological study of Conrad's fiction to ethical criticism, but Robin draws more on the tradition of poststructuralist theory than Phelan's rhetorical model does.

Genre

Conrad was not just a novelist whose narrative techniques were creative and innovative; he was a writer whose innovations redrew the borders between different genres and thus transformed generic conventions.

J. H. Stape's contribution shows how Conrad sought to give the essays that comprised *A Personal Record* coherence by adapting the conventions of autobiography and epic, while attempting to satisfy both the demand that he reveal himself and his own desire that he do no such thing. One of Conrad's moves, Stape suggests, is to establish a heritage that is less familial (as the genre of autobiography would require) and more literary. Another is to lay claim to a maritime parentage. Elsewhere, as Stape puts it, the self-imposed task of talking about himself is deflected by talking about others. It is striking how much the Joseph Conrad described by J. H. Stape resembles the Charles Marlow described by Zdzisław Najder: both are men to whom the reader feels close, but both are men who deny the reader that final openness of naked intimacy. For us, both men are real because of their public voices, not because of their willingness to display their innermost privacies.

In the final essay in the volume, Jakob Lothe argues that the formation of the narrative discourse of *Lord Jim* is inseparable from Conrad's enrichment of this particular novel—and the novel as a genre—by his creative importation of elements taken from a range of other fictional subgenres such as "the sketch, the tale, the fragment, the episode, the legend, the letter, the romance, and the parable" (236). For Lothe, Conrad's modernism is in part constituted by his generic experimentations and innovations: *Lord Jim* is a major modernist novel not least because it includes elements borrowed from a range of sources and incorporated in the text in ways that are "novel" and that thus become part of the generic resources of "the novel." Moreover, as Lothe shows, although many critics have recognized that Conrad's fiction straddles a number of boundaries (in Thomas Moser's terminology, for example, "adventure story" and "complexly wrought 'art novel'"), this recognition has often stopped short of the understanding that this straddling does not mean that a novel such as *Lord Jim* is half traditional and half modernist, but rather that its essential modernism is inseparable from its combination of generic elements.

As should already be clear, this collection of essays seeks to present the reader with a considerable variety of approaches to Conradian narrative. Yet although the approaches vary, they share a common premise and a common aim: aided and inspired by narrative theory, they discuss the intricate and fascinating ways in which Conrad, writing at the turn of the twentieth century, used and experimented with narrative in order to give aesthetic shape to his ideas, impressions, thoughts, doubts, and fears. Conrad is a modernist author, and modernist fiction presents a particular challenge to the study of narrative: it is the product of the epistemic break at the turn of the century, which generated an aesthetic break and a problematization of realistic narrative premises. As the following essays show, Conrad's narrative art both illustrates and responds to this break in ways that make him a most rewarding author to read and study in the twenty-first century.

Works Cited

Armstrong, Paul B. "Reading, Race, and Representing Others." In *Heart of Darkness,* 4th ed., edited by Paul B. Armstrong. New York: Norton, 2006. 429–44.

Berthoud, Jacques. *Joseph Conrad: The Major Phase.* Cambridge: Cambridge University Press, 1978.

Bonney, William. *Thorns and Arabesques: Contexts for Conrad's Fiction.* Baltimore: Johns Hopkins University Press, 1980.

Brooks, Peter. *Reading for the Plot: Design and Intention in Narrative.* Oxford: Oxford University Press, 1984.

Conrad, Joseph. "The Partner." In *Within the Tales.* Dent Collected Edition. London: Dent, 1950. 89–128.

———. *Chance: A Tale in Two Parts.* Edited by Martin Ray. Oxford World's Classics. Oxford: Oxford University Press, 1988.

———. *Heart of Darkness and Other Tales.* Edited by Cedric Watts. Oxford World's Classics. Oxford: Oxford University Press, 2002.

———. *Lord Jim: A Tale.* Edited by Thomas Moser. 2nd ed. New York: Norton, 1996.

———. *Lord Jim: A Tale.* Edited by Jacques Berthoud. Oxford World's Classics. Oxford: Oxford University Press, 2002.

———. *An Outcast of the Islands.* Edited by J. H. Stape. Oxford World's Classics. Oxford: Oxford University Press, 2002.

Erdinast-Vulcan, Daphna. *Joseph Conrad and the Modern Temper.* Oxford: Clarendon Press, 1991.

———. "Some Millennial Footnotes on *Heart of Darkness.*" In *Conrad in the Twenty-First Century,* edited by Carola Caplan, Peter Mallios, and Andrea White. New York: Routledge, 2005. 55–66.

GoGwilt, Christopher. *The Invention of the West: Joseph Conrad and the Double-Mapping of Europe and Empire.* Stanford: Stanford University Press, 1995.

Guerard, Albert J. *Conrad the Novelist.* Cambridge, MA: Harvard University Press, 1958.

Hawthorn, Jeremy. *Joseph Conrad: Narrative Technique and Ideological Commitment.* London: Edward Arnold, 1990.

Knowles, Owen, and Gene Moore. *Oxford Reader's Companion to Conrad.* Oxford: Oxford University Press, 2000.

Lothe, Jakob. *Conrad's Narrative Method.* Oxford: Clarendon Press, 1989.

MacIntyre, Alasdair. *After Virtue: A Study in Moral Theory.* 2nd ed. London: Duckworth, 1997.

Miller, J. Hillis. *Poets of Reality: Six Twentieth-Century Writers.* Cambridge, MA: Harvard University Press, 1966.

———. *Fiction and Repetition: Seven English Novels.* Oxford: Blackwell, 1982.

———. "*Heart of Darkness* Revisited." In *Conrad Revisited: Essays for the Eighties,* edited by Ross C. Murfin. Tuscaloosa: University of Alabama Press, 1985. 31–50.

———. "Should We Read *Heart of Darkness?*" In *Conrad in Africa: New Essays on Heart of Darkness,* edited by Attie de Lange and Gail Fincham. New York: Columbia University Press, 2002. 21–40.

Najder, Zdzisław. *Conrad in Perspective: Essays on Art and Fidelity.* Cambridge: Cambridge University Press, 1997.

Peters, John. *Conrad and Impressionism.* Cambridge: Cambridge University Press, 2001.

Richardson, Brian. "Conrad and Posthumanist Narration: Fabricating Class and Consciousness on Board the *Narcissus.*" In *Conrad in the Twenty-First Century,* edited by Carola Caplan, Peter Mallios, and Andrea White. New York: Routledge, 2005. 213–22.

Said, Edward. *Joseph Conrad and the Fiction of Autobiography.* Cambridge, MA: Harvard University Press, 1966.

———. *Beginnings: Intention and Method.* Baltimore: Johns Hopkins University Press, 1975.

———. "Conrad: The Presentation of Narrative." In *The World, the Text, and the Critic.* London: Faber and Faber, 1984. 90–110.

Schorer, Mark. "Technique as Discovery." *Hudson Review* 1 (1948). Rpt. in *The Theory of the Novel,* edited by Philip Stevick. New York: Free Press, 1967. 65–84.

Senn, Werner. *Conrad's Narrative Voice: Stylistic Aspects of His Fiction.* Berne: Francke Verlag, 1980.

Stape, J. H., ed. *The Cambridge Companion to Joseph Conrad.* Cambridge: Cambridge University Press, 1996.

Todorov, Tzvetan. "Connaissance du vide: *Coeur des ténèbres.*" In *Les Genres du discours.* Paris: Seuil, 1978. 161–73.

Van Ghent, Dorothy. *The English Novel: Form and Function* (1953). New York: Harper and Row, 1961.

Watt, Ian. *Conrad in the Nineteenth Century.* Berkeley: University of California Press, 1980.

Watts, Cedric. *Conrad's "Heart of Darkness": A Critical and Contextual Discussion.* Milan: Mursia, 1977.

White, Andrea. *Joseph Conrad and the Adventure Tradition: Constructing and Deconstructing the Imperial Subject.* Cambridge: Cambridge University Press, 1993.

I

Voice

1

The Personal Voice in Conrad's Fiction

ZDZISŁAW NAJDER

Critical literature about Conrad is, to use one of his favorite words, immense. This immensity should not, however, discourage us from asking, occasionally, simple and perhaps even elementary questions, the answers to which may reveal patterns otherwise difficult to discern. One may also note that, in the thick tissue of scholarship, often very fine, there remain thinner patches. Remarkably enough, although Conrad was a multi- (or cross-) cultural writer, the terms of interpretation applied to his work refer more frequently to psychology than to semiotics. Even more remarkable is another neglected patch. It is well known that Conrad was a writer deeply concerned with establishing emotional and intellectual contact with his readers. Moreover, for an artistically innovative and challenging writer he has been over the years exceptionally popular. But studies of Conrad applying the reader response approach continue to be very rare. I keep on dreaming of a scholar who would ask the question about the implied (in Wolfgang Iser's) or intended (in Erwin Wolff's terminology) reader of Conrad's works.

In my tentative essay I want to steer our attention—gently, without much specialist terminology—in these two neglected directions.

Personal narratives, as we all know, are one of Conrad's trademarks. What stylistic means and structural devices does Conrad use in the texts of his personal narrators to make them actually sound like personal narratives? How and to what extent do his narrators learn and tell us about the psychology of other protagonists? Or to put it even more simply: how do Conrad's texts justify the fact that the narrator knows what he tells about? Of course, all these questions have been asked before—but usually in more specific forms.

The use of personal narrators by Conrad is commonly explained in terms of the author "distancing" himself from the narrative point of view, or "placing a screen" (in the shape of a teller) between himself and the written text. Both concepts are psychological. The former term begs the question whether indeed in every instance we have to do with "distancing"—moving farther rather than, as may be the case sometimes, with closing up, narrowing the distance (emotional or intellectual) to the content. The latter formulation is obviously metaphorical, with all the advantages and disadvantages of this figure of speech. Both clearly entail the idea of "subjectivity."

An omniscient, a nonpersonal narrator ("authorial voice"), an unnamed frame narrator, and every personal narrator, whether quoted directly or indirectly—the appearance of each of them is bound up with a discrete language, constituted by words, phrases, whole conceptual networks, and an implicit consciousness. Do personal narrators augment the component of subjectivity? Not necessarily, and not prima facie. The sense data registered by our consciousness may be justly called "subjective."[1] But once we want to communicate them in words (or other signals), they have to become conceptualized and conventionalized, that is, converted into intersubjective signs. Languages—systems of communication—cannot, by definition, be "subjective" in the basic sense of the term (= idiosyncratic, not implicitly shared by other persons). In fact, using personal narrators is—from a semiotic point of view—not a step in the direction of "subjectivity," that is of egotism and uniqueness,[2] but rather the opposite: it is to use a technique of open identification of the code used (with the concreteness of identification depending on the degree in which the given narrator is characterized).[3] This happens because the facts as told have to be conceptualized twice: once from the perspective of the communicated content as imagined "factually," that is in a interpersonal language of comprehensible description, the second time from the specific perspective of the given teller. A case of "delayed decoding" (in Ian Watt's terminology) may serve as a good if macabre example: the author has to visualize how the corpse of the

---

1. I skirt here the whole epistemological controversy whether they are indeed "basic," that is, unmixed with innate ideas, and free from the components of expectation.

2. As suggests John G. Peters in his *Conrad and Impressionism* (2001), 135, 158.

3. Captain Mitchell in *Nostromo*, with his ostentatiously stressed conventionality of thought and expression, is a good example, see Senn 1980, 153.

wretched Señor Hirsch, killed by Colonel Sotillo, would look and then imagine how it could have been perceived by an ignorant observer (*Nostromo*, 427). In "indirect speech"—a form very often used by Conrad—the languages of the primary and secondary speakers are superimposed, offering a scintillating mixture of semantic perspectives.

When Marlow complains in *Heart of Darkness* about the impossibility of conveying "the life-sensation of any given epoch of one's existence" (*Youth: A Narrative, and Two Other Stories*, 82), he refers at the same time to two problems: the first is a chasm between the experience and the word, the bane of all writers aiming at authenticity;[4] the second is the practical difficulty in finding—creating—a language in which one may communicate with an audience for which the facts described are even more novel and exotic than to Marlow himself. Conrad, unlike Joyce in *Finnegans Wake*, was never interested in creating a "private language"; on the contrary, he wanted "to hold up . . . the rescued fragment [of life] before *all* eyes," to make us "see," that is, to reconstruct and share his original experience (preface, *Nigger of the "Narcissus"*, x; my emphasis). This is why using the device of personalized narrative was for him so natural. It meant to evoke different conceptual networks, to look at the same objects from various and clearly defined points, or to set mirrors which refract under different angles. It was analogous to Conrad's use, notably in *Lord Jim*, of components belonging to various literary genres: the adventure story, the novel of education, the chivalric tale, tragedy—components stemming from a number of traditional conventions, appealing to a wealth of different associations and ultimately creating an effect of artistic polyphony.

After these rudimentary preliminaries I pass on to my questions. Looking for answers I shall limit myself to three tales and one novel with personal narrators: "Amy Foster," *Heart of Darkness*, "Falk," and *Lord Jim*, and then juxtapose the results with two novels where personal narratives occur only sporadically, *Nostromo* and *The Secret Agent*.

I begin with "Amy Foster," as it is the simplest, and represents what seems to me a paradigmatic case. The story has two personal narrators. One, unnamed and identified only as an inhabitant of Kent who had spent some time abroad, introduces and repeats a tale told by Kennedy, the local doctor. The frame narrator's function is to characterize Kennedy (formerly a surgeon in the Navy, traveler, and learned specialist in exotic fauna and flora) and to vouch for his intelligence, humanity, and an "inexhaustible patience in

---

4. This chasm has been known to Joseph Conrad from his early readings of Adam Mickiewicz, who in his "Great Improvisation" (in *Dziady* [*Forefathers' Eve*, 1834]), spoken by Konrad, to whom Conrad owed his given name, complains about words "which belie the thoughts, and vibrate over them as the earth over an underground, invisible river."

listening to [people's] tales" (*Typhoon and Other Stories*, 106). Kennedy's report is of a synthetic character, and its veracity is never put in question either by the doctor himself or by the frame narrator.

The narrative begins from the end: we first meet Amy Foster, during one of the frame narrator's rides through the country in Kennedy's company, as a widow, tending the son of the late Yanko Gooral. Then Kennedy begins his almost chronological tale—almost, because, very naturally, he supplements and elucidates his reminiscences with his knowledge about Yanko, acquired at later stages of their acquaintance.

The focal theme of the piece is one of cultural and psychological divides. The eponymous protagonist is a young, mentally limited woman, plain and dull, who nevertheless turned out to have "enough imagination to fall in love" (107) and to show pity for the wretched castaway Yanko, victimized by the local peasantry (121). Amy is difficult to communicate with, and thus both narrators, and consequently the reader, are deprived of any possibility to follow her thoughts. And while Amy's mind remains impenetrable because there is so little of it, Yanko's is at first inaccessible not only because he does not know English, but also because he operates within a very different cultural code and system of values. He is initially characterized by the movements of his body, "lithe, supple and long-limbed"; by his "long elastic stride that made him noticeable at a great distance" (111); and by his voice. The language of his body, his gestures, are fairly easy to interpret (134, 138), but to understand them requires, we learn, a receptive attitude, a readiness to accept him as human. As we know, the tragedy of Yanko stems from the local villagers' refusal to recognize his fundamental humanity, from the fact that they (and in the end Amy herself) identify his otherness with madness.

In the course of "two or three years" Kennedy learns enough from Yanko to reconstruct his origins and the story of his shipwreck. This reconstruction is couched mostly in free indirect discourse, allowing the reader to follow at the same time the workings of Yanko's indigenous conceptual framework (notably his social, cultural, and religious notions) as well as Kennedy's subtle juxtaposing of them with the local Kentish customs. Yanko's wonder at the hostile and plainly inhuman attitudes of most of his new neighbors is evidently shared by Kennedy; in the end the reader is more likely to identify with the strange castaway from the Eastern Carpathians than with the English folk around him. The question, however, of why Amy is capable of showing initial sympathy for Yanko and then refuses to understand him in his illness—remains unanswered.

The scope of the information passed by the narrators to the reader is clearly circumscribed. Kennedy unobtrusively though repeatedly signals that he presents hypotheses and results of investigation: "no doubt" (118), "I should say" (118), "maybe" (119), "looks as if" (123), "I suppose" (127). Elements of introspection appear solely in free indirect speech, and are expressed in Yanko's own terms. In fact, almost the entire psychology of the story is grounded in behavioral observation. This is fully justified in view of the characters of Amy and Yanko, but still significant and, I believe, characteristic of Conrad's general authorial attitude: to identify the language in which one can understand a given person one begins with behavioral scrutiny.

In *Heart of Darkness* the role of the wretched Yanko is, in a way, played by the Africans. They seem incomprehensible, but Marlow—unlike the "pilgrims"—has no doubt that they are human and that he is simply unable to decode their signals: " . . . a bit of white worsted round his neck . . . was it a badge—an ornament—a charm—a propitiatory act?" (*Youth: A Narrative, and Two Other Stories,* 67). Of course, *Heart of Darkness* is much more complex, both in its content and structure, but it raises the same dual problem of communication. This problem consists, first, of understanding the psychology, individual (of Kurtz) and collective (of the Africans), evidently unconventional by the standards of the observer; and second, to find a language to convey to the audience (and the reader) the results of the investigation. The basic structure is also analogous to that of "Amy Foster" (written two years later): there is an unnamed frame narrator, who introduces and comments upon a story told this time by Charlie Marlow. The frame narrator provides little factual information about Marlow (in "Amy Foster" we learn more about doctor Kennedy); we are to find out much more from Marlow himself (about his seagoing past, his Continental connections, fluency in French, some knowledge of German, etc.). But the frame narrator recommends Marlow as a storyteller and even offers a clue on how to interpret his tales (Lothe 1989, 26–28). Marlow interrupts his tale from time to time, which gives the frame narrator opportunities to insert comments: on Marlow's posture and face, on the behavior of other listeners, on the very scene of storytelling. One of these comments is particularly significant; to Marlow's appeal for consent: "You see me, whom you know . . ."—the narrator reacts by saying that "[i]t had become so pitch dark" that for a long time Marlow had been for them "only a voice" (83). The function of these interruptions is, of course, to put Marlow in relief as a protagonist, and not merely the teller of a story: he not only recites the narrative, but responds to the reactions of the audience.

For the sake of brevity, I shall look only at the two main objects of Marlow's psychosemiotic scrutiny: the Africans and Kurtz. His visit to Brussels alerts Marlow that in the Congo he will be met by a discrepancy between appearances and reality. When in the Congo, he is faced with two concurrent challenges: one is the country itself, completely novel to his experience, the other a glaring contrast between the colonialist ways of describing Africa— and reality. He reacts by adopting a radically empiricist attitude: facts, not declarations; things, not words; designates, not signs are his guide (e.g., 65, 71, 76–77). "There was surface-truth enough [he says about his concentration on his work on the riverboat] in these things to save a wiser man" (97), and he resolutely prefers surface-truth (silently supplemented by his human solidar- ity) to lofty slogans.

As to the black Africans, he is painfully aware of failing to understand not only their speech, but also their behavior (107). But, as I have already noted, he admits and respects their humanity—which not only sets him apart from local white officials and the "pilgrims" from Europe, but insulates him against the rhetoric of Kurtz, to whom he stands at the opposite cognitive pole. While Kurtz "has kicked himself loose of the earth," carried away by the magic of his own words (116–18), Marlow has stuck to simple facts. This humane empiri- cism constitutes the basis for his moral authority.

Marlow's consistent psychological behaviorism and the concomitant reti- cence to speculate enhance his image as a personal narrator. And so do his complaints about the difficulty of finding an adequate language in which he can convey the gist of his experiences (82, 116–17). The flow of his narrative is by and large chronological, with scattered, naturally occurring elements of *prolepsis* (115) and *analepsis* (as when he sums up his information about the background of Kurtz, 117). Extended analytic fragments in which he accounts for his observations alternate with fragments in reporting, conversational style (e.g., 51, 53, 65, 70) and with pieces of introspection (e.g., 65, 97, 119). There are even rhetorical addresses to his listeners ("I hear," "you wonder," 97). All in all, one of the great strengths of *Heart of Darkness* lies in Marlow's convincing role as a narrator, although if we try to recapitulate what we know about him, we find that it does not amount to much. He comes to life through the story he tells and the way he tells it, but to visualize him the reader must rely entirely on his own uninstructed imagination (what height? hair? eyes? age? accent? origins?). He is, in fact, mainly his voice.

The narrative structure of "Falk" (more than twice the length of "Amy Foster" and a little shorter than *Heart of Darkness*), written two years later, is again analogous: a frame narrator introduces a tale, told by the main narrator. But this time the frame narrator uses the first person plural, speaking in the name of "several of us, all more or less connected with the sea"; the main nar- rator remains unnamed, and his story in not put in quotation marks. There is an initial dialogue between the frame and the main narrators (*Typhoon and Other Stories,* 147), but one detects no difference of attitudes or perspectives:

they are evidently all linked by the companionship of the sea. About the main narrator we first hear only that he is a man "of more than fifty, that had commanded ships for a quarter of a century" (147); later, from his own tale, we learn that at the time of the action he was less than thirty and in his first, fortuitously obtained command of a sailing ship.

He tells us how, in the course of his efforts to have his ship tugged out to sea, he was compelled to act as an intermediary and a psychological interpreter within the triangle: Hermann, captain of the German steamer the *Diana*—his niece—and the "centaur" Falk, the owner of the sole tugboat in the port. We may note that the silent niece takes pity on Falk (236) analogously to Amy Foster's compassionate treatment of Yanko; but the analogy stops here, and in the niece-Falk case the motive of sexual attraction is made fairly obvious.

Although the narrator does not, of course, have a direct access to the thoughts and feelings of other protagonists, he does not seem to encounter essential difficulties in understanding their motives and actions. There is a language gap between him and Hermann's family, jokingly remembered, but it turns out to be of no practical importance. No knowledge, factual or intuitive, of other cultures seems required from the narrator. Once Falk's secret—gruesome, but apparently of only external consequence (217)—is revealed, all mysteries of the situation disappear. The narrator's moral convictions seem to be seriously engaged only once, when he questions Falk's Darwinian equating of "toughest" and "best." In telling his story, he follows the chronology of the events virtually throughout. Utterances by other protagonists are by and large given in reported speech, which increases the immediacy of action, but at the same time makes the narrator as a person redundant and increases the effect of theatrical conventionality; only occasionally, and notably in rendering Falk's tale, the more "digested" indirect speech is used. In his dealings, the narrator displays self-avowed cunning (as he says, in the interest of his ailing crew) and common sense, but no discernible personal traits. The location where the story is being narrated is described precisely and vividly (if somewhat acerbically), the place of the action itself is not named (although Bangkok is clearly suggested), and the main narrator is even unsure whether the eponymous protagonist was "a Dane or perhaps a Norwegian" (161). There is no dialogue between the frame narrator(s) and the unnamed young captain, and the story ends without the frame narrator's farewell.

Unlike "Amy Foster," which is a story about Yanko Gooral, brought to life by the voice of the compassionate and sagacious doctor Kennedy, and *Heart of Darkness,* which is a story as much about the Congo and Mr. Kurtz as about Charlie Marlow—"Falk" reads like a yarn about just one of the narrator's adventures which did not engage his own personality. Marlow confesses that his African experience has changed him; Kennedy is moved to reflect on the difference between Yanko and the Kentish villagers (111), and the reader has no doubt that Kennedy's attitude to the latter has been modified. In "Falk" the related story seems to be just an expanded anecdote, grist for "a vague tale still going about town" (240); it does not endow the teller with any recognizable individuality. But the unnamed narrator's noncommittal attitude fits the content: the reverberations of Falk's story of his survival-by-cannibalism are amply rendered by the contrasting reactions of his listeners in the story.

The narrative structure of *Lord Jim,* a novel four times the length of *Heart of Darkness,* is unique within Conrad's opus by its coupling of the introductory "authorial," omniscient narrative with the subsequent long (and technically very complex) narration of Marlow. About the Marlow of *Lord Jim* we know, in fact, rather less than about that of *Heart of Darkness.* They share their seaman's experience, their knowledge of French and German; the protagonist of *Lord Jim* has, also, more opportunity to display his classical education; but about his past we know less than about Stein's or even the French lieutenant's. His British and/or continental background is left unelaborated. This is quite remarkable for the main teller of a major and convoluted story, who plays the role of arbiter between other personal points of view.

I appreciate Jakob Lothe's argument about the authorial narrative in *Lord Jim* as "diverse, edited personal narration" (Lothe 1989, 133) (in fact, when it returns, momentarily in chapters VIII, IX, and XXXVII, and extensively at the beginning of chapter XXXVI, it is in an openly personalized form), but I consider it based on a sophisticated specialist analysis. What must strike the common reader is the immediate contrast between the omniscience (even if limited) displayed in the authorial narrative of the first four chapters, where we get an easy access to Jim's thoughts and dreams, and the distinctly circumscribed and personalized knowledge of Marlow and his subsequent interlocutors. The initial form of the narrative puts Marlow as a personal narrator into sharp relief: he knows about Jim much less than the reader, who listens to Marlow's report about collecting information and opinion from other personal sources, as he proceeds in his inquiry.

His quest has two objectives. Initially, Marlow wants to find out what happened onboard the *Patna* and why Jim behaved as he did. Later, and what turns out to be much more complicated and problematic (both for Marlow himself and for the critics, analyzing the novel), he attempts to understand the evolution of Jim's posttrial attitude and his behavior, especially in Patusan. Marlow's primary source is, of course, Jim himself: Marlow watches him very closely, registering his movements, gestures, and tone of voice, and not only listens attentively to his confession, but enters into a polemic with him.

Not less importantly, he carefully collects information from other sources and adduces their evidence and opinion either in reported or (more often) in free indirect speech. Apart from Jim himself, there are no fewer than eleven secondary personal narrators; in the order of their appearance: Jones (Captain Brierly's first mate), Brierly himself, the French lieutenant, Chester, Marlow's friend Denver, Egström, Stein, Cornelius, Jewel, Brown, and Tamb'Itam. They are all carefully scrutinized, as Jim is at all times, by Marlow, who displays the same inquisitive and behaviorist attitude which we know from *Heart of Darkness*. They all enter with their physical and psychological characteristics, their idioms (Gallicisms of the Frenchman, Chester's Australian colloquialisms, Egström's primitive grammar, Stein's Germanisms, etc.), their specific points of view, and their autonomous judgments; they use different descriptive and evaluative languages. The reader has to take into account not only facts reported (and retold by Marlow), but also the evaluative slant of the informants: their values determine their judgments and color their descriptions. It ought to be obvious that "Gentleman" Brown wants Jim to feel with him the double solidarity of a white man and an outcast; but we receive no indication that Jim feels that way. When we hear about Cornelius's opinion that Jim "is just like a child," we ought to remember that that "child" has been for a few years a shrewd ruler of the country, and conclude that for Cornelius being an adult implies readiness for treachery. When we hear Jewel's accusation that Jim is a traitor, we must realize that it echoes analogous emotional charges expressed by innumerable bereaved mothers and widows against their sons and husbands who had lost their lives while doing what they thought was their duty to their king or nation. When in *Chanson de Roland* Olivier tells Roland that his foolhardiness will cost him the hand of Olivier's sister Oda—the gist of the reaction is the same.

I comment more extensively on these instances because I wish to highlight the fact that what is problematic for Marlow and his interlocutors (and hence for the reader) are not Jim's actions as such, nor even his feelings, but the ethical categories by reference to which they ought to be understood. This, by the way, makes Marlow's quest more intensely personal: "there was no incertitude as to facts," we hear (56); and only persons can evaluate. Furthermore, there are in Marlow's expressed opinions both uncertainties—he repeats that he has not fully understood Jim—and discrepancies, which additionally signal his role of an engaged protagonist.

When Marlow asks Jim "what advantage [he] can expect from this licking of the dregs" (153) after the trial, or wonders why he attaches so much importance to "his disgrace, while it is the guilt alone that matters" (177)—he reveals that he is unaware that the ethics of shame and the ethics of guilt

constitute two distinct traditions in the history of European moral ideals. No
wonder that his talk with the French lieutenant ends in mutual incomprehension. Marlow, attached to the rigid seaman's code, but at the same time
a member of the nation which has given birth to Utilitarianism, tries—like
many others—to combine the ethics of principles with the ethics of results. In
practice, they may, with luck, coincide; but they are grounded in contradictory
systems of values. The code disregards psychology: duty, fidelity, and honor
are ideals binding irrespective of emotional circumstances[5] (the fact which
Jim does not initially accept). The antithesis of Jim's reasonable jump from the
deck of the doomed *Patna* is Bob Stanton's futile and heroic death.

It is noteworthy that the two of Marlow's interlocutors who quite readily
find the words—and whole conceptual frameworks, well grounded in concrete
traditions—to describe Jim's predicament haven't encountered him before:
they talk about a paradigmatic case. Both the French lieutenant, a figure
straight from the pages of Alfred de Vigny's *Servitude et grandeur militaires,*
and the former romantic revolutionary Stein, see Jim's situation in terms of
an ethics which considers practical consequences irrelevant in the face of "the
fixed standard of conduct" (35). The instinctively practical Marlow has doubts
about the "sovereign power" of such a standard: in what does this power
reside? Indeed there is, on the horizons of *Lord Jim,* no transcendental power
to endorse it; the "certain" but simple faith of Jim's father (5) does not seem
to reach that far. The rules of the code of honor are man-made and grounded
solely in the history of human communities. Therefore, for breaking them the
main punishment is shame—not the guilt a sinner feels.

Marlow reports on the extensive and probing investigation which concerns, as I have remarked, the language and hue of evaluation rather than the
specifics of description of Jim's character and deeds. The investigating team
consists of men, and one woman, of diverse background and equally varied
axiological attitudes. Thus their points of view are clearly individualized and,
as assembled by Marlow, augment the personal character of his own tale as
well. The reader witnesses the process of gathering and juxtaposing information and is asked—indeed, compelled—to participate in it actively, as during
a personal encounter.

This multifarious tissue of reports and opinions is spread on the highly
complicated time-framework of the novel. I once called *Lord Jim* a treatise
in practical epistemology (Najder 1965, 100); this referred both to the mul-

5. A good illustration of this point is to be found in *Nostromo,* when Dr Monygham's
"conception of his disgrace" is described: "It was a conception eminently fit for an officer and a
gentleman. . . . It was a conception which took no account of physiological facts or reasonable
arguments" (375).

tiplicity of sources and to the reconstruction of the sequence in which the data are collected. Jim's history is recorded from different perspectives and in many temporal segments. (Adopting an arbitrary rule that any bunch of events described at the length of at least one page is given a separate number, I calculated that there are in *Lord Jim* at least fifty-three such clusters.)[6] Thus the first cluster (Stein's youth) emerges in chapter XX, the last (the privileged man reading Marlow's letter in London) in chapter XXXVI. Out of forty-five chapters, only in fifteen is the narrative by and large chronological. However, while remarking the complexity, the reader does not have an impression of artificiality: time-shifts come quite naturally, as they chronicle a natural process of accumulating and conveying information. The notoriously convoluted time-structure of *Lord Jim* reflects the common course of our piecemeal learning about facts and evaluating actions we haven't ourselves witnessed. By the same token it serves to underscore, again, the personal character of the narrative: in an authorial telling there would be scant empirical justification for such lack of chronological continuity in the narrative. I referred above to Jakob Lothe's observation that the restraints within the formally authorial narrative in *Lord Jim* in the first four chapters create the impression that it constitutes in fact an "edited" personal narration, that there is somebody behind it. When the "Privileged Man" of chapters XXXVI and XXXVII (an undisguised racist, by the way; see 338–39) takes over as the audience of Marlow's narration, he may leave the reader with a vague feeling that this most attentive listener to Marlow's yarn merges somehow with the "authorial" voice of chapters I to IV, the source privy to the initial inside information on Jim's past. This feeling would be, of course, irrational. What remains certain, however, is that the preponderance of personal points of view, and the lack of a central narrative command, invite the reader to be uncommonly active, weaving together the multiple narrative threads to work out a coherent whole. This enforced cooperation between the reader and the author was, I am convinced, Conrad's conscious aim. To achieve it, he uses ostensibly contrasting ruses.

Nostromo is—formally—a novel written by an unnamed, omniscient authorial narrator. Within its text, overtly personal narratives are scarce; only three stand out: Captain Mitchell's yarns about the recent past of Costaguana

---

6. In the order of chapters, they appear as follows: I–p. 22, 35, 2, 3; II–p. 4, 5, 6, 7; III–p. 7, 8; IV–p. 16, 9; V–p. 16, 14, 15; VI–p. 16, 20, 37, 17; VII–p. 17, 9; IX–p. 9, 10, 17; X–p. 11, 17; XI–p. 17; XII–p. 17, 12, 13, 25; XIII–p. 25, 23, 36, 17; XIV–p. 16, 18; XV–p. 19; XVI–p. 39, 19; XVIII–p. 21, 22; XIX–p. 23, 24; XX–p. 26, 1; XXI–p. 26, 35; XXII–p. 29, 37; XXIII–p. 27, 28; XXIV–p. 39, 29; XXV–p. 39, 30; XXVI–p. 39, 35; XXVII–p. 35, 39; XXVIII–p. 39, 38; XXIX–p. 39, 31; XXX–p. 39, 31, 32; XXXI–p. 39, 33; XXXII–p. 32, 39; XXXIII–p. 39, 34; XXXIV–p. 39; XXXV–p. 39; XXXVI–p. 53, 52; XXXVII–p. 51, 50; XXXVIII–p. 40, 41, 42; XXXIX–p. 42, 43; XL–p. 43; XLI–p. 45, 51, 40; XLII–p. 44, 51, 46; XLIII–p. 45, 46; XLIV–p. 47; XLV–p. 48, 49, 50 (Najder 1978, XLVIII–L).

and about his own experiences, Decoud's letter to his sister, and the story of
Dr. Monygham's imprisonment and torture, told in free indirect discourse.
But *Nostromo*'s time structure is no less complex than that of *Lord Jim:* after
the majestically slow, panoramic chapter I we move to what will turn out to
be late events, and then proceed to jump backwards in chapters II to VIII.[7]
And in subsequent chapters the course of the narrative is more often analeptic
than proleptic, with several loops (as on pp. 539–51, in the midst of the scene
in which Dr Monygham and Nostromo look at the body of Hirsch). Cedric T.
Watts, who has meticulously charted both the chronology of events within the
story and the sequence in which they are told, proposes four reasons for what
he calls narrative "deviousness:" to endow fictional events with a stereoscopic
plausibility; to enhance the text's ironies; to suggest that history is repetitive, or
even cyclical; and to challenge the reader with "resistances to overcome"(Watts
1982, 152–53).

These are very perceptive comments, but they concern not so much the
reasons for, as the artistic consequences of Conrad's technique. There is, in
fact, no prima facie justification for an omniscient narrator *not* to tell the story
straight from the beginning to the end. Apart from the four effects listed by
Watts, by means of such an intensive use of time-shifts Conrad contributes to
a more general, elusive, and at the same time all-pervasive impression: that we
have to do with a person who handles the flow of the narrative. As Ian Watt
puts it, "the frequent changes of time and place must have an assumed directing narrator" (Watt 1988, 43). This is, however, not the only and not the main
factor at work which aims at achieving the same effect.

The authorial narrator of *Nostromo* does not behave like a purveyor of
possessed information, but rather like an investigator and interpreter, deci-
phering data and often hesitating about the categories that can be used to
understand what he has learned and what he is currently witnessing. Thus we
find here the same actively inquisitive attitude which we have noted in "Amy
Foster" or *Lord Jim*. The multiplicity of possible meanings of narrated facts
is signaled by the very ambiguity of the main protagonist's name (527). The
difference between appearances, "bare" facts—as in the description of men
and horses running patternlessly on the plain, which Giorgio Viola observes
(26–27)—and facts decoded is revealed over and over again and forms the
epistemological leitmotif of the novel.

And if the unnamed main—authorial—narrator is nominally omniscient,
he usually refrains from introspection and watches his protagonists from the
outside, like a true behaviorist; Cedric Watts talks even about his occasional

7. For a thorough analysis of chronology in relation to narrative, see Watts's Everyman
edition of *Nostromo*, 1995.

"solipsism" (Watts 1982, 79). Particularly attentive to physiognomies, the main narrator reads the eyes and faces of protagonists for their moods, feelings, and intentions: thus, for instance, Sotillo's eyes shine to him "with rapacity and hope" (343).[8] This investigative attitude is, naturally, shared by personal narrators, such as Decoud and Captain Mitchell, who extensively report on their behaviorist psychological findings; we find an excellent example on pages 487–89, in a fragment where the Captain studies the hidden emotions of Nostromo. To recognize and interpret different cultural and individual codes of behavior (and implicit evaluative languages) constitutes a recurrent motif; the story of Mr. Gould-father and a Finance Minister residing in Sta. Maria offers a grotesque example (54–55); another example would be Charles Gould's meaningful silences (203).

Three subjects of scrutiny stand out: Nostromo, Dr. Monygham, and Costaguana as a whole. The differences in the perspectives on the eponymous protagonist of the novel are obvious; and it is perhaps only worth noting that Nostromo himself changes his conception of his own personality (523–24). Dr. Monygham is variously decoded by the engineer-in-chief, Nostromo, and Emilia Gould. But perhaps most remarkable is the diversity of perspectives on the country where the action takes place: we have the contrasting general opinions of the older Mr. Gould, Charles Gould, Emilia Gould, Captain Mitchell, Father Romàn (398–400), Don Pépé (89), Martin Decoud, Antonia Avellanos, her father; not to mention the implicit views of figures like Señor Fuentes, Pedrito Montero, or Sotillo. (Even the Goulds' parrot makes its contribution [69]). Their judgments and their conceptual frameworks are, to a certain extent, sorted out by the main narrator. But there is no reason to treat his tangential, usually implicit, and often caustic comments as more authoritative than the opinions of the protagonists: he does not seem to possess a treasure trove of facts known only to himself, nor, more importantly, does he possess the moral authority of, say, Doctor Kennedy of "Amy Foster" or the French lieutenant of *Lord Jim*. It is the reader who has to contribute the essential component of evaluative order: the reader in collaborative dialogue with the main narrator.

This last, maintaining the discursive tone of narration, seems constantly in search of an interlocutor. He is eager to express judgments about particular protagonists; for example, a deflating assessment of Decoud (153) who, at the same time, seems very close to his own point of view (Lothe 1989, 210). The narrative easily oscillates between the authorial and definitely personal (i.e., of the particular protagonist's) point of view (cf. 26–31). Very frequent modalization of the text by the use of words like "seem," "appear," "like,"

8. See Senn 1980, 74, 85–86 for other examples.

"look," and above all "as if" strengthens the personal component of the narrative: Werner Senn, who provides a painstaking analysis of Conrad's use of this
stylistic device, notes that "whatever seems, seems so to somebody"; the same
applies to "appear"; while "as if" implies seeing objects from two perspectives
at the same time (Senn 1980, 145, 148, 150, 157–58). This constant shimmer-
ing of narrative colors makes the single, sudden, and momentary transition
from the third to the first person singular (95) sound unsurprising: the reader
has been mentally prepared for such open admission of individuality, because
he or she is conscious of the constant interplay of angles of vision, which can
be justified only by the presence of personal participants.

In such a context also the very extensive use of the free indirect speech
(and thought) mode, which permits the easy introduction of the words or
thoughts of a protagonist but implies the mediation of a narrator "who selects
the most telling and salient features and embeds them in his own narrative"
(Senn 1980, 169), strengthens the impression of a person, hidden behind the
ostensibly impersonal text. Such an implicit person enters more naturally into
dialogue with the reader than an abstract, unnamed, disembodied entity, represented by the authorial narrator. Such dialogue engages, and obliges, the
reader to pay attention ("to keep us guessing," as Ian Watt says [Watt 1988,
31]). Consequently, the consistent personalization of the narrative in *Nostromo* results in making the reader a companion, or even an accomplice of the
anonymous teller. It makes the reader of *Nostromo,* like the reader of *Lord Jim,*
co-responsible for the assembling of temporal and thematic elements of the
whole structure.

In comparison with *Lord Jim* and *Nostromo, The Secret Agent* is indeed "a
simple tale," as it is coyly named in its subtitle. Sparse in its style, it is frugal
even in the number of characters: although the place of its action is much
more populous than Patusan and Costaguana put together, it has few protagonists. And the action itself is, by any comparison, economic. But there is yet
another difference, more important from the point of view of my subject: the
text of *The Secret Agent* does not involve its readers emotionally in a way and
to the degree found in the other two Conrad novels. The narrative preserves
a consistently ironic distance and, apart from the Assistant Commissioner,
there is in this story—in which only the poor Stevie is not a double (or treble)
agent—no other character with whom the reader could identify. Both *Lord
Jim* and *Nostromo* abound in such women and men; indeed, I have argued
elsewhere that the number of decent protagonists in *Nostromo* is the strongest
argument against the novel's alleged pessimism (Najder 2005).

However, the answer to the question: to what extent does the authorial
form of narration in *The Secret Agent* engage the reader in such a way as to

give the impression of a personal intercourse?—is anything but simple. We may note that the time structure of the novel (the plot) is both complex and far from following the chronology of events (the story) described; this may be an indication of a personality at work. Decoding the protagonists' behavior, both interactive (as for instance in the conversations between Verloc and Mr. Vladimir, or Chief Inspector Heat and the Assistant Commissioner, or—the most fatally deficient—between Winnie and her husband) as well as filtered through the narrator, is the main motif (both semiotic and psychological) of the novel. The macabre examination of the remnants of Stevie (87–88) is just one—and the most memorable—example of the investigative approach prevailing in the narrative. Charles Jones is certainly right when he writes that "[m]uch of the novel's strength and attractiveness lies in the shifting of the reader's viewpoint brought about by his constant uncertainty of the nature of the linguistic data confronting him—i.e., whether it represents the author's narration, a particular character's direct or reported utterance, or a mixture of all three" (Jones 1968, 165). Thus we find in *The Secret Agent* salient semiotic and structural elements, identified in *Lord Jim* and *Nostromo* as engendering the personal coloring of the narrative.

On page 13 the narrator, hitherto conventionally anonymous and omniscient, suddenly shifts gears and appears as a reflexive and doubting "I" ("I am not sure . . . For all I know"). The reader may feel startled and ignore the intrusion; as Jakob Lothe says, this grammatical self-identification "probably does not make the narrative as a whole appear less authorial" (Lothe 1989, 231). And indeed, throughout the text the variation of angles of vision seems tightly controlled by the central narrative authority, preserving most of the time an archly ironical posture. "Authorial," however, does not equal impersonal. Lothe's analysis of the complex and sometimes evolving relation of the narrator to his main protagonists, particularly to Winnie and Stevie (1989, 253–59), indicates that the narrator displays the traits of a concrete person, with shifting, unstable psychological attitudes.

Thus the problem of the "personalization" of the narrator in *The Secret Agent* (or of an instinctive search for a person behind the authorial narration) seems to concern not so much the structural symptoms of individuality, which *are* present in the text, as the mental qualities of such a person. To put it in simple terms: it is a great challenge to the reader's empathy to imagine, to get a feel of the teller as a concrete human being. And although there have been attempts to identify the unnamed narrator of *The Secret Agent* (notably with the Assistant Commissioner himself!)—for all the reasons briefly listed above the plea for his existence is psychologically less urgent than in the case of *Nostromo*.

A conclusion of this tentative and unsystematic inquiry must begin with the banal statement that Conrad's art does not easily submit to generalizations: each of his major works is structurally distinct. And if his attitude toward his reader remains clear and constant—Conrad always wants to engage, involve, activate his readers—he does not repeat his techniques, he uses different strategies to achieve this end.

The idea that in Conrad's prose we can hear a peculiar "voice" has been put forward for a long time and in many versions. For Albert Guerard it was audible "to some extent regardless of the narrative point of view and whether or not a fictional personage is speaking or writing" (Guerard 1976, 7). This voice was, for Guerard, "unmistakably a speaking voice" (Guerard 1958, 1). Werner Senn echoes this opinion when he writes that "an interpreting, ever active, infinitely flexible human voice is [in Conrad's prose] of central importance . . . above all in that area where fiction and reality meet and intersect, in the pragmatic relationship between reader, narrator and author" (Senn 1980, 179). The positioning of that voice has been variously understood: it appears in personal, or in authorial narratives, or both; Guerard could hear it in all forms of Conrad's prose (explaining this mainly by resemblance to the spoken word); others (as, e.g., Senn 1980, 176) concentrated on the speech of personal narrators.

Conrad's recurrent use of personal narrators has been usually ascribed to the necessity or compulsion to put a "psychological distance" between himself as author and the contents of his fiction. My experience as biographer has taught me to shun such hypotheses. They are, on the one hand, impossible to prove, on the other—useless in artistic analysis and irrelevant to the common reader, who in most cases knows little or nothing about Conrad himself. Maybe Conrad found it emotionally easier to tackle certain themes by making them handled by clearly individualised protagonists different than himself; maybe, but I don't know a way to prove or disprove such a thesis; and—so what? That Conrad's writing strategies consistently aim at engaging the attention and emotions of the reader is not a psychological, but a critical thesis, which can be supported—quite apart from references to Conrad's own programmatic statements—by textual analysis. The impulse to be in contact, to activate, to consort with the reader as a person—this goal is, I believe, to be recognized as an (if not the most) important organizing principle of Conrad's style and narrative techniques.

It has seemed to me worthwhile to take a closer (if cursory) look at the means Conrad uses to convince his reader, or rather to make him feel instinctively, that while reading his prose he communicates with other persons, other human beings, who talk to her or him about their experiences and reflections.

But this is not all. In the tales and novels I have concentrated upon, and especially in "Amy Foster," *Lord Jim,* and *Nostromo,* there exist (or seem to exist) an unnamed supernarrator, who offers us the narratives of others. This implicit narrator possesses the qualities of a person. And his chief human quality is to encourage the reader to be just as inquisitive and sensitive, semiotically and emotionally, as he is. The metanarrator creates for the reader the potentiality to assemble the whole fictional universe.

I would not identify this metanarrator with the "author." That would oversimplify the structures and at the same time hamper the reader in pursuing the task to which she or he has been invited. I believe Conrad's unspoken objective—and the internal artistic logic of his works—is that the reader, in search of the countenance of the metanarrator, sees his, or her, own face in the mirror.

Works Cited

All references to Conrad's works are to the Dent Collected Edition, London, 1946–54.

Berthoud, Jacques. *Joseph Conrad: The Major Phase*. Cambridge: Cambridge University Press, 1978.

Conrad, Joseph. *Lord Jim*. Edited by Zdzisław Najder. Wrocław: Ossolineum, 1978.

Guerard, Albert J. *Conrad the Novelist*. Cambridge, MA: Harvard University Press, 1958.

———. "The Conradian Voice." In *Joseph Conrad: A Commemoration,* edited by Norman Sherry. London: Macmillan, 1976. 1–16.

Jones, Charles. "Varieties of Speech Presented in Conrad's *The Secret Agent*." *Lingua* 20 (1968): 162–76.

Lothe, Jakob. *Conrad's Narrative Method*. Oxford: Oxford University Press, 1989.

Najder, Zdzisław. *Nad Conradem*. [Reading Conrad]. Warsaw: PIW, 1965.

———. "A Century of *Nostromo*." Lecture delivered in New York, 12 March 2005, at a conference arranged by the Joseph Conrad Society of America.

Peters, John G. *Conrad and Impressionism*. Cambridge: Cambridge University Press, 2001.

Said, Edward W. *The World, the Text and the Critic*. Cambridge, MA: Harvard University Press, 1983.

Senn, Werner. *Conrad's Narrative Voice: Stylistic Aspects of his Fiction*. Berne: Francke, 1980.

Watt, Ian P. *Conrad in the Nineteenth Century*. Berkeley: University of California Press, 1979.

———. *Conrad: Nostromo*. Cambridge: Cambridge University Press, 1988.

Watts, Cedric T. *A Preface to Conrad*. London: Longman, 1982.

2

"'I affirm nothing.'"

Lord Jim and the Uses of Textual Recalcitrance

Jim's Character and Experience as an Instance of the Stubborn

JAMES PHELAN

Lord Jim is justly famous for both its artistic achievement and the difficulty it presents to interpreters. These two qualities of the novel have attracted many astute commentators who have offered significant insights into many of its techniques and strategies (e.g., Watt and Lothe). The novel's difficulty has also meant that critical consensus about some central issues of the novel has never been achieved. Two very astute commentators in the 1980s nicely represent the spectrum along which most critical opinion falls. At one end of the spectrum, J. Hillis Miller argues that the novel is ultimately indeterminate: "The indeterminacy lies in the multiplicity of possible incompatible explanations given by the novel and in the lack of evidence justifying a choice of one over the others. The reader cannot logically have them all, and yet nothing he is given determines a choice among them. The possibilities, moreover, are not just given side by side as entirely separate hypotheses. They are related to one another in a system of mutual implication and mutual contradiction. Each calls up the others, but it does not make sense to have more than one of them" (1982, 40). At the other end of the spectrum, Ralph Rader sees the novel as determinate but built on a principle of "unambiguous ambiguity," by which he means that Conrad incorporates what Marlow calls "the doubt of the sovereign power enthroned in a fixed standard of conduct" (1989, 37) into the representation of

Jim's movement toward his eventual fate. In Rader's view, the novel traces Jim's development within the frame of both the fixed standard and the inescapable doubt. Rader argues that Conrad both endorses Jim's final decision to take the death of Dain Waris on his own head (in that decision Jim is living up to the fixed standard) but stops short of making that decision heroic because the doubt about the rightness of that standard persists.

In this essay, I want to say "yes, but" to both Miller's and Rader's accounts of the novel, and in so doing, to advance the conversation about the relation between the novel's artistic achievement and its difficulty. Indeed, I want to link those two elements even more tightly than Miller's and Rader's analyses do. If we were to accept fully Miller's view of the ultimate indeterminacy of the novel, we would have to significantly revise most of our claims for the novel's artistic achievement. Within Miller's deconstructive view the novel's achievement is not finally in its representation of Jim's struggles and Marlow's efforts to comprehend them but rather in the way literary language inevitably immerses its readers into the deconstructive element. On the other hand, if we were to accept fully Rader's view of the ultimate determinacy of the novel, we would be shortchanging the novel's difficulty, its way of using Marlow's narration to underline the way Jim's life resists definitive interpretation. In my view, Conrad's artistic achievement is interwoven with this resistance, because he succeeds in making that resistance serve a larger narrative purpose. Furthermore, that purpose is best described not simply in thematic terms such as some statement about the fixed standard of conduct, but even more importantly with reference to the affective and ethical consequences of Marlow's—and ultimately Conrad's own—telling about it. To put these points another way, I propose to investigate *Lord Jim* as Conrad's fascinating experiment with a particular kind of textual recalcitrance that I call *the stubborn*. By "the stubborn," I mean textual recalcitrance that will not yield to our efforts at interpretive mastery but that nevertheless functions intelligibly within a larger artistic design. I distinguish the stubborn from the much more common kind of textual recalcitrance that does yield to interpretation, what I call *the difficult*. I shall begin, first, by clarifying the nature of *Lord Jim*'s stubbornness by comparing it to some other examples of the phenomenon, and then by examining some key features of the novel's progression, especially ones related to Marlow's role as narrator.

I first proposed the concept of the stubborn in an essay on Toni Morrison's *Beloved* that attempted to come to terms with the multiple and ultimately incompatible identities of the title character (see chapter 9 of *Narrative as Rhetoric*, 1996). Beloved is Sethe's slain daughter reincarnated; the woman who escaped from the cabin of a white man found dead around the time of her arrival at 124 Bluestone Road; a survivor of the Middle Passage; and Sethe's murdered African mother. It is impossible to meld all these identities into the figure of a single coherent character, but Morrison makes the incoherence function as part of her narrative argument that her audience needs to counter the continuing effects of slavery in American culture.[1] A second example of the stubborn is the character of Sarah Woodruff in *The French Lieutenant's Woman*, whom John Fowles represents as both an unfortunate Victorian woman who is grateful for the love of the Victorian gentleman Charles Smithson and a forerunner of the New Woman who is far too independent to want the kind of conventional domestic happiness that Charles envisions for the two of them. Sarah's stubbornness enables Fowles to write two different endings to the novel and to have his narrator plausibly insist that the reader should not yield to the tyranny of linear order and accept the second ending, in which Sarah remains independent, as the "real" ending. The two endings, by contrast, are an instance of the difficult rather than the stubborn: each is intelligible in itself and together they yield to our efforts at interpretation. As a unit, they provide Fowles with an effective conclusion to his narrative case about the differences between the culture and fiction of 1867 and the culture and fiction of 1967.

In both these cases, the novelist builds the stubbornness into the representation of the character and leaves the reader to discover it. Conrad's use of the stubborn is different because through Marlow he makes an interpreter's unsuccessful effort to overcome the recalcitrance of a phenomenon a prominent part of the narrative. And rather than signal that this interpreter is too obtuse or otherwise deficient to grasp the situation, he uses Marlow's inability to overcome the recalcitrance of Jim's experience as a guide to our similar experience.[2] Unlike *Beloved* and *The French Lieutenant's Woman*, which do not

1. In the history of the criticism on *Beloved* most early commentators treated Beloved only as the reincarnation of Sethe's murdered daughter, but then Elizabeth House made the case that Beloved was actually the woman who had escaped from the dead white man's cabin and that Morrison therefore was working with a plot about mistaken identity. In my terms, the early critics and House were all treating Beloved as yet another instance of the difficult; over time critics have come to recognize her as an instance of the stubborn (though of course they typically don't use that term).

2. One of Jim's traits of character is of course stubbornness, and Conrad not only shows that trait in action but also has Marlow refer to Jim as "stubborn" eight times. In this way Conrad's representation of Jim's trait is very clear and, thus, from the perspective of readerly understanding, qualitatively different from the textual stubbornness surrounding the meaning and significance of Jim's life. In addition, I believe it is good interpretive practice to be cautious, if not entirely suspicious, about hanging major interpretive conclusions on connections that are made primarily on the basis of terminology. (If I'd called the textual recalcitrance I find in *Beloved*, *The French Lieutenant's Woman*, and *Lord Jim* "the intractable" rather than "the stubborn," I might not be writing this note.) With these caveats in mind, I still want to suggest that Conrad invites us to reflect on the similarities and differences between Jim's stubbornness of character and the stubborn recalcitrance of the whole novel.

foreground the stubbornness of their characters, *Lord Jim* wears its stubbornness on its sleeve. But at the same time *Lord Jim* is more than just Marlow's telling about his unsuccessful effort to master the significance of Jim's experience; it is Conrad's telling about Marlow's telling, which is itself contained within the telling of a heterodiegetic narrator, a telling that is not stubborn. I shall return to these points after a brief discussion of the framework within which they are most intelligible: the rhetorical theory of narrative and its concept of narrative progression.

A Sketch of the Rhetorical Approach to Narrative

The rhetorical approach starts with a definition of narrative as a rhetorical action: somebody telling somebody else on some occasion and for some purpose—or purposes—that something happened. In fiction this rhetorical action is at least double-layered, as the author tells her audience about the narrator telling his audience that something happened. This conception of narrative differs from most other accounts because they regard narrative as a fixed object or a product rather than an action—for example in classical narratology a synthesis of story and discourse or in cognitive narratology a mental model of relating characters and actions in time and space. The rhetorical conception is not opposed to these other models—indeed, it is indebted to many of their findings—but it places particular emphasis on tellers, audiences, and effects. More specifically, in both fiction and nonfiction, it notes that the rhetorical action of narrative generates a multilayered communication, one that involves the authorial audience's cognition, emotions, and ethical values.

`When we have a telling situation in fiction such as the one in *Lord Jim* with a clearly identified character narrator and set of narratees, then we have one text with at least two distinct audiences and at least two distinct sets of purposes: those of the narrator, on the one hand, and those of the author on the other. As I have argued in *Living to Tell about It*, character narrators, like other narrators, have three main functions: to report about facts, characters, and events in the story world; to interpret those reports; and to offer ethical evaluations of the characters and their behavior. Much of the art of character narration involves the author's ability, while restricted to the same text as the narrator, to signal his convergence with or divergence from the narrator's reports, interpretations, and evaluations. From the rhetorical perspective, the ethical dimension of the narrative is constituted by the dynamic interaction of the telling, the told, and the audience's ethical evaluations of both. That is, the ethical dimension includes the ethical quality of the characters' actions;

the ethical evaluations of those actions offered by the narrator and author; the ethical quality of the narrator's treatment of both the characters and the audience; and the ethical quality of the author's treatment of the narrator, the characters, and the audience. The final element of the ethical dimension of narrative is the way individual readers' ethical values intersect with the ethical dimensions of the telling and the told.

The rhetorical approach also postulates that the progression of a narrative, that is, the logic of its movement from beginning through middle to end, is governed by its purposes and, therefore, that a good way to determine those purposes is through an analysis of that progression. More specifically, I define progression as the synthesis of two sets of narrative dynamics. The first set is what I call *textual dynamics,* the means by which the narrative generates its internal movement through the introduction, complication, and resolution (in whole or in part) of instabilities (unstable relations among characters) and/or tensions (unstable relations among authors, narrators, and audiences as in fictions with unreliable narrators). The second set is what I call *readerly dynamics,* the developing responses of the authorial audience to the textual dynamics. These developing responses, in turn, are tied to the judgments that the audience makes, because these judgments deeply influence our cognitive, affective, and ethical experience. More generally, then, narrative progression is the synthesis of two kinds of movement and change: that which occurs in the story world and that which occurs in the audience. The practical consequences of the rhetorical approach will become clear as I turn to examine the progression of *Lord Jim.*

Marlow's Narration as Rhetorical Action

The most striking general feature of *Lord Jim* is the double quality of its progression. It combines, on the textual level, two main sequences of instability-complication-resolution: the first involving Jim as character and the second involving Marlow as narrator who seeks to come to terms with Jim's story. One of the functions of Conrad's breaking Marlow's narration in two is to emphasize Marlow's ongoing effort; having told the incomplete story "many times," Marlow feels compelled to tell the most interested listener the rest of the story, and that means, as he says, that he has had to build a complete picture from fragmentary information. This act of construction raises the possibility that Marlowe can move from the uncertainty he openly acknowledges at the end of the oral narration to some determinate interpretation and evaluation of Jim's life.

The textual dynamics of Jim's story, though marked by multiple anachronies, follow the standard pattern of instability-complication-resolution: he has dreams of heroism inspired by light holiday literature; he fails to live up to those dreams in his jump from the *Patna,* and suffers as a consequence; he is given another chance in Patusan where he succeeds for a time until Brown arrives and reminds him of his past failure; as a result, he misjudges Brown badly, which leads to the death of many Bugis natives, including Dain Waris, and for that misjudgment Jim pays with his life. The readerly dynamics associated with the progression of Jim's story, however, are much harder to specify because they are so deeply influenced by the textual dynamics of Marlow's progression, which of course ends without any clear resolution. (It is worth noting that a later modernist novelist, F. Scott Fitzgerald, works with the same kind of double progression in *The Great Gatsby,* but Fitzgerald allows—indeed, needs—Nick Carraway to succeed with his quest to come to terms with Gatsby.)

What we can say about the readerly dynamics of Jim's story at this point is akin to what Albert Guerard said long ago: Marlow's narration generates a dynamic interaction between sympathy and judgment in our responses to Jim. In addition, in responding to the textual dynamics, we cannot help but recognize the pattern of repetitions—both in the oft-noted two-part structure of the novel (divided between the *Patna* incident and the Patusan events) and in Marlow's repeated efforts to comprehend Jim. As the narrative progresses, however, the repetitions add to rather than remove the recalcitrance of Jim's experience to our full understanding, and in that way, add to the novel's ultimate stubbornness. Finally, it is also helpful to distinguish between Marlow as character and Marlow as narrator. As character, Marlow consistently aids Jim even as he conducts his own inquiry into Jim. That habit of inquiring carries over into both halves of his narration about Jim.

This outline of the progression allows me to reformulate one of my earlier points: since Conrad constructs Marlow as a figure who undertakes within the world of the novel an interpretive activity much like the one that as Conrad's audience we undertake outside that world, we must perform a double decoding. We must puzzle through Marlow's puzzling over Jim in order to reach our own decisions about the meaning and significance of Jim's story. For this reason, in what follows, I will focus much more on Marlow than on Jim, considering both Marlow's narration as a rhetorical action and his specific execution of that action.

The heterodiegetic narrator introduces Marlow's narration with two salient comments: (1) "And later on, many times, in distant parts of the world, Marlow showed himself willing to remember Jim, to remember him in detail and audibly" (24); (2) "and with the very first word uttered Marlow's body, extended at rest in the seat, would become very still, as though his spirit had winged its way back into the lapse of time and were speaking through his lips from the past" (25). Taken together, these two comments reveal not only Marlow's great interest in Jim's story (why else tell it many times in detail all around the world?) but also his effort to enter once again into the time of the action; his effort, in other words, to reimagine and even reexperience the events of Jim's life. But the larger consequences of these comments become clear only at the end of the oral narrative, when Conrad has Marlow comment on what he makes of Jim and then has the heterodiegetic narrator return to describe the immediate aftermath of Marlow's telling.

It is worth noting here that the heterodiegetic narrator's telling does not involve any stubbornness. His narration, though holding back information about "the fact" that keeps the adult Jim "a seaman in exile from the sea" (4), offers an otherwise clear view of Jim's character as flawed and limited, overly affected by his reading of light holiday literature, not able to handle the harsher demands of the sea. Strikingly, however, the heterodiegetic narrator's view does not make Conrad's audience infer that Marlow's uncertainties about Jim are a result of special pleading. Instead, because Conrad makes Marlow so earnest and scrupulous in his effort to come to terms with Jim and because Marlow narrates events that are much more complicated than those narrated by the heterodiegetic narrator, Marlow's view of Jim ultimately has more weight for Conrad's audience.

Here is Marlow at the end of his oral tale describing and reflecting on his last look at Jim: "He was white from head to foot, and remained persistently visible with the stronghold of the night at his back, the sea at his feet, the opportunity by his side—still veiled. What do you say? Was it still veiled? I don't know. For me that white figure in the stillness of coast and sea seemed to stand at the heart of a vast enigma. . . . And suddenly, I lost him. . . ." (244). In light of the heterodiegetic narrator's descriptions of Marlow as he begins the oral narrative, the two most prominent sentences here are the two are in the present tense. "What do you say?" and "I don't know." Despite Marlow's deep interest in Jim and despite Marlow's many efforts to reimagine and reexperience the events of Jim's story, he is not yet able to come to terms with Jim's life. The reference to the "still veiled" opportunity by Jim's side recalls Marlow's earlier report that as Jim first entered Patusan, "his opportunity sat veiled by his side like an Eastern bride waiting to be uncovered by the hand of the master" (177). His uncertainty about whether the opportunity is still veiled and his direct address to his audience constitute a confession that he is unable to render a clear interpretation of the meaning of Jim's success in Patusan.

Moreover, accompanying Marlow's interpretive hesitation is his inability to render a clear ethical judgment about Jim. If Jim's jump from the *Patna,* whatever the mitigating circumstances, is an ethical failure that calls into question the whole ideal of conduct upon which Marlow's life has been based, does Jim's current success constitute an appropriate atonement, however partial, for that failure? Is it enough to restore Marlow's firm belief in the ideal and that those like him are fit to live up to it? At this stage, the best Marlow can answer is "I don't know."

Furthermore, Conrad has not given his audience sufficient grounds to answer the questions any better than Marlow can. Although Conrad does not make Marlow a wholly reliable narrator—I shall shortly examine some instances of his unreliability—he does not do anything to undermine Marlow's conclusion that Jim existed at the heart of an enigma. As Marlow ends his oral narration, then, Jim is moving from being an instance of the difficult to being an instance of the stubborn.

At the same time, however, Conrad uses Marlow's direct address to his narratees as a way to highlight his audience's active engagement in trying to interpret and evaluate Jim's success in Patusan. When Marlow asks his audience, "What do you think?" we in Conrad's audience can't help but feel he is asking us the same question. In addition, with the commentary of the heterodiegetic narrator about Marlow's narratees at the beginning of chapter XXXVI Conrad extends an invitation to his audience that Marlow is unaware of and thus unable to control.

> With these words Marlow had ended his narrative, and his audience had broken up forthwith, under his abstract, pensive gaze. Men drifted off the veranda in pairs or alone without loss of time, without offering a remark, as if the last image of that incomplete story, its incompleteness itself, and the very tone of the speaker, had made discussion vain and comment impossible. Each of them seemed to carry away his own impression, to carry it away with him like a secret. (245)

Since Marlow's narratees are barely characterized, they function as figures for Conrad's readers. Consequently, the report that each has his own secret impression not only implies that many are able to decide upon interpretations and evaluations of Jim's story but also authorizes us to do the same.

That this invitation is just an extension of Marlow's "What do you think?" also reveals an important element of the ethics of the telling by both Marlow and Conrad. Marlow, despite his own conclusion that Jim stands at the heart of an enigma, remains open to the idea that his listeners can and should have other thoughts. Conrad goes further and invites us to have those other thoughts—though it is just as important that he does not yet articulate specific alternatives. At the same time, because the narrative is, as the heterodiegetic narrator says, "incomplete," any answers we might give at this stage will be provisional. Nevertheless, as Conrad breaks Marlow's narration in two here, he simultaneously calls attention to the stubborn quality of his representation of Jim and to his invitation that each of us get beyond that stubbornness by rendering our own interpretations and ethical judgments of him. Before I consider how Marlow's written narrative builds on these effects, I want to offer a broader look at where the progression stands at the end of Marlow's oral narration and to do that I need to say a little more about the concept of progression.

In some recent work (*Experiencing Fiction*), I have been trying to refine the concept of progression by proposing that beginnings, middles, and endings each have four aspects, two of which are primarily related to textual dynamics and two of which are primarily related to readerly dynamics. Here is a sketch of the overall model, though, for my purposes in this essay, what it suggests about middles and endings are most important.

BEGINNINGS

Exposition	including front matter and any other information about setting, character, and other contexts for the action
Launch	introduction of first global instability or tension
Initiation	introduction to author-narrator-audience communication
Entrance	the tacit hypothesis about the overall configuration and signification of the narrative formed at the point of launch

MIDDLES

Exposition	same as above, minus front matter
Voyage	the complication of the instabilities and tensions
Interaction	the developing relationships among author-narrator-audience
Intermediate configuration	the tacit and evolving hypothesis about the overall configuration and signification of the narrative

ENDINGS

Exposition/ Closure	same as above for exposition; closure designates signals for ending independent of the resolution of instabilities or tensions
Arrival	the resolution (which may be more or less complete, more or less open-ended) of the instabilities and tensions
Farewell	the final exchanges among author-narrator-audience
Completion	the final configuration and signification of the whole narrative

By breaking Marlow's narration in two at the point of Marlow's last meeting with Jim, Conrad marks a distinct intermediate stage in both tracks of his progression, as we can see by examining the interactions in chapters XXXIV and XXXV among Conrad, Marlow, and Conrad's audience. The key element of that interaction is the combination of authority, unreliability, and limitation that Conrad gives to Marlow. When Marlow reports that Jim has become Lord Jim and brought peace and stability to both Patusan and his own life, we take the report as fully reliable, and we recognize that the complications of Jim's progression have now reached a point of temporary stasis. At the same time, Conrad invites us to see, more clearly than Marlow does, that Jim's progression is "incomplete." When Marlow interprets Jim's situation in Patusan as evidence that he has mastered his fate, Conrad invites us to regard the interpretation as too hasty, more motivated by Marlow's desire than by the larger narrative logic. Conrad's audience cannot yet see Jim as having mastered his fate because Jim himself will only go as far as saying that he was "satisfied . . . nearly" (236) and because Jim has not yet had to confront the past whose return had always previously made him flee. Indeed, Marlow's own concluding comments show that he himself moves away from this interpretation.

Similarly, when Marlow remarks that, because Jim regards himself as "satisfied . . . ," "it did not matter who suspected him, who trusted him, who loved him, who hated him—especially as it was Cornelius who hated him" (236), Conrad's audience cannot trust Marlow's interpretation. We cannot trust it because it, too, stems from Marlow's own desire for Jim's success, because Cornelius, however defeated he currently seems, is still an enemy who comes from the world from which Jim has fled. We also cannot trust Marlow's interpretation because his formulation of it sets in the motion the operation of what I'll call—in the manner of another rhetorical theorist Peter J. Rabinowitz—the Rule of Hubris, namely, that a character's unquestioning confidence about a happy future is a sure sign that the future will not be so happy.

The other significant instability that remains in Jim's progression involves his relationship with Jewel. Although they live and work together with mutual devotion and love, and although both Jim and Marlow assure her that Jim will never leave, Jewel's fear cannot be assuaged. Conrad links this instability with the one about the possible return of Jim's past not only to make such a return more likely but also to raise the stakes of his response to it. What will be at stake now is not just his own fate but also that of the woman he loves. At this stage of intermediate configuration in the narrative, then, because of Marlow's treatment of Jim as both character and narrator, we come to share Marlow's hope and desire that he will ultimately master—and be satisfied with—his fate, even as the pattern of action and Marlow's own occasional unreliability cue us to expect that our hope and desire will not be fulfilled.

Marlow's Narration and Farewell in the Written Narrative

As *Lord Jim* makes the transition from Marlow's oral to his written narrative, Conrad introduces one specific interpretation and evaluation of Jim's life— that made by the privileged man. I will return to the details of the privileged man's view of Jim later, but for now I want to focus on Marlow's prefatory comments about his own final view of Jim.

> I affirm nothing. Perhaps you may pronounce—after you've read. There is much truth—after all—in the common expression "under a cloud." It is impossible to see him clearly—especially as it is through the eyes of others that we take our last look at him . . . ; there shall be nothing more [from him]; there shall be no message, unless such as each of us can interpret for ourselves from the language of facts that are so often more enigmatic than the craftiest arrangements of words. (246–47)

These comments constitute a startling move in the track of the progression involving Marlow's efforts to understand Jim and the audience's response to those efforts. Marlow's "I affirm nothing" significantly changes our relation to Marlow's narrative: rather than being immersed in following his efforts to understand Jim, we now know the outcome of those efforts. Consequently, our readerly interest shifts from *whether* Marlow will finally be able to come to terms with Jim to *why* he will be unable to. At the same time, Conrad uses Marlow's "perhaps you may pronounce," to reiterate his own invitation to us to reach judgments beyond Marlow's. This time, however, the invitation comes with explicit attention to the difficulty, though not the ultimate stubbornness, of the evidence: "perhaps" we may pronounce, but only if we can interpret the enigma contained within the language of facts. Marlow's concluding comments link up with these prefatory ones, but before turning to them, I want to look more closely at some differences between his oral and his written narration and what these differences reveal about why he is unable to come to terms with Jim.

In Marlow's oral narration, he is frequently featured as a character—and not just because he recounts his many interactions with Jim. When he brings in the perspectives of other characters such as Brierly, Jones, Chester, and the French Lieutenant, he typically focuses on his interactions with those characters and his responses to their opinions and ideas. This method is central to Conrad's establishing the double progression of Jim's story and to tracing Marlow's developing responses to Jim's story. In the written portion of the narrative, Conrad largely confines Marlow's role as character to his cover letter to the privileged gentleman, where he describes his visit to Stein's house and his interactions with Tamb' Itam, Jewel, the Bugis trader who took them to Stein's, and Stein himself. These descriptions both establish a tension of unequal knowledge between Marlow and Conrad's audience—we know that Jim has died but not how or why—and they emphasize the negative effects of that death on the other characters, Jewel's conviction that Jim has betrayed her, and the mystery that still surrounds Jim in the eyes of Tamb' Itam and the Bugis trader. These too are matters I will return to; for now I want to keep our attention on the way Marlow's role as character gets greatly diminished in the longer narrative he writes.

Another of Marlow's prefatory remarks is that "[m]y information was fragmentary, but I've fitted the pieces together and there is enough of them to make an intelligible picture" (249). This situation opens the door for him to continue his habits in the oral narrative, that is, narrating his interactions with the characters who gave him the fragmentary information as he also tells Jim's tale. Instead, however, he keeps the focus on Jim and Brown. When Marlow does refer to his encounter with Brown, he almost never records how he responded at the time to what Brown told him. As a result, the function of these returns to that scene are not to involve Marlow the character in the events but rather to have Brown serve as commentator on the picture that Marlow the narrator is putting together.

Here is a report that occurs early in the written narrative, shortly after Brown's arrival in Patusan, and immediately after Marlow tells the narratee that Kassim, accompanying Cornelius on a visit to Brown, has brought food for Brown and his men:

the three drew aside for a conference. Brown's men, recovering their confidence, were slapping each other on the back, and cast knowing glances at their captain while they busied themselves with preparations for cooking. (266)

This report is notable because Marlow has made it up out of whole cloth: Brown is the only possible source for this information about his men, but he has left them to confer with Kassim and Cornelius. That his drawing aside takes him out of their eyesight is suggested by Conrad's choice of the phrase "cast knowing glances at their captain" rather than, say, "exchanged knowing glances with" him. This passage indicates that, as Marlow pieces his fragmentary information together, Conrad not only continues to make him a reliable reporter but also extends his authority to matters that he does not have any sources for.[3] And in this particular case, Conrad uses Marlow's extended authority to flesh out his portrait of Brown as someone who, though currently in a bad situation, nevertheless inspires considerable confidence in his men and who is therefore more resourceful and more dangerous than anyone Jim has had to deal with in Patusan.

Marlow's remark about piecing together fragmentary information and this example of his reporting beyond what his sources have told him also underline his active work in reconstructing Jim's story. And the extent of that work is given further support by what we can infer about the interval between Marlow's meeting with Brown and his sending the written narrative to the privileged man. Marlow meets Brown "eight months" (251) after getting his initial fragments of the story from Tamb' Itam, Jewel, and the Bugis trader at Stein's, meetings that occur shortly after Jim's death. Marlow's cover letter to the privileged man comments that the final events of Jim's life occurred "in the year of grace before the last" (249), that is, not in the previous year but the one before that. Since up to two years may have passed since Jim's death, and Marlow met Brown about nine months after that death, it seems fair to conclude that it took Marlow approximately a year to compose his narrative. That is certainly time enough for him to use the new information about Jim to come to a determinate interpretation and judgment of him. Consequently, at this stage, Marlow's statement that "I affirm nothing" seems more rather than less puzzling.

3. In the Introduction to *Living to Tell about It,* I discuss this type of character narration by introducing a distinction between disclosure functions (the character narrator's role in communicating between the implied author and the authorial audience) and narrator functions (the narrator's role in communicating to the narratee) and the principle that disclosure functions trump narrator functions.

Let us turn to a passage of Marlow's narration in which he does render interpretations and evaluations. I choose one from chapter XL shortly after his report, based on Brown's testimony itself, that while waiting for Jim and negotiating with Kassim, "the lust for battle was upon him" (269).

> No doubt the natural senseless ferocity which is the basis of such a charac-
> ter was exasperated by failure, ill-luck, and the recent privations, as well as
> by the desperate position in which he found himself; but what was most
> remarkable of all was this, that while he planned treacherous alliances, had
> already settled in his own mind the fate of the white man, and intrigued
> in an overbearing, offhand manner with Kassim, one could perceive that
> what he had really desired, almost in spite of himself, was to play havoc
> with that jungle town which had defied him, to see it strewn over with
> corpses and enveloped in flames. Listening to his pitiless, panting voice I
> could imagine how he must have looked at it from the hillock, peopling it
> with images of murder and rapine. (269–70)

Marlow is interpreting Brown here because he is going beyond anything Brown told him directly. Marlow is evaluating here because those interpreta-tions are inextricably connected to his ethical assessment of both Brown's character (its natural senseless ferocity) and his desire (his imaginative peo-pling of his surroundings with "images of murder and rapine"). In a sense, this passage shows Marlow doing at the level of interpretation and evaluation what he does at the level of reporting in the previous passage: he leaps beyond the information provided by Brown to his own conclusions about what is driving Brown and about what Brown most desires. And again, although Con-rad could have used the evidence of Marlow's leap as a sign that we should not fully trust his interpretation and evaluation, Conrad does nothing in the passage to cast doubt on them and then he dramatically confirms them by Brown's later actions. In short, the interpretation and evaluation are reliable, authoritative, and significant. Indeed, I can find no instances of Marlow being an unreliable interpreter or evaluator in this section of the narrative.

But now consider another passage of Marlow's interpretation, this one occurring in chapter XLIII, after his report that most of the Bugis agreed to Jim's proposal to let Brown go free because they "believed Tuan Jim." "In this simple form of assent to his will lies the whole gist of the situation; their creed, his truth; and the testimony to that faithfulness which made him in his own eyes the equal of the impeccable men who never fall out of the ranks" (287).

Initially, Marlow's interpretation is both reliable and authoritative, as he sums up the "whole gist" of Jim's situation in Patusan; but when Marlow moves to interpret the larger significance of Jim's "faithfulness," he actually switches from interpreting to reporting, as he veers away from offering his own view of Jim's faithfulness and instead giving Jim's. Given Marlow's broad authority as reporter and as interpreter of Brown and of the motives of the Bugis members of the Council, his limitation as interpreter of Jim stands out—though the passage itself does not help us come any closer to understanding the gap between his narratorial powers with everyone else and his narratorial powers with Jim. I turn for a possible answer to the novel's ending, especially Marlow's long farewell.

Before that farewell, Marlow reliably reports Jim's arrival at the end of his progression, his following through on his promise to take "on his own head" (302) the consequences of his misjudgment of Brown. But once again, Marlow is unable to make the move from reliable reporting to determinate interpreting and evaluating.

And that's the end. He passes away under a cloud, inscrutable at heart, forgotten, unforgiven, and excessively romantic. Not in the wildest days of his boyish vision could he have seen the alluring shape of such an extraordinary success! For it may very well be that in the short moment of his last proud and unflinching glance, he had beheld the face of that opportunity which, like an Eastern bride, had come veiled to his side.

But we can see him, an obscure conqueror of fame, tearing himself out of the arms of a jealous love at the sign, at the call of his exalted egoism. He goes away from a living woman to celebrate his pitiless wedding with a shadowy ideal of conduct. Is he satisfied—quite, now, I wonder? We ought to know. He is one of us—and have I not stood up once, like an evoked ghost, to answer for his eternal constancy? Was I so very wrong after all? Now he is no more, there are days when the reality of his existence comes to me with an immense, with an overwhelming force; and yet upon my honour there are moments, too, when he passes from my eyes like a disembodied spirit amongst the passions of this earth, ready to surrender himself faithfully to the claim of his own world of shades.

Who knows? He is gone, inscrutable at heart, and the poor girl is leading a sort of soundless, inert life in Stein's house. Stein has aged greatly of late. He feels it himself, and says often that he is "preparing to leave all this; preparing to leave . . ." while he waves his hand sadly at his butterflies. (303–4)

The first effect of this farewell is to give the greatest possible emphasis to Jim's ultimate stubbornness: not only Marlow but "we" ought to know whether

Jim was satisfied, whether he was eternally constant, whether he is an ongoing immense force or just a shadowy presence who never fully emerges into light. But we don't because he remains inscrutable at heart. This emphasis on the stubbornness sheds some retrospective light on the discrepancy between Marlow's narratorial powers with regard to Brown and everyone else, on the one hand, and with regard to Jim on the other. Marlow "affirms nothing" because his own identification with Jim means that by his own code of ethics he must be as scrupulous as possible in interpreting and evaluating him. Since Jim's case raises for Marlow, as it does for Brierly and others, the question of what it means for "one of us" to act as Jim does, Marlow wants his answer to be as rigorous about and as responsible to the full evidence of Jim's life as possible. Consequently, Marlow's own commitment to an ethics of interpretation and an ethics of telling leaves him unable to overcome Jim's stubbornness.

Although Marlow cannot reach any determinate judgment, his farewell does implicitly rule out some other interpretations and evaluations, especially the one offered by the privileged man at the end of the oral narrative. Marlow writes in his cover letter,

> I remember well you would not admit that he had mastered his fate. You prophesied for him the disaster of weariness and disgust with acquired honour, with the self-appointed task, with the love sprung from pity and youth. . . . You said also . . . that "giving your life up to them" (*them* meaning all of mankind with skins brown, yellow, or black in colour) "was like selling your soul to a brute."

Marlow's farewell eliminates this response as a viable option not only because the privileged man's prophecy does not come true, but also because neither Marlow nor Conrad shares his blatant racism. Indeed, if Marlow shared that attitude, he could not entertain the possibility that in his final acts Jim achieves a satisfactory heroism. In this connection, it is worth noting that the farewell's simultaneous emphases on the textual stubbornness surrounding Jim and on the inadequacy of the privileged man's view of him also explain why Conrad does not return to the frame provided by the heterodiegetic narrator and record the privileged man's response. Such a return would diminish both effects because Marlow's uncertainty would surely allow the privileged man to maintain his basic position.

More importantly, the conclusion of Marlow's letter to the privileged man functions as a highly effective way for Conrad to complete his novel because of its affective and ethical consequences. Although Conrad does not provide any textual basis for us to convert Jim from an instance of the stubborn to an instance of the difficult, he does push us beyond Marlow's formulations because Conrad uses those formulations as one means to enhance the affective power of the ending even as they underline the narrative's ultimate stubbornness. To put this point another way, although Conrad's narrative does not allow us to settle on a final interpretation and evaluation of Jim, that very uncertainty contributes to the sense that in his death something—and someone—significant has gone out of the world, and this sense makes his death deeply moving. The uncertainty contributes to this effect because it means that we can enter into the disparate views of Jim held by all who knew him well, and, thus, can recognize the wide-ranging consequences of his death on the lives of those people. Conrad constructs Marlow's last paragraph to call attention to Jim's effects on Jewel and on Stein. It is striking that here, at the end, the emphasis is not on Jewel's anger and outrage but on what these emotions have previously covered over, her sorrow and emptiness now that Jim has gone out of her life. It is also striking that Jim has such a powerful effect on Stein, who has previously been represented as capable of rising above any situation. And above all Conrad insists that we pay attention to Jim's powerful effect on Marlow, to the way that Jim's story has turned Marlow, first, into a version of the Ancient Mariner, and then into an active and imaginative historian who, because he still remains uncertain, remains in the grip of Jim's inscrutability.

Indeed, it is in the realm of the affective that we perceive the greatest gap between Marlow's conclusions and our own, because we see both Marlow and Jim within the larger frame of Conrad's construction. For Marlow, Jim and his life are above all inscrutable; for Conrad's audience, Jim and his life are not just inscrutable but also very moving. The affective power of the ending keeps us, like Marlow, fascinated by Jim, but also, I submit, even more tempted than Marlow to solve the riddle of Jim's character. And while Conrad does use Marlow's direct address and his many rhetorical questions to invite us to keep seeking our own answers, he also trusts his audience not to settle on any determinate answer. In other words, the ethics of his own telling, an ethics he invites us to share, involve a commitment to a kind of negative capability: he unequivocally makes the case that Jim's life is worthy of Marlow's and of the authorial audience's quest for its meaning without allowing Marlow or us to complete that quest by arriving at any definitive formulation. Flesh-and-blood readers, like many of the characters in the novel, may find themselves reaching conclusions about Jim, converting his stubbornness into difficulty. Indeed, if, as Albert Guerard suggests, each of has a *Patna* incident in our lives, then we may find ourselves needing to come to some determinate judgment about Jim, and, indeed, about Marlow's inability to reach such a judgment. Nevertheless, precisely because Conrad ends by underlining Jim's stubbornness, we are likely to find that any determinate interpretive and ethical judgments that we make of Jim will be subject to revision as our own lives progress.

Attending to the affective and ethical consequences of Jim's stubbornness also sheds light on the overall completion of the progression. These consequences help us explain why the ending, despite its qualities of indeterminacy and open-endedness, remains aesthetically satisfying. The affective power points to Conrad's ability to combine the resolution of the action in Jim's strand of the progression with the lack of resolution in Marlow's narrative quest to produce an emotionally appropriate conclusion. Conrad's handling of the ethics of both Marlow's telling and his own telling enhances our ethical engagement and ethical admiration for the open-endedness. In achieving these effects, Conrad has also demonstrated how foregrounding the stubbornness of major elements of a narrative can paradoxically enhance its power.

Works Cited

Conrad, Joseph. *Lord Jim: A Tale.* Oxford: Oxford University Press, 2002.

Guerard, Albert. *Conrad the Novelist.* Cambridge, MA: Harvard University Press, 1958.

Lothe, Jakob. *Conrad's Narrative Method.* Oxford: Oxford University Press, 1989.

Miller, J. Hillis. *Fiction and Repetition: Seven English Novels.* Cambridge, MA: Harvard University Press, 1982.

Phelan, James. *Narrative as Rhetoric.* Columbus: The Ohio State University Press, 1966.

———. *Living to Tell about It: A Rhetoric and Ethics of Character Narration.* Ithaca: Cornell University Press, 2005.

———. *Experiencing Fiction: Judgments, Progression and the Rhetorical Theory of Narrative.* Columbus: The Ohio State University Press, 2007.

Rader, Ralph. "*Lord Jim* and the Formal Development of the English Novel." In *Reading Narrative: Form, Ethics, Ideology,* edited by James Phelan. Columbus: The Ohio State University Press, 1989. 220–35.

Watt, Ian. *Conrad in the Nineteenth Century.* Berkeley: University of California Press, 1979.

3

"To make you *see*"

Narration and Focalization in *Under Western Eyes*

GAIL FINCHAM

Prolegomena: Narrative Design and Historical Context

The phrase "to make you see" comes from Conrad's Preface to *The Nigger of the "Narcissus"*: "My task which I am trying to achieve is, by the power of the written word to make you hear, to make you feel—it is, before all, to make you *see!*" (Conrad 1979, 147). Jeremy Hawthorn has drawn attention to the authorial compulsion implicit in this often-quoted sentence, noting that coercive looking in *The Nigger of the "Narcissus"* is "matched by an element of coercion at the level of . . . narrative technique" (2001, 296). My essay starts with a similar yoking together of authorial/narratorial coercion and narrative design. I argue that in *Under Western Eyes* the author orchestrates the double ruse of constructing a "Western" reader and a narrator acceptable to that reader. This double ruse persuades the reader to "see" what the narrator has slowly and painfully learned to see in the daunting process of "translating" Razumov's story for a Western readership. The reader's learning to "see" anew is enabled by shifts in narrative perspective and in focalization.

Where other critics have found Conrad's creation of the language teacher narrator either inept or duplicitous,[1] I argue that the narrator's mediation is

---

1. "The schoolteacher simply will not do as a narrator," objects Edward Crankshaw. Irving

essential to the reader's understanding of this novel of ideas.[2] The language teacher presents himself as a commonsense empiricist, lacking gifts of imagination or creativity in "translating" Razumov's story based on the diary composed on the Isle Jean-Jacques Rousseau. Such faith in rationality was of course crucial to the Enlightenment. Equally important to the Enlightenment was the role of sympathy in founding ethics, as was the preoccupation with vision or lucidity in the *siècle des lumières*. I will argue that the *textual* strategies of *Under Western Eyes*—the shifts between rationality and sympathy, narration and focalization—are also *contextual* strategies, linking the novel's thematics and narrative techniques to the Enlightenment's preoccupation with the interdependence of rationality, sympathy, and lucidity. The novel may be read as demonstrating Conrad's conviction that reason without imagination is individually, socially, and politically suspect. Where Tony Tanner contends that the narrator should be seen as the mouthpiece of European complacency against Russian nightmare, I suggest that, on the contrary, he is caught in a precarious and uncomfortable mediation between the two. I shall argue that, through the circumstances under which he undertakes to tell Razumov's story, the narrator is forced into positions where his Western rationality—and the pragmatism to which he is verbally attached—is overwhelmed by a capacity for sympathetic identification with the subject of his narrative.

In the Author's Note to *Under Western Eyes*, Conrad writes: "I needed also a sympathetic friend for Miss Haldin" (2003, 282); of Razumov "[he] is treated sympathetically" (282); of the whole cast of characters bar Peter Ivanovitch, Madame de S—, and their cronies: "Nobody is exhibited as a monster here" (282). To translate that sympathy into narrative immediacy he needs a voice more human, fallible, impassioned, erring, and involved than the authorial narrators of *The Secret Agent* or *Nostromo*. The language teacher is elderly, pedantic, imaginative (although he denies this), and manipulative, torn between logophilia and logophobia, Westernizing rationality and Slavophile emotionality, between the irrational fervor of a lover and the control of a writer. Conrad requires somebody like the English language teacher, as opposed to Marlow or his authorial narrators, because he is perfectly placed to capture the Western reader's confidence: "The old teacher of languages . . . was

---

Howe similarly protests that "the narrator is not simply an awkward intrusion, he signifies a wish on Conrad's part to dissociate himself from his own imagination" (quoted in Laskowsky 1992, 170).

2. I concur with Zdzisław Najder and Henry J. Laskowsky that *Under Western Eyes* is a "novel of ideas." Najder remarks that comparing Conrad with Rousseau involves, among other things, "an exploration in the history of certain ideas" (Najder 1997, 139). Laskowsky's position is that "the drama of *Under Western Eyes* comes directly from the fact that it is most importantly a novel of ideas—an epistemological novel as well as a political one" (Laskowsky 1992, 172).

useful to me and therefore . . . must be useful to the reader both in the way of comment and by the part he plays in the development of the story" (282). This is a good example of authorial coercion. Conrad doesn't invite the reader to consider what kind of narrator might best tell this story. Rather he insists that the language teacher *must* be useful to the reader, *because he was useful to the author.* If Conrad "had never been called before to a greater effort of detachment" (281), he had never before created a narrator so adept at manipulating the reader's response. The psychic urgency of the author's situation and the narrator's control of the reader are causally related.

An obvious inspiration for *Under Western Eyes* is Jean-Jacques Rousseau, on whose island in Geneva[3] Razumov composes his diary.[4] Rousseau's concerns are echoed in the question Jeremy Hawthorn asks: "What are the respective claims of self-interest, social duty and common humanity? To whom, or to what, do we owe the first allegiance: to ourselves, to our social group or nation, or to the particular claim of another individual who, in extreme circumstances, asks for help?" (Conrad 1983, vii). Critics like Najder and Fleishman who discuss Conrad's relationship to Rousseau have concentrated on *The Social Contract,* drawing attention to significant contrasts between Rousseau's and Conrad's political philosophies. But Najder characterizes Conrad's relationship with Rousseau as an "opposition obsession" and maintains that "the ideas [Conrad] condemned left on him an indelible imprint . . . he saw radical social change, the modern nation-state, and democracy itself in characteristically Rousseauan terms"[5] (Najder 1997, 146).

3. If my argument about the rootedness of *Under Western Eyes* in the Enlightenment triad reason-sympathy-lucidity is correct, the novel is a good example of what Alan Palmer calls the "intersubjective" as opposed to the "subjective" presentation of fictional minds. Palmer is concerned to move beyond "the self-communings [that] lend themselves to the highly verbalized, self-conscious form of thought that is known as inner speech" (Palmer 2004, 9). He believes that "fictional minds [must be] seen not as private, passive flows of consciousness, but as engaged, social processes of mental action" (246). These processes, he maintains, are best revealed, in the analysis of fiction, by what he calls "thought report" as opposed to the "speech categories" which concentrate on individual consciousness. But *Under Western Eyes* is strikingly anomalous. It uses the "speech categories" to dramatize thinking, but never in purely subjective terms. The novel's "intersubjectivity" is established by its drawing on the shared intellectual and cultural context of Enlightenment thought. Conrad's use of Geneva as a social environment in *Under Western Eyes* demonstrates the "intersubjective" elements theorized by Palmer. Historical site of Western democracy but peopled by complacent citizens, home to Russian revolutionaries and other foreigners like the language teacher, it is a rich source of diverse social interaction.

4. As Peter Knox-Shaw has pointed out to me, Rousseau himself spent a lonely sojourn on the Isle Saint-Pierre in the lake of Bienne, and described this in the fifth section of his *Reveries du promeneur solitaire.*

5. It seems to me characteristic of Conrad that he anticipates the debate around representation which preoccupies us as readers today. Jacques Derrida in *Of Grammatology* builds an entire interpretation of Rousseau on his essay *On the Origin of Languages,* arguing that it proves

A characteristically Rousseauan notion foregrounded in *Under Western Eyes* is the role of compassion or sympathy in balancing rationality. This has received little critical attention, except from Lorrie Clark, who discusses the tension between compassion and skeptical detachment in Conrad's depiction of Axel Heyst in *Victory:*

> This tension between pity as an egalitarian sentiment (a form of non-judgmental compassion or fellow-feeling) and as an aristocratic aloofness from sentiment (a form of judgmental contempt) mirrors the oft-noted tension between democratic and aristocratic—or progressive and reactionary—elements in Conrad's politics. This indicates Conrad's profound awareness of the extent to which political institutions must be grounded on, and consistent with, our understanding of human nature. It also ... reveals the profundity of Conrad's understanding of modernity, and in particular, of its acknowledged father, Rousseau. It is Rousseau who defined pity as "the democratic sentiment"—who grounded his revolutionary ideal of political democracy in a "universal humanity" characterized by natural, instinctual compassion and fellow-feeling, a natural, pre-political brotherhood of "solidarity" of sentiment on the basis of which corrupt political institutions could be reformed or overthrown. (Clark 1999, 121)

The "politicization" of compassion referred to by Clark is particularly striking in Rousseau's *On the Origin of Languages,* where imagination is celebrated as the cornerstone of civil society:

> We develop social feeling only as we become enlightened. . . . How am I to imagine ills of which I have no idea? How would I suffer in seeing another suffer, if I know not what he is suffering, if I am ignorant of what he and I have in common. . . . He who imagines nothing is aware only of himself; he is isolated in the midst of mankind. (Rousseau [1852] 1966, 32)

Sympathy was also taken to be a founding ethical principle among the British Enlightenment writers and politicians Smith, Shaftesbury, and Hutcheson,[6]

Rousseau's logocentrism and his attachment to a metaphysics of presence rooted in the authentic speaking self. Paul de Man completely disagrees: "Rousseau escapes from the logocentric fallacy precisely to the extent that his language is literary" (de Man 1983, 139). Whatever Conrad found interesting in Rousseau, it was not the idea that speaking is somehow more authentic than writing (if indeed that is Rousseau's position). For Conrad speaking and writing can be equally unreliable. *Under Western Eyes* is full of phony orators and phony texts.

    6. I am once again indebted to Peter Knox-Shaw, whose *Jane Austen and the Enlightenment* (2004) makes extensive references to British thinkers of her time.

and the driving force behind a whole school of radical and "sentimental" fiction inspired only in part by Rousseau. So the narrator, as an English intellectual, *might* have encountered the notion of sympathy as a founding principle of ethics in his own culture. But it is through his telling of *Razumov's* story—that story based on a journal written on the Isle Jean-Jacques Rousseau—that he moves closer to the fusion of rationality and sympathy which the Enlightenment celebrated in its espousal of lucidity. Lucidity, with its multiple connections with light and vision, may be related to the novel's frequent (obsessive, even) references to sight, vision, and gaze, and these again return us to Rousseau. Martin Jay notes that "Jean-Jacques Rousseau['s] . . . ocular preoccupations evinced a passionate personal dimension. His search for transparency sought not merely to reveal the truth of the world, but also to make manifest his own internal truth, his own authentic self" (Jay 1989, 90). Struggling for "crystalline limpidity," Rousseau dreamed of "a new social order in which humans would be utterly open to each other's gazes, a utopia of mutually beneficial surveillance without reprobation or repression" (Jay 1989, 92). In *Under Western Eyes,* there are dozens of references to sight. I shall argue that the novel's foregrounding of the visual has a cumulative effect, heightening the reader's capacity for sympathetic identification both with the narrator and with Razumov, while simultaneously informing the reader's judgment.

Attempting to bring together Conrad's conception of the Enlightenment triad rationality-sympathy-vision with his narrative strategies in *Under Western Eyes,* my argument closely follows the novel's narrative design. In Part 1 the narrator engages the reader's sympathy for Razumov's situation by reconstructing and interpreting events in Russia which he has not witnessed. Part 2 is set in Geneva and the narrator now becomes a protagonist. I show how his sympathy for Natalia Haldin infuses his worldview. Part 3 builds toward the climax of Razumov's story as double agent, and in this section the narrator partially removes himself from the story so that Razumov's thoughts can be presented in his own words. Finally, in Part 4, the narrator reenters active authorship, though now his account is complicated by a new level of self-irony.

A feature common to all four sections makes the language teacher unlike any other Conradian narrator: narration (who speaks) and focalization (who sees)[7] are nearly always disjunct. Two of the most spectacularly visualized sequences in the novel take place in Part 1 where scenes are linked in their imbrication of the physical/visual with the psychological/cognitive. The first

---

7. I follow Shlomith Rimmon-Kenan in meaning by focalization the perceptual, emotive, cognitive, and ideological angles from which the story is told. See Rimmon-Kenan 1983, 71–85.

is an episode in which Razumov furiously beats the drunken peasant Ziemi-anitch; the second is a mock-epiphany sequence in which a transfigured Razumov "sees" the frozen wastes of Russia as a *tabula rasa* on which the Perfect Autocrat of the future will inscribe his name. These two sequences have an extraordinarily vivid quality for the reader. As well as attesting to the narrator's graphic—though always denied—powers of imagination, they stand out from the surrounding text as so exaggerated as to seem grotesque. Time is arrested.[8] These tableaux powerfully impress themselves upon the reader's consciousness, so that although it is the narrator who speaks of what he imagines a character seeing, that section of text is equally focalized by the reader. The narrator's descriptions activate in us both a perceptual response (we "see" what is depicted) and a cognitive response (we understand that Razumov's perceptions are linked to his emotional needs). Forcing the reader not only to *see* but to *understand* is a powerful aspect of the novel's focalization, and another example of authorial coercion.

The way in which the language teacher characterizes Razumov's focalization draws attention to the link between conscious choice and unconscious impulse in Razumov's momentous decision to betray Haldin. Yet the narrator has witnessed neither scene,[9] and is at pains to explain the difficulties he has in comprehending the Russian psyche. That these episodes leave an indelible impression on the reader suggests the imaginative power of the narrator's focalization, and its successful "translation" into the reader's response.

Problems in focalization are not confined to Part 1, where the narrator reconstructs a story in which he has played no part: they are conspicuous in the subsequent Geneva sections of the novel where he has become a protagonist. Here the distance between what Ford calls the informed storyteller and the naive or uninformed observer[10] is also the distance between narration and focalization; none of the perceptions recorded are being experienced for the first time. This is of course true of all retrospective protagonist narration,

8. As in the murder sequence in *The Secret Agent* where the recumbent Verloc has time to see in minute detail the shadow on the wall of Winnie's arm and hand about to descend, wielding the carving knife, but not enough time to defend himself. The reader "sees" this sequence in slow motion and graphic detail. This scene, and the focalized sequences in the Ziemianitch-beating and epiphany episodes in *Under Western Eyes*, are striking examples of the expansion of the moment—the capacity to suspend or stretch time—which Cohn sees as a powerful tool of psychonarration.

9. "Theory helps illuminate narrative texts even as elements of those texts challenge theory and lead to its extension or revision," notes James Phelan (2005, Preface, x). The language teacher as what Phelan calls a "character narrator" exemplifies this two-way process. He simultaneously enacts and problematizes the narrative processes which constitute his subjectivity. Both protagonist and observer, his focalization of what he *does not* see is as significant as what he *does* see.

10. Boris Ford, ed., Introduction and Notes. In Conrad 1985, 26.

but in *Under Western Eyes* the focalization/narration disjunction is even more complex.

As narrator and focalizer[11] the English language teacher's personality is cunningly characterized. Master of rhetoric (though he denies this), he insists on his rationalist convictions. Craving impartiality, he frequently stands revealed to the reader as vulnerable and bewildered. These contradictions conspire to endear him to the reader, who instantly recognizes his involvement in the drama he unfolds. The language teacher's congeniality is essential to the success of the narrative, the success, that is to say, of Conrad's design upon us. However much the reader is aware of factual implausibilities, (s)he must identify emotionally with the narrator's account.

Enlisting the Reader's Sympathy

Since the narrator casually remarks that the diary entries "proper" only begin after Razumov's encounter with Councillor Mikulin, on what does he base his detailed knowledge of the previous events that took place in Part 1? This opening section is Conrad's—and the narrator's—tour de force. Using the language teacher to construct, interpret and interact with Razumov's story so as to predispose the reader to suspend judgment, Conrad shifts between third person narrative modes. Hawthorn suggests that "What Conrad seems most concerned to display with regard to Razumov is the verbal nature of his thought processes, his use of words to argue with himself. In the depiction of these thought processes FID [= Free Indirect Discourse] constitutes a variation from the use of Direct Speech" (1990, 57). Equally important, however, is the mediation of a narrator ideally placed to understand and influence a Western reader.

Conrad creates transitions between what Dorrit Cohn describes as *psychonarration, narrated monologue* and *quoted monologue*.[12] These transitions

11. Jakob Lothe draws attention to the narrator's dual role for the reader: "Anticipating the predominant position of Razumov as a character by drawing attention first to his name and then to his diary, the beginning [of the novel] also hints that the language teacher is to perform a crucial function not only as a narrator in the technical sense (as teller of a story) but also as a reflective observer. His function, it is suggested at once, is not merely narrative but thematic as well" (Lothe 1989, 266).

12. I have retained Dorrit Cohn's term "narrated monologue" although FID (Free Indirect Discourse) is currently the standard term used for this narrative mode. The advantages for my argument of using this term are twofold. First, "narrated monologue" draws attention to the narrator's text *as a translation*—Cohn's "transposed thought-quotations" (1978, 105). Second, it distinctively colors the emotional register of the narration: "no matter how 'impersonal' the tone of the text that surrounds them, narrated monologues themselves tend to commit the narrator to attitudes of sympathy and irony" (117).

register the mechanisms of the rationalizing mind, moving almost imperceptibly from incontrovertible fact to highly suspect interpretation. In Cohn's definition psychonarration is "the narrator's discourse about a character's consciousness." Old-fashioned in including the perspective of the author or narrator, it is modern in dealing with the unconscious—an area over which by definition the conscious subject has no control. Quoted monologue is at the other extreme. Signaled by quotation marks, it records a speaker's own words in an imaginary conversation. The third mode of narrated monologue is somewhere "between the immediacy of quotation and the mediacy of narration" (Cohn 1978, 106). Here the language a character uses when talking to her/himself is cast into the narrator's grammatical forms.

In Part 1, strategic modulations between narrative modes occur in key passages that sometimes highlight and on other occasions conceal the tensions between the narrator and Razumov, the West and Russia. Psychonarration[13] is frequently used to establish a shared set of values with the reader. "Razumov was one of those men who, living in a period of mental and political unrest, keep an instinctive hold on normal, practical, everyday life" (8) we read. The normalizing subtext implicates both narrator and reader as though it read: "we all agree that maintaining a sense of reality is what keeps us sane."

Figural preoccupations are glimpsed but they are quickly edited. We are given Razumov's greatest ambition in narrated monologue in words he might use when talking to himself: "a celebrated professor was a somebody. Distinction would convert the label Razumov into an honoured name" (11). But the narrator swiftly intervenes with a universalizing perspective: "There was nothing strange in the student Razumov's wish for distinction. A man's real life is that accorded to him in the thoughts of other men by reason of respect or natural love" (11). The impact of these words is of course to justify individual ambition by relating it to communal values in a formulation no Western reader is likely to contest.

The next instance of narrated monologue virtually erases the distinction between facts and their interpretation: "This evening's doings could turn up against him at any time as long as this man lived and the present institutions endured" (16), the narrator remarks, evidently "translating" Razumov's own thoughts. But his next comment: "They [the present institutions] appeared to him rational and indestructible at that moment" signals, in its changed

---

13. Palmer, whose book (2004) registers the limitations of the speech category modes in narrative theory, acknowledges that Cohn considers what she calls "psychonarration" (and he calls "thought report") to be as important as the speech category modes. Drawing on Cohn, I argue that it is precisely through the *alternation* of psychonarration with the speech category modes that Conrad, through the narrator, dramatizes the shift between individual consciousness and communal responsibility that the whole novel demonstrates.

pronouns and altered tense, a shift back into what is clearly the narrator's perspective. His observation about life under autocracy as opposed to democracy makes inevitable—and somehow therefore acceptable—Razumov's political conservatism. Bridged through concepts the Western reader values—rationality and indestructibility—the narrative now moves back inside Razumov's mind. A new aesthetic register—emotionally coercive but logically suspect—is introduced: "They had a force of harmony—in contrast with the horrible discord of this man's presence" (16). This prepares the reader for the heightened rhetoric of the epiphany sequence where political betrayal is figured in pseudo-religious terms.

In the Ziemianitch beating scene the transition to narrated monologue is just as striking. Initially the episode is rendered from the outside with visual and emotional detachment: "Except for the violent movements of Razumov nothing stirred, neither the beaten man nor the spoke-like shadows on the walls. And only the sound of blows was heard. It was a weird scene" (22–23). The narrator moves swiftly to explain Razumov's feelings: "Ziemianitch's passionate surrender to sorrow and consolation had baffled him. That was the people" (23). The phrase "that was the people" again returns us to Razumov's consciousness, acting as a verbalized rationalization to himself of the hopelessness of democracy. We remain in Razumov's mind in the next sentences: "Between the two [the people and Haldin] he was done for. Between the drunkenness of the peasant incapable of action and the dream-intoxication of the idealist . . . [i]t was a sort of terrible childishness. But children had their masters" (23). In these statements, the frustration that has been building in Razumov since Haldin's fateful appearance is very clear. Yet they are infiltrated by the narrator's rationalist assumptions. He has as little sympathy for drunken peasants and dreamy visionaries as has Razumov.

Such shifts in Part 1 take place with great rapidity, sometimes within the same sentence, as in the heightened language of the epiphany sequence: "Razumov stamped his foot—and under the soft carpet of snow felt the hard ground of Russia, inanimate, cold, inert, like a sullen and tragic mother hiding her face under a winding-sheet [psychonarration]—his native soil!—his very own—without a fireside, without a heart!" [narrated monologue] (24). The switch between authorial and figural language is facilitated by the image of Mother Russia. The commentator is acutely aware of the pathos of Razumov's situation, caught as he is between Russia and Geneva; despite weeks of successful play-acting, he is quickly disarmed by the silent grief of the mother of the man he betrayed. On a first reading this passage about Russia as mother seems to move naturally from physical description to mental image. It is, in fact, carefully constructed by a narrator who knows the story of Razumov's psychological journey, and who interprets Part 1 in terms of Part 4.

The narrator shares Razumov's vision of revolutionary activity as covert and sinister, and he understands the mechanisms by which Razumov replaces emotional need with intellectual certainty. Because the Haldin episode belongs to a dark underworld which must be repressed at all costs, Razumov mounts a bullying pulpit from which he hopes to convince an imaginary audience, or perhaps himself:

> What's a man to do? What must be must be. Extraordinary things do happen. But when they have happened they are done with. . . . And the daily concerns, the familiarities of our thoughts swallow it up—and the life goes on as before with its mysterious and secret sides quite out of sight, as they should be. Life is a public thing. (40)

In this quoted monologue and elsewhere in the betrayal sequence the reader is apparently reassured, but actually swept into an emotional vortex of extremism whose logical consequences are too frightening to contemplate. I end my discussion of Part 1 by emphasizing two points. In the public realm—following the form of an imagined conversation with others—the rationalizing mind confirms its own prejudices. And in this realm, with its associations of fair play and verbal exchange based on consensus, the Western reader feels most at home.

Imaginative Seeing

Conrad's strategy in Part 1 is to elicit the reader's sympathy for Razumov and we have seen how he achieves this by filtering different third-person narrative modes through the perceptions of the narrator. In Part 2 Conrad's design upon the reader takes a different form. Here we are exposed to anomalies within the account of the language teacher, who has now become an actor in the events he is recording, and is therefore positioned to tell the story from firsthand knowledge.

Part 2 opens with the familiar pretense that the narrator's account is guided by fact rather than by imagination, moves through Razumov's query, "How can you tell the truth from lies?" and culminates in Razumov's hanging over the parapet, staring down at the water below in search—it would seem—of a Rousseauan transparency. This section can be read as exploring the psychologically fluid nature of a protagonist's focalization.

The narrator's first aberrant moment in relation to seeing takes place in Switzerland in the context of a discussion with Natalia about class conflict. She has remarked on Occidentals' failure to understand Russia. He speaks of practical forms of political liberty and objects that concord cannot be achieved through "blood and violence." Natalia rejects his rationalism as myopic: "[t]he whole world is inconceivable to the strict logic of ideas" (79). The speakers are conceptually miles apart. Despite this challenge to Natalia's ideas, the narrator is already focalizing Geneva through Russian eyes—Natalia's eyes. He sees "the Chain of Jura covered with snow, like a white wall closing the end of the street" (77). His reaction to the setting of the Haldin women's apartment is similarly empathetic. After breaking the news of Haldin's death to Natalia, he is overcome by his inability to console her: "I could get hold of nothing but . . . commonplace phrases, those futile phrases that give the measure of our impotence before each other's trials" (84). Appalled at the depressing transformation in Mrs. Haldin, the narrator now sees the Boulevard des Philosophes as "a singularly arid and dusty thoroughfare" and as "empty" (86). He has found an objective correlative[14] for his sense of the limitations of Western values. Perceiving a mismatch between himself and Natalia he remarks: "The most precise of her sayings seemed always to me to have enigmatical prolongations vanishing somewhere beyond my reach" (88).

At the Château Borel a further shift takes place—and another example of the narrator's design on the reader. The subject of the transformation is Natalia. The story is told by the narrator in a "reconstructed" section based on her account of the Château Borel—where the language teacher has never set foot. They meet in "the unattractive public promenade of the Bastions." In a distractingly interrupted narrative the reader is exposed to a reconstructed episode "founded on [Natalia's] narrative . . . not so much dramatized as might be supposed" (119). Devoted as he is to her, the narrator recognizes a momentous change in Natalia after the Château Borel and he signals this to the reader.

The authenticity of Tekla who tells the story of her own life contrasts with the decay and fraudulence experienced by Natalia at the Château Borel. The narrator chooses direct speech, though the context of reconstruction would make represented speech a logical choice. He clearly believes it is essential for Tekla to speak in her own voice. No longer silenced or instrumentalized, she opens her heart to Natalia:

> I am indebted for my salvation to an old apple-woman, who had her stall under the gateway of the house we lived in. She had a kind wrinkled face, and the most friendly voice imaginable. One day, casually, we began to talk about a child, a ragged little girl we had seen begging from men in the streets at dusk; and from one thing to another my eyes began to open

14. Bakhtin's notions of "character zones" and "speech zones" are apposite here.

gradually to the horrors from which innocent people are made to suffer in this world, only in order that governments might exist. After I once understood the crime of the upper classes, I could not go on living with my parents. (111)

The effect of these words on Natalia is now foregrounded: "And Miss Haldin seemed to see for the first time, a name and a face upon the body of that suffering people whose hard fate had been the subject of so many conversations between her and her brother in the garden of their country house" (113). These words, the narrator's reformulation of what he has been told, have a double effect. They register both the new processes of vision now opening out to Natalia, and the narrator's own recognition of the momentous implications of such insight. Tekla's experience converts Natalia's convictions into action, and it is no coincidence that by the end of the novel both Tekla and Natalia return to Russia to work amongst the most destitute of their compatriots.

By the end of Part 2, then, the narrator appears to have adopted Natalia's focalization, as Natalia has adopted Tekla's. He is now so estranged from Geneva that he feels, in Natalia's company, "like a traveller in a strange country" (125). Descriptions of Geneva and Genevans are consistently negative as he begins to see Razumov in the way she sees him. At the opening of the novel the narrator's description of Razumov stressed lack of definition: "It was as if a face modelled vigorously in wax (with some approach even to a classical correctness of type) had been held close to a fire till all sharpness of line had been lost in the softening of the material" (4). Now the portrait takes on a sharp clarity:

He had an air of intelligence and even some distinction quite above the average of the students and other inhabitants of the *Petite Russie*. His features were more decided than in the generality of Russian faces; he had a line of the jaw, a clean-shaven, sallow cheek; his nose was a ridge, and not a mere protuberance. (132)

The contrast is striking. The influence of Natalia on the narrator is profound.

Verbalizing Solipsism

Part 3 foregrounds speaking. It contains a high incidence of quoted monologue—the words Razumov uses in conversation with himself—to present the mental pressures which drive him inexorably toward confession. Trapped in words, his survival dependant on lying, Razumov's solipsistic loquacity increases as his frustration and loneliness escalate.

Razumov's speech has becomes symptomatic of unresolved conflict. Simultaneously reckless—teetering on the verge of confession—and duplicitous, it conceals as much as it reveals. Psychologically convincing as this verbal activity is, Conrad's effort to "show" rather than "tell" what is happening in Razumov's mind inevitably creates narrative tensions. As readers we know that the story is told retrospectively by a controlling narrator, but his insights as orchestrator of the story jar with our acceptance of the narrator as an involved—and frequently confused—protagonist.

So Razumov's quoted monologue "What is the meaning of all this? . . . Why has that meddlesome old Englishman blundered against me? And what is this silly tale of a crazy old woman?" (146) is less convincing to the reader than the presentation of speech in dialogues. In this section the conversations between Razumov, Peter Ivanovitch, and Sophia Antonovna are effectively orchestrated demonstrations that social language between practitioners without a common context is futile. Razumov remarks that "cartloads of words and theories" (156) could not bridge the "chasm between the past and the future" (156); to Sophia Antonovna he protests wearily "I will not be played with." The next sentence, "He had spoken such words before" (197) sounds like the narrator, but could equally be Razumov's own self-ironizing perception, since the paragraph ends by rendering his thoughts in free indirect discourse.

Ironizing dialogues convince where quoted monologue does not for two reasons. On the level of plot plausibility, it is not impossible that the narrator could have reconstructed them from Razumov's notebooks. Perhaps more importantly, they ring true psychologically, since every reader has experienced social interactions built on obliquity and half-truth. When a speaker is driven by conflicting impulses both to share and to withhold information, the narrator's comment that speech seems "given to us for the purpose of concealing our thoughts" (192) is apposite. But conversations that are simultaneously symptomatic and transgressive cannot be sustained forever. In these dialogues there are perhaps two (linked) levels of "being convincing." The first has to do with narrative plausibility ("are we convinced that these thoughts or words would have gone through the mind of the character?"). The second has to do with our acceptance of the narrator's understanding of Razumov's thought processes and emotional reactions. This might be formulated: "Is it convincing that the narrator would know enough to be able to present these thoughts in this way?" It seems to me that Conrad's design upon the reader ensures the second response. As in many other instances in the novel, we suspend disbelief in an unrealistic plot construction because we are asked to endorse the narrator's psychological qualifications to enter into the story he is telling.

Razumov's mental turmoil is cast into real and imaginary conversations through the direct speech modes of quoted monologue and dialogue. These monologues and dialogues, conveyed by the characteristically sympathetic narrator, are instigated by Razumov himself. He attempts to exorcise the demons of his own divided consciousness through constant enactments of verbal charades. Word games, however, only exacerbate his unease. The narrator speaks of the silence which Razumov, caught up in bitter word play, secretly craves: "he felt the need of perfect safety, with its freedom from direct lying, with its power of moving amongst [the revolutionaries] silent, unquestioning, listening, impenetrable" (205). At the end of Part 3 his yearning for solitude and silence has been resolved by his withdrawal to the Isle Jean-Jacques Rousseau where he writes the diary. Despite the setting's bathos this activity soothes Razumov. On the Island he has only to listen to the sound of water around him: "All the other sounds of this earth brought contamination to the solitude of a soul" (291).

The narrator's observation here indicates an understanding of, and sympathy with, Razumov's plight. But his attitude toward Razumov seems to have changed dramatically in the closing paragraph which immediately follows this. In dissonant psychonarration, and using maximal distance between authorial and figural consciousness, he comments:

> This was Mr. Razumov's feeling, the soul, of course, being his own, and the word being used not in the theological sense, but standing, as far as I can understand it, for that part of Mr. Razumov which was not his body, and more specially in danger from the fires of this earth. And it must be admitted that in Mr. Razumov's case the bitterness of solitude from which he suffered was not an altogether morbid phenomenon. (215)

The tone of sardonic pedantry is reminiscent of that of the narrator in *The Secret Agent*, even to the ponderous distinction drawn between the protagonist's body and his soul. (See the description of Verloc's return from his interview with Vladimir in *The Secret Agent*, chap. 2, p. 33.) It seems out of character with the compassionate presenter of Razumov's secret thoughts in Part 1. The most obvious explanation is that the predominance of direct speech in Part 3 demonstrates the more negative aspects of Razumov's personality. The narrator wishes to dissociate himself from this abuse of reason through compulsive and destructive wordplay.

Imagination, Bewilderment, and Self-Irony

The reasons why Razumov engages in verbal hyperactivity are made clear by the narrator in Part 4. Over and above the guilt generated by his betrayal of Haldin (already evident in Part 1), Razumov feels he has become "the helpless prey" of the Russian autocracy. Far from being able to resume a normal life now that Haldin is out of the way, he is embroiled in secrecy and pretence from which there is no escape. And he is conscious of another betrayal: "madcap Kostia" is turned from a buffoon into a thief by Razumov—an act of instrumentalization that is as callous and premeditated as the initial betrayal of Haldin was unsought.

In Part 4 Razumov moves toward the ultimate authenticity of his confession to Natalia. The narrator now resumes an authorial role, shifting back to a mode that will once again predispose the reader toward sympathy. The section begins with the reminder that "Razumov's youth had no one in the world" which the narrator insists "is but a statement of fact from a man who believes in the psychological value of facts" (216). Claims to reliability notwithstanding, the narrator takes liberties with the construction of the story just as he did in Part 1. As the authorial role partially suspended in Part 3 becomes reestablished, his capacity for sympathetic identification continues to expand, as seen in his relationship with the Haldin women and with Sophia Antonovna.

Prominent among many examples of consonant psychonarration is the narrator's insight into Mrs. Haldin's suffering: that what is for the West "mere liberalism" is for her "a heavy trial of fortitude, a matter of tears and anguish and blood" (234). To Natalia he remarks gently: "You think of the era of concord and justice" (243)—concepts attacked in Part 2 as being hopelessly utopian. He even introduces a theological register into his pleas for tolerance from the Western reader. Mikulin is not to be seen as "the Enemy of Mankind . . . holding subtly mendacious dialogues with some tempted soul" (224), nor is Sophia Antonovna to be demonized for her revolutionary views. Her "inquiring glance" is "curiously evil-less . . . I may say . . . un-devilish" (240).

Part 4 has many instances of the narrator's sympathy for Razumov, and it also retains much Conradian self-irony. When Razumov confesses to Natalia, there are three people—Razumov, Natalia, and the language teacher—present. The setting is described pictorially and dramatically, as a camera obscura and as a theater set. The narrator has become invisible; the younger protagonists are too preoccupied with each other to notice him. A "silent spectator" (253), situated outside the psychological and ideological space which constitutes the "sombre horizon," "boundary," or "prison" (253) of their discourse, he sees Razumov and Natalia as actors fully lit on stage, while he sits in the darkened auditorium. They are in the spotlight, powerful; he is passive and forgotten.

Yet the desire to stage-manage the proceedings lingers in the narrator, who wishes to direct the actors: "standing thus before each other in the glaring light, between the four bare walls, they seemed brought out from the confused immensity of the Eastern borders to be exposed cruelly to the observation of my Western eyes" (254). Marginal and insecure as he feels in a context where he has no speaking role, he still wants to be Master of Ceremonies. In the scene that follows, where the narrator is no more than an eavesdropper, by turns bewildered, frightened, and indignant, he is revealed to the reader as both vulnerable and absurd. Unable to comprehend what is unfolding before his eyes, when at last his turn comes to speak he turns the tragedy into a melodrama: "That miserable wretch has carried off your veil!" (261). In this scene, the play is allowed to unfold without rearrangement. The language teacher could so easily have assigned himself a more dignified part, rather than revealing his impotence. That he does not rearrange the telling bespeaks self-irony—an implied recognition that he is psychologically and culturally out of his depth.

Bewildered by the events that he witnesses, the narrator is back in control when it comes to interpreting the cryptic fragment that is Razumov's diary—a mere "page and a half of incoherent writing" (262). He recognizes in its halting quality Razumov's first encounter with "the novelty and the mysteriousness of that side of our emotional life to which his solitary existence had been a stranger" (262). The diary, according to the narrator, is of quite a different order from anything else Razumov has ever penned:[15] "In this queer pedantism of a man who had read, thought, lived, pen in hand, there is the sincerity of the attempt to grapple by the same means with another profounder knowledge" (262). Sincerity, then, is not to be confused with the surface eloquence that Razumov as a word-child has always been able to command. The recognition that writing can militate against profound self-knowledge highlights new levels of insight and self-irony in the narrator. Penn Szittya remarks, "the old teacher of languages shows us the possibility of human knowledge which is sophisticated enough to know some of its limitations. . . . Neither Razumov or

---

15. Jennifer Fraser relates this halting style of writing to the work of grief discussed in Derrida's *Specters of Marx*. She remarks: "Much as Razumov speaks 'with difficulty' and in 'strangled phrases' when he tries to express grief . . . Derrida sees mourning as the breakdown of language; in grieving for a friend, he anticipates that his address will 'traverse speech at the very point where words fail us'" (Fraser, 2005, 254, quoting from Jacques Derrida, *The Work of Mourning*, ed. Pascale-Anne Braut and Michael Nass [Chicago: University of Chicago Press, 2001], 200).

[*sic*] the old professor is a novelist, but together they express the novelist's (and Conrad's) double relation to his fiction: it both is and is not about himself; it is both a confession and a disguise" (Szittya 1992, 202).

Conclusion

The language teacher is simultaneously external focalizer, controlling all the temporal dimensions of the story (past, present, and future) and internal focalizer, confined like the characters to their present. In other words, he is both cognitively privileged and cognitively limited. Moving from external to internal focalization generally involves changing from "objective" to "subjective" registers. But the early sections of the novel argue a close identification with the student Razumov that is hardly objective. And though in the Geneva sections the narrator's perspective is undoubtedly subjective, the consistently negative depiction of Switzerland and the Swiss is ideologically at odds with what he says to Natalia about democracy. What he *says* and how he *sees* are thus entirely different.

In my reading, Conrad's separation of narration and focalization is a deliberate strategy. Discussing Conrad's use in this novel of Free Indirect Discourse—the sliding between authorial and figural perspectives—Jeremy Hawthorn notes: "The potentiality of FID to 'lose the narrator' is useful to Conrad; it allows the narrative of *Under Western Eyes* to flow smoothly, with the reader being reminded of its technical origin or chain of delivery only when it suits the author" (Hawthorn 1990, 58–59). But FID also conveniently allows the narrative to lose Conrad as author while drawing attention to *the authorship of the narrator.*

The authorship of the narrator is crucial in this novel which turns on the narrative convention of paralepsis. This is not a fictional *donné,* but a *choisi,* an authorial strategy that has a palpable design on the reader. We must accept the language teacher's narrative not because it is factually plausible, but because it is psychologically appealing.

What is implied in my account now needs to be spelled out: the author's concealed presence behind his narrator. The fact that the reader frequently forgets this ghostlike authorial presence attests to Conrad's skill in creating a narrator who draws us into his story as though he alone were its author. We become aware of the author in the wings only sporadically, as in the *camera obscura* sequence already discussed, in which the narrator as both *voyeur* and eavesdropper witnesses Razumov's confession to Natalia. Here a revealing tension between authorial irony and narratorial self-irony arises. Conrad has composed the scene in such a way that the narrator is given a minor role, offstage and in the dark, while Razumov and Natalia are center-stage, emblazoned in light. Although the language teacher, inspired by his love for Natalia, has increasingly moved from a rationality-dominated discourse to one infiltrated by sympathy, here his acute jealousy renders him incapable of sympathy. He cannot begin to understand what Razumov is struggling to say. At the same time, he has moved so far away from pedantic self-aggrandizement that he gives an unedited account of his own confusion. The author as controlling force behind the narrator's failed attempt at control in this scene is signaling that the equilibrium sought by the Enlightenment between rationality sympathy and lucidity is precarious, and can only be achieved erratically.

Several critics have drawn attention to doubling mechanisms in *Under Western Eyes,* pointing out that the narrator's characterization often parallels Razumov's, and that both the narrator and Razumov can be read as reflecting Conrad's own situation. These metafictional elements, in conjunction with the authorial ironies which frame the narrator's account, complicate the distinction between those sections of the text mediated by the narrator's imagination which have been the focus of this essay, and those sections which purport to be "rationally" or "factually" derived. "How can [we] tell the truth from lies?" the reader may ask, reiterating Razumov's question. The answer, I think, lies not in distinguishing different degrees of constructedness in this multiply mediated text, but in relating the trajectory of the novel's plot to Conrad's—and Rousseau's—concerns with rationality, sympathy, and lucidity. "The century of the Enlightenment . . . looked at things in the sharp clear light of the reasoning mind whose processes appear to have been closely akin to those of the seeing eye," remarks Starobinski.[16] But for Rousseau, and for Conrad, this connection between reason and lucidity is inadequate. It is the capacity for imagination that truly conduces to vision, linking the ethical to the political as it links the individual to the collective. In *Under Western Eyes* Razumov the Cartesian rationalist[17] has elevated the capacity for thought into a private religion. Lonely, reclusive, and introverted, he is "aware only himself" and therefore is initially "isolated in the midst of mankind." At the end of the novel, he has retained his intellectual independence, declaring to Natalia "I am not

---

16. Jean Starobinski quoted in Jay 1993, 85.

17. Roderick Davis comments: "There are elements of Descartes' thought in Razumov's recurring sense of his life as a dream, one haunted by apparitions and demons" (1991, 162). The Cartesian first-person view ("that one takes meaning from one's own case and then extrapolates it to others") is the reverse of what Palmer theorizes in his explorations of fictional minds' intersubjectivity. This intersubjectivity is, I believe, built on the sympathy which I have tried to demonstrate in the narrator's and Razumov's "doubly embedded" narratives.

converted." Yet he has come to recognize his connection to others: he now acknowledges that in betraying Haldin he has betrayed himself. Mirroring this move from intellectual control to imaginative identification, the initial rationalism of the narrator in *Under Western Eyes* is cumulatively eroded by the sympathy required to tell Razumov's story to Western readers.

Works Cited

Bakhtin, M. M. *The Dialogic Imagination.* Edited by Michael Holquist. Austin: University of Texas Press, 1981.

Clark, Lorrie. "Rousseau and Political Compassion in *The Nigger of the 'Narcissus.'*" *Conradiana,* 31.2 (Summer 1999): 120–30.

Cohn, Dorrit. *Transparent Minds: The Representation of Consciousness in Fiction.* Princeton, NJ: Princeton University Press, 1978.

Conrad, Joseph. *The Nigger of the "Narcissus."* Edited by Robert Kimbrough. Norton Critical Edition. New York: Norton, 1979.

———. *Under Western Eyes.* Edited by Jeremy Hawthorn. Oxford World's Classics Edition. Oxford: Oxford University Press, 1983.

———. *Under Western Eyes.* Introduction and Notes by Boris Ford. Harmondsworth: Penguin, 1985.

———. *The Secret Agent.* Edited by Bruce Harkness and S. W. Reid. Cambridge: Cambridge University Press, 1990.

———. *Under Western Eyes.* Edited by Jeremy Hawthorn. Oxford World's Classics Edition. Oxford: Oxford University Press, 2003. (All quotations from this text are taken from this edition unless otherwise indicated.)

Davis, Roderick. "Crossing the Dark Roadway: Razumov on the Boulevard des Philosophes." In *Joseph Conrad's "Under Western Eyes": Beginnings, Revisions, Final Forms,* edited by David R. Smith. Hamden, CT: Archon Books, 1991. 155–73.

de Man, Paul. *Blindness and Insight: Essays in the Rhetoric of Criticism.* London: Routledge, 1983.

Derrida, Jacques. *Of Grammatology.* Translated by Gayatri Chakravorty Spivak. Baltimore: Johns Hopkins University Press, 1976.

Fleishman, Avrom. *Conrad's Politics: Community and Anarchy in the Fiction of Joseph Conrad.* Baltimore: Johns Hopkins University Press, 1967.

Fraser, Jennifer. "'A Matter of Tears': Grieving in *Under Western Eyes.*" In *Conrad in the Twenty-first Century,* edited by Carola M. Kaplan, Peter Lancelot Mallios, and Andrea White. London: Routledge, 2005. 251–65.

Hawthorn, Jeremy. *Joseph Conrad: Narrative Technique and Ideological Commitment.* London: Edward Arnold, 1990.

———. "Power and Perspective in Joseph Conrad's Political Fiction." In *Conrad at the Millennium: Modernism, Postmodernism, Postcolonialism,* edited by Gail Fincham and Attie De Lange. Boulder: Maria Curie-Sklodowska University Press /Social Science Monographs, 2001. 275–307.

Jay, Martin. *Downcast Eyes: The Denigration of Vision in Twentieth-Century French Thought.* Berkeley: University of California Press, 1989.

Knox-Shaw, Peter. *Jane Austen and the Enlightenment.* Cambridge: Cambridge University Press, 2004.

Laskowski, Henry. "Conrad's *Under Western Eyes:* A Marxian View." In *Joseph Conrad: Critical Assessment,* vol. 3, edited by Keith Carabine. Mountfield: Helm Information, 1992. 170–84.

Lothe, Jakob. *Conrad's Narrative Method.* Oxford: Clarendon Press, 1989.

Najder, Zdzisław. *Conrad in Perspective.* Cambridge: Cambridge University Press, 1997.

Palmer, Alan. *Fictional Minds.* Lincoln: University of Nebraska Press, 2004.

Phelan, James. *Living to Tell about It: A Rhetoric and Ethics of Character Narration.* Ithaca, NY: Cornell University Press, 2005.

Rimmon-Kenan, Shlomith. *Narrative Fiction: Contemporary Poetics.* London: Methuen, 1983.

Rousseau, Jean-Jacques. *On the Origin of Languages.* 1852. Translated, and with an afterword, by John Moran and Alexander Gode. Chicago: University of Chicago Press, 1966.

Szittya, Penn R. "Meta-Fiction: The Double Narration in *Under Western Eyes.*" In *Joseph Conrad: Critical Assessments,* vol. 3, edited by Keith Carabine. Mountfield: Helm Information, 1992. 185–204.

Tanner, Tony. "Nightmare and Complacency—Razumov and the Western Eye." In *Critical Assessments,* vol. 3, edited by Keith Carabine. Mountfield: Helm Information, 1992. 137–55.

II
Sequence

4

Life Sentences

Linearity and Its Discontents in Joseph Conrad's *An Outcast of the Islands*

JEREMY HAWTHORN

In the second volume of his autobiography, Leonard Woolf describes how his wedding to the then Virginia Stephen was disrupted by her sister Vanessa:

> [O]ur wedding ceremony was provided with an element of comic relief (quite unintended) characteristic of the Stephens. In the middle of the proceedings Vanessa interrupted the Registrar, saying: "Excuse me interrupting; I have just remembered: we registered my son—he is two years old—in the name of Clement, and now we want to change his name to Quentin—can you tell me what I have to do?" There was a moment of astonished silence in the room as we all looked round sympathetically and saw the serious, slightly puzzled look on Vanessa's face. There was a pause while the Registrar stared at her with his mouth open. Then he said severely: "One thing at a time, please, Madam." (Woolf 1964, 70)

"One thing at a time" sums up the fundamental constraint imposed by convention not just on marriage ceremonies but also on narratives. However much we experience life as did Leonard Woolf—as multiplicity, interruption, and even astonished silence—our narratives must transpose this complexity into a unilinear succession of signs of some sort or another. In the quoted passage, on the level of the sjužet, we do indeed get "one thing at a time"; on the level of the fabula, however, we experience simultaneity and rupture—a rupture mirrored in the jerky syntax of Vanessa's interruption.

Our sense of an already lived life, whether it is our own life or someone else's, frequently takes the form of a narrative. While we live, unself-consciously, we seem to be swimming around in a sea of events, feelings, and thoughts. But as soon as we come to represent the progress of a life we typically choose the model of a linear progression from one point to another. The English language does not lack for metaphors to depict our sense of life as a linear and unidirectional progression from a beginning to an end: "Life's rocky road," "the story of my life," "my journey from childhood to understanding," "the final full-stop of his death." The road, the story, the journey and the sentence—all can be made to model aspects of our experience of life by representing temporal succession ("one thing after another") by means of spatial movement ("from one place to another"). Certain narratives make use of such culturally familiar parallels without exploring—or exploiting—their limitations. John Bunyan's *Pilgrim's Progress* does not draw the attention of the reader to the ways in which becoming a Christian and reaching heaven is *not* like making a journey through difficult terrain.

Modernist writers such as Virginia Woolf typically attempt to expose and foreground the contrast between living, and representing, a life. In the case of Woolf she explicitly theorizes this contrast in her essays, and in her fiction she consistently draws attention to the way in which such organizing metaphors impose an order upon experience that misrepresents its actuality. Her first published novel, *The Voyage Out* (1915), famously has no voyage back for its heroine, whose death interrupts a return that both she and Woolf's reader might have expected. For Woolf's admired predecessor Joseph Conrad, the voyage from A to B may represent a convenient metaphor for a phase of life in his earlier fiction, but its too neat misrepresentation of life's digressions, interruptions, false starts, and unexpected endings is the focus of Conrad's overt critique in his later work. Thus, whereas *The Nigger of the "Narcissus"* (1896) opens as the ship sets sail and ends soon after the completion of its voyage, *The Shadow-Line* (1917) begins with the narrator unexpectedly leaving his ship, and terminates in mid-voyage, with the narrator planning to sail further on the following day, thus presenting the reader with a mismatch between the structuring logic of the "life-as-voyage" metaphor and the more messy reality of the many lives that it maps.

However, if Conrad's early novels individually present the reader with more conventional forward-moving chronologies, taken together they display some decidedly unconventional attitudes toward temporal progression.

Conrad's "Malay trilogy"—*Almayer's Folly* (1895), *An Outcast of the Islands* (1896), and *The Rescue* (published 1919–20 but begun 1896) share common characters and the same fictional world, but their story chronology is the reverse of their publication chronology. *An Outcast of the Islands* details events that occur before those narrated in *Almayer's Folly*, while *The Rescue* details events that occur before those narrated in *An Outcast of the Islands*. If the deferral of closure is, by common consent, a standard element in modernist fiction, right from the start of his writing career Conrad seems intent on establishing that all openings, all beginnings, are provisional.

And indeed, Conrad's second published novel contains a foregrounding of the inadequacy of those conventional metaphors that invite us to see a life as a road, a journey, a sentence—or even a narrative. In *An Outcast of the Islands* it is in part by displaying the differences between certain of these varied life-metaphors—the path, the sentence, the narrative—that such foregrounding takes place. The reader of *An Outcast of the Islands* is recurrently led to expect that the life of the outcast, Peter Willems, will be presented by means of a number of well-known analogues—travel along (or away from) a path or road, the construction of a sentence, or the reading of a narrative (a "tale")—only to find that these different analogues interrogate and expose one another's limitations and shortcomings. What is more, the fact that Willems's life is compared to a tale introduces a self-referential element into the novel that forces the reader to relate the experience of his or her reading of the text of *An Outcast of the Islands* to Willems's living of his life—and also to Conrad's *writing* of the novel.

In a short article on Guy de Maupassant that Conrad wrote to introduce a selection of the Frenchman's tales translated into English by Ada Galsworthy (it is reprinted in *Notes on Life and Letters* [1904]), Conrad draws admiring attention to Maupassant's ability to resist the temptation to leave the path of unilinear narrative development. "The inherent greatness of the man consists in this, that he will let none of the fascinations that beset a writer working in loneliness turn him away from the straight path, from the vouchsafed vision of excellence. He will not be led into perdition by the seductions of sentiment, of eloquence, of humour, of pathos; of all that splendid pageant of faults that pass between the writer and his probity on the blank sheet of paper, like the glittering cortège of deadly sins before the austere anchorite in the desert air of Thebaïde" (2004, 26).

Conrad's religious terminology here may remind us that lurking in the shadows of his early fiction another related metaphor for life—that of the "book of life" written prior to one's birth—is often to be found. In all of Conrad's fiction this phrase appears only in *An Outcast of the Islands*. The first time it is used in a semisecular context. At the start of chapter 2 in Part 1 of the novel there is mention of the "old sea," "whose servants were devoted slaves and went from youth to age or to a sudden grave without needing to open the book of life, because they could look at eternity reflected on the element that gave the life and dealt the death" (Conrad [1896] 2002, 14). But in the chapter following, Willems finds things in the book of life that have been written by the Devil himself. There is, moreover, what Conrad may intend as a more specifically Islamic sense of the book that is associated with characters such as Babalatchi and Abdulla. At the start of chapter 3 in Part 2 of the novel, for example, we are told that for "upwards of forty years Abdulla had walked in the way of his Lord," and that later on "it became clear that the book of his destiny contained the programme of a wandering life" (85). But a firm sense of predestination and the fact that he "bore himself with the humility becoming a Believer, who never forgets, even for one moment of his waking life, that he is the servant of the Most High" (85–86) do not prevent "his ability, his will— strong to obstinacy—his wisdom beyond his years" from forcing his family to recognize him as its leader (85). Whereas Abdulla displays tenacity and deter- mination while walking along a road he believes to be mapped out in advance in the divinely written book of his life, Willems is convinced that he is showing initiative and independence in leaving the path of his peculiar honesty but is, actually, incapable of any form of independent, creative endeavor.

The opposition between the "straight path" and the "seductions" that lead to "perdition" that Conrad details in the essay on Maupassant is in *An Outcast of the Islands* applied not to the writer but to Willems, the epony- mous "outcast." The novel opens as follows. "When he stepped off the straight and narrow path of his peculiar honesty, it was with an inward assertion of unflinching resolve to fall back again into the monotonous but safe stride of virtue as soon as his little excursion into the wayside quagmires had produced the desired effect. It was going to be a short episode—a sentence in brackets, so to speak—in the flowing tale of his life: a thing of no moment, to be done unwillingly, yet neatly, and to be quickly forgotten" (7). These opening words present us with a complex double-metaphor that establishes links and associa- tions that persist and are amplified throughout the length of the work. Even though the "path" referred to in the novel's first sentence is that of the as-yet unnamed protagonist's "peculiar honesty" (a collocation that undercuts itself: honesty is not honesty if it is peculiar to an individual), the metaphor feeds off a long tradition of representing an individual's temporal progression through life, or his or her adherence to a code of moral behavior, as physical move- ment along a path or road—in other words a transposing of the dimension of experience-in-time to that of movement-in-space.

While the novel's opening sentence describes the protagonist's life of "peculiar honesty" in terms of the physical movement of an individual along a defined path, the sentence that follows extends this metaphor so as to associate a stepping aside from this path with the temporary abandonment of straightforward narrative progression: "It was going to be a short episode—a sentence in brackets, so to speak—in the flowing tale of his life." Here the imaginary bracketed sentence performs a function comparable to that performed within a tale by an episode, or within a single sentence by an appositional noun phrase; it betokens a break in unilinear progression. This second sentence has a curiously disorienting effect on the reader as he or she experiences the tenor of the second metaphorical association not only being evoked but also—almost—demonstrated. In this sentence the words that are enclosed by the two dashes do not technically form a bracketed sentence but an appositional noun phrase; nevertheless, they effect what the critic F. R. Leavis was wont to dub an "enacting" of the semantic force of the words. Where dashes are used to mark the insertion of such a phrase, they must, like brackets, be used in pairs. The first dash or bracket thus implies the unavoidable use of a second one, and accordingly brings with it a sense of formal inevitability. The reader associates this sense of formal inevitability with what the man who we later learn is named Willems assumes: that his life will inevitably return to its established "path" once his brief trip through the wayside quagmires has "produced the desired effect"—although it is presumably the narrator rather than Willems himself to whose ironic vision we must attribute the term "peculiar honesty."

But what Willems considers to be the "flowing tale" of his life, unlike the linear progression of the sentence's syntactical structure, is actually never resumed or brought to (for him) a satisfactory conclusion. As Willems remarks to himself toward the end of the novel: "I am a lost man" (260). The "sentence in brackets" of his dishonesty closes only with his death and he never clambers out of the wayside quagmires and back on to the path. The "episode" takes over the "tale" and, as we and he are to learn, it is a tale that is not authored by himself. According to Eric Partridge (1958) there are interesting etymological links between the words "path" and "episode." He points out that words such as episode, exodus, method, and synod all derive from the Greek *hodos,* a way, a road, hence a journey, accordingly also a way, manner, means of doing something. The etymology of "episode" thus involves the sense of "a coming in besides," although Willems's episode is more a "going off to the side."

Willems understands too late that the human control represented by either a unilinear progression governed by the geography of a path, or the syntax of a sentence, has been replaced by a solitary backwards-and-forwards drifting movement far away from the helpful markers of a preordained order. "He had a terrible vision of shadowless horizons where the blue sky and the blue sea met; of a circular and blazing emptiness where a dead tree and a dead man drifted together, endlessly, up and down, upon the brilliant undulations of the straits. No ships there. Only death. And the river led to it" (253). A dead tree in a river may be hindered or delayed, but it cannot of its own volition change its movement.

The two opening sentences of *An Outcast of the Islands,* then, introduce four different examples of unilear progression: travel along a predetermined physical route (path, road, or river); the writing or reading of a sentence; the living of a life; and the writing or reading of a narrative—"the flowing *tale* of his life" (my emphasis—and note how "flowing" brings with it the idea of a river). The inserted phrase in the novel's second sentence is thus richly suggestive, as its arresting and unsettling stylistic force provides the reader with an interruption to the straightforward linear progression that represents what Willems hopes will be like his own interruption to his linear progression along the path of his "peculiar honesty": temporary. The sentence does indeed move back from completed noun phrase to conclude its dominant syntactical pattern, but Willems finds that the sentence in brackets of his dishonesty cannot be concluded to allow a return to the desired tale of his life. The "sentence in brackets" swallows up the tale of his life.

Used as a model for the temporal progress of a human life, the act of composing a sentence draws attention to different aspects of living a life from those highlighted by the metaphor of walking along a path. The act of composing or reading a sentence, like reading a narrative, can proceed only in one direction, whereas a path can be walked along in both directions, or abandoned. Moreover, a path is there already: the traveler has choice only to the extent that he or she chooses either to follow or to abandon it—or to mark out a new one.

Writing a sentence involves a succession of determining and irreversible choices: each word that is chosen closes off some possibilities and opens up others. Instead, then, of a single path, there is a network of verbal possibilities spreading out like a family tree from every word chosen. We can usually see where a path goes, but knowing which life choices one should make is not normally so obvious. Comparing the syntactical generation of a sentence to a succession of life choices is better: each syntactical choice changes the options available for the next choice, whereas a path stays there whether one sticks to it or crashes off into the undergrowth. Furthermore, paths do peter out—a fact of which, as we shall see, other characters are more aware than is Willems. The novel contains no examples of Willems's "cutting" or "charting" a new path; when he leaves literal and metaphorical paths and encounters wayside quagmires or brambles, he is incapable of maintaining an ordered progression but instead abandons himself to their disorder. In chapter 6, Part I, Willems can leave his canoe and follow "chopped-out pathways," but when the path that he has chosen ends "abruptly in the discouragement of thorny thickets" (52), he gives up.

In *An Outcast of the Islands* the collapse of what Willems thinks of as the flowing tale of his life is reflected at the end of the novel in the collapse of syntactical order, both for himself and for the object of his desire, Aïssa. While Aïssa is begging Lingard to display mercy toward Willems in the closing pages of the novel, her speech seems to dissolve like a river flowing into uncharted sea. Willems's "sentence in brackets" has swallowed up more than the tale of his own life. "The fragments of her supplicating sentences were as if tossed on the crest of her sobs; of sobs long, rolling, and deep like the waves of the open sea under the tormenting breath of strong winds; the miserable wreckage of her passion, her thoughts, her desires rising and falling and beating, black, sinister and torn up, in the white foam at the foot of hard rocks that belong to the solid and motionless earth" (194). Instead of the unilinear sentence we have utterances dissolving into fragments that are at the mercy of the waves of her preverbal sobs, no longer under her control, and powerless in the face of hard realities that she cannot influence. Instead of the finite linear path of the sentence, with a formal structure that includes a beginning and an end, we have the repetitive and unending motion of the sea and the fragments of sentences that are tossed about on her sobs like flotsam.

Because a sentence and a narrative must both conventionally be completed, while a road may be abandoned before its end, sentences, narratives, and roads have a different metaphorical force when used to represent a single life. Conrad indeed draws ironic attention to the fact that roads can be abandoned, when he writes of Willems: "In his conviction of having made her happiness in the full satisfaction of all material wants he never doubted for a moment that she was ready to keep him company on no matter how hard and stony a road" (23). The introduction of all of these metaphors in *An Outcast of the Islands* has two important effects on the reader's experience of the text. First, the differences between them make it impossible for the reader to view any single one of them as a full and unproblematic model of what living a life is like. (If the syntax of a life is like the syntax of a sentence, then it cannot be quite the same as walking along a road.) But, second, because these different metaphors are presented in the narrative that is *An Outcast of the Islands,* and one of these metaphors is that of a tale, or narrative, the reader's experience of reading the novel is made more self-conscious, and is enriched and interrogated by other models of unilinear progression. Most important, the reader's passivity and sense of predestination ("the novel has already been written, neither I nor anyone else can change the text") is undermined by a sense of how Willems's belief in his own predestined success turns out to be confounded. In a manner that we have learned to view as typically modernist, the novel undermines the reader's security by repeatedly making it clear that the predictabilities of the conventional realist novel stand in contrast to the unpredictabilities involved in living a life.

Throughout *An Outcast of the Islands* the reader is forced to confront a binary opposition that is linked to the metaphor of travel along a road: on the one hand, predictability = safety (keeping to the straight and narrow); on the other hand, unpredictability = excitement (wandering off the beaten track). For a long while the reader comfortably assumes that the novel is underwriting the former coupling, only to discover that it opens up the possibility that the latter pairing is perhaps to be preferred. The novel's ambivalence here seems to represent an ambivalence with regard to narrative itself on the part of its author: on the one hand "straightforward and under control" and on the other hand "seduced into abandonment and life." Thus in a letter to Carlo Placci of 26 October 1911, Conrad writes: "In that involved form of narrative which so often seduces me away from the straight path what I am looking for is the effect of the *living word*. That quest fascinates me against my better judgement. And yet you who know my work with such completeness—you know that I can also do the other thing. What leads me astray is the ineradicable conviction that it is in the living word que l'on saisit le mieux la forme du rêve" (Karl and Davies 1990, 494; original emphasis). Here the word "seduces," like "seductions" in the essay on Maupassant, implies that an abandonment of unilinear narrative represents a moral failing on the part of the writer of fiction, almost as if the narratorially meandering Conrad is in some ways guilty of a lapse equivalent to that of the morally meandering Willems when he steps off the straight and narrow path of his peculiar honesty.

The most important model of unilinear progression in *An Outcast of the Islands* is that of progression along a path and road. But this metaphor is itself undercut by making it clear—and on the first page of the novel—that there are other worlds beyond the edges of the road. In this novel examples of predefined linear progression associated with the dimension of space—the road, the path, the track, the safe route up a river that is the basis of Lingard's fortune—are repetitively set against forms of physical spatiality that confront, negate, or threaten such ordered forms of progress: the virgin forest, the sea, the uncharted river; lush vegetation consisting not of a single line but of creepers, tendrils, tangled undergrowth, mazes of branches, "the wild luxuriance of riverside thickets" that make linear progression impossible. Against the hard surface of the road are contrasted surfaces that do not sustain an ordered forward progression but that trap and engulf the would-be traveler: mud, slime, swamp. Against the restraint and control symbolized by progression along a preordained path that is fixed, is set the luxuriance of the forest in which growth and change are permanent, and in which a man—and especially a white man—can become entangled or even lose himself. And if the "seductions" that threaten the writer are metaphorical, those that tempt Peter Willems are very literal and erotic.

In Willems's case the loss of self is also literal: on repeated occasions throughout the novel he observes himself as if he were witnessing another person—a stranger. Early on in the narrative, Willems shouts "hooray!" and then asks, "Who shouted hooray?" (11). After being sacked by Hudig, Willems considers his indiscretion: "He did not recognise himself there" (21). Looking back on his assault on his wife's relative, Willems thinks "It was some other man. Another man was coming back. A man without a past, without a future, yet full of pain and shame and anger" (26). After meeting Aïssa for the first time Willems experiences a rush of emotions, including that of "the flight of one's old self" (54). Lying in Aïssa's arms he sees another man: "There was something familiar about that figure. Why! Himself!" (112). Perhaps most dramatically Willems even experiences his own death as happening to another man: "His mouth was full of something salt and warm. He tried to cough; spat out. . . . Who shrieks: In the name of God, he dies!—he dies!—Who dies?—Must pick up—Night!—What? . . . Night already. . . ." (275). If the loss of a unitary self is a commonplace of modernist fiction, Conrad importantly associates this loss with the condition of being an outcast—with the abandonment of the group in terms of which a self is defined.

Given that the opening of the novel has explicitly compared progress along a path with progress along a tale or narrative, the reader must stop to consider whether his or her own moments of mental wandering in the fiction's created world after the book is laid down and the pages stop being turned are like Willems's abandonment of his peculiar honesty, or are like leaving a safe path for the seductive and luxuriant but dangerous thickets. And as we stop to think such thoughts, we realize that the very act of thinking them is itself what we are thinking about: an abandonment of forward unilinear progression for a more meandering abandonment to marginal seductions. Although a narrative may involve strict unilinear progression, reading a narrative is punctuated by bursts of extralinear exploration as the reader muses about the narrated events. This geography of the reading experience is mirrored by the geography of *An Outcast of the Islands*.

The rice clearing within which Lakamba lives is "framed on three sides by the impenetrable and tangled growth of the untouched forest, and on the fourth came down to the muddy river bank" (40), and the denial of linear progression represented by this tangled growth is symbolically reproduced in a wisp of Willems's wife's hair and then, as he is overcome by his desire for Aïssa, by his own "long, tangled hair that stuck in wisps on his perspiring forehead and straggled over his eyes" (69). (Recall Marlow's comment in *Lord Jim*: "Woe to the stragglers!"[(1900) 2002, 162].) Willems's entrapment within the uncharted and nonlinear entanglement of the forest is shared by his fellow victim Aïssa who, although she "followed as well as she could," at times feels "lost like one strayed in the thickets of tangled undergrowth of a great forest" (190).

Mikhail Bakhtin has traced the "chronotope" of the road back to *The Golden Ass* of Apuleius, noting that it is "specific, organic and deeply infused with folklore motifs" (Bakhtin 1981, 120). He further notes that "[t]he concreteness of this chronotope of the road permits *everyday life* to be realized within it. But this life is, so to speak, spread out along the edge of the road itself, and along the sideroads. The main protagonist and the major turning points of his life are to be found *outside everyday life*. He merely observes this life, meddles in it now and then as an alien force" (120–21). The key difference between Conrad's novel and the fiction with which Bakhtin is here concerned is that Conrad is writing about a reality transformed by colonialism. One of the metaphorical "roads" that Willems leaves is not just that of everyday life, but the life of the privileged European settler. Indeed, as he steps off this particular road there is a sense in which Willems steps *in to* another "everyday life"—the everyday life of the colonized. Willems becomes an "alien force" in not just one everyday life but in two: the everyday life of Europeans that he has abandoned, and the everyday life of the colonized that he has entered—but entered as an outsider. European control does not replace "native" topography: it forces the "native" to recede, but never to disappear. On either side of the European road the conquered but still fertile past waits for European victims to stray into its kingdom.

Peter J. Rabinowitz has suggested that the narratological distinction between story and discourse (in another terminology, fabula and sjužet) needs to be supplemented by a third term: *path*. Rabinowitz's "path" metaphorically represents the order in which a protagonist experiences events, as against (i) the order in which events happen (story or fabula) or (ii) the order in which a narrator presents events (discourse or sjužet) (2005, 182–83). Conrad's *An Outcast of the Islands* provides a neat illustration of the usefulness of Rabinowitz's distinction; as the first sentence of the novel tells the reader, the path of Willems's honesty is *peculiar* to him, it is not common to any community. But

Conrad's novel further suggests that the limitation of "path" as a metaphor for the narrative of a life is that it implies a looking-back perspective; it assumes that the path is complete. As Rabinowitz's article makes clear, "path" is a useful way of modeling a character's experience of events *from the perspective of an observer looking at that experience once it is completed.* Such an observer might well be, for example, a narratologist analyzing a given fictional narrative. But to the character him- or herself in the middle of the novel—just as to any one of us at any point in our lives apart from that point before an imminent and perceived death—what we see is a path behind us and waste ground ahead on and through which a path must be constructed.

One of the key things that we learn about Peter Willems at the start of *An Outcast of the Islands* is that he thinks that a road exists that will carry him forward to a happy and successful future. A few pages into the novel we follow him on his way home from a successful game of billiards, unaware of the calamity that awaits him: "He walked faster, jingling his winnings, and thinking of the white stone days that had marked the path of his existence" (10). Here each day is a milestone, pointing the way forward along the metaphorical path of the man's existence. But the form of the verb—"had marked"—has an ominous ring to it: the white markers do not spread out along the path that leads into the future. Later on in the novel Aïssa—the "native" woman with whom the man we come to know as Willems will become besotted—is portrayed watching her father's servant Babalatchi. "Aïssa looked with respect on that wise and brave man—she was accustomed to see at her father's side as long as she could remember—sitting alone and thoughtful in the silent night by the dying fire, his body motionless and his mind wandering in the land of memories, or—who knows?—perhaps groping for a road in the waste spaces of the uncertain future" (47). The final observation is an example of hypothetical focalization, and attributing it to a particular consciousness is not easy; it could be either that of Aïssa, Babalatchi, or an extradiegetic narrative consciousness associated with the novel's third-person narrator. But it bears witness to a belief that the future is not marked out by helpful white stone days: it is a succession of "waste spaces" on and through which a road has to be built, not found. Willems is later to learn what Aïssa and her father appear to know, that our futures are not mapped out for us by convenient markers. When the cunning Babalatchi tells Willems that he, Babalatchi, has the power to remove Aïssa so that Willems will have to live without her, Willems "gasped and started back like a confident wayfarer who, pursuing a path he thinks safe, should see just in time a bottomless chasm under his feet" (97). It is at such points that *An Outcast of the Islands* is at its most modernist, jolting the reader into an appreciation of the fact that if one of the comforts of reading a novel is

that of following the living of a life without having to make any hard or decisive choices, actually *living* a life is not like this. The reader knows that for him
or her, Willems's life is mapped to its conclusion not by white stone days but
by white pages. But the reader is also made to realize that from the perspective
of Willems's understanding—from his "path" in Rabinowitz's sense—this life
has to be lived through unmarked waste spaces.

One of the most striking examples of the metaphor of a path used to represent the willed, or unthinking, progression of an individual life in this novel
involves not Willems but Captain Lingard. Although the following passage
starts by generalizing its message to apply to "men," it shades almost imperceptibly into discussion of "the man of purpose," and is succeeded by a paragraph
that opens with the sentence: "Lingard had never hesitated in his life." Retrospectively, therefore, we read the paragraph not as a description of all men, but
as a description of men who, unlike Willems, have *not* stepped off the straight
and narrow path of their honesty. After all, if the description applied to all
men, how could we look over the hedges at "other human beings"?

> Consciously or unconsciously, men are proud of their firmness, steadfast-
> ness of purpose, directness of aim. They go straight towards their desire, to
> the accomplishment of virtue—sometimes of crime—in an uplifting per-
> suasion of their firmness. They walk the road of life, the road fenced in by
> their tastes, prejudices, disdains or enthusiasms, generally honest, invari-
> ably stupid, and are proud of never losing their way. If they do stop, it is
> to look for a moment over the hedges that make them safe, to look at the
> misty valleys, at the distant peaks, at cliffs and morasses, at the dark forests
> and the hazy plains where other human beings grope their days painfully
> away, stumbling over the bones of the wise, over the unburied remains of
> their predecessors who died alone, in gloom or in sunshine, half-way from
> anywhere. The man of purpose does not understand, and goes on, full of
> contempt. He never loses his way. He knows where he is going and what
> he wants. Travelling on, he achieves great length without any breadth, and
> battered, besmirched, and weary, he touches the goal at last; he grasps
> the reward of his perseverance, of his virtue, of his healthy optimism: an
> untruthful tombstone over a dark and soon forgotten grave. (152)

If the reader anticipates a positive presentation of the life of those who, unlike
Willems, do *not* lose their way, he or she is disappointed. So far as staying
between the hedges that make us safe is concerned, the final quoted sentence
suggests that we are damned if we do and damned if we don't.

In one sense this is a puzzling passage, one that seems to undercut the novel's consistent criticism of Willems for his abandonment of the path of his own peculiar honesty. It is possible that the passage represents one of those pessimistic and despairing outbursts that Conrad indulges frequently in his letters and occasionally in his fiction. Whatever the case, the puzzlement that the passage induces in the reader adds to the novel's consistent sabotaging of the reader's sense of comfortable security and thus to its modernist ability to disturb the reader's preconceptions. If the early pages of the novel lull the reader into a sense of smug superiority ("Willems is a fool, the narrator and I view his conceited dishonesty with contempt, I would never do what he does"), this passage causes us to wonder whether our conventional refusal to leave the straight and narrow may guarantee us no better life than that obtained by Willems ("Lingard and I stick to the straight and narrow while people like Willems have all the fun").

According to Milan Kundera, "since its very beginnings, the novel has tried to escape the unilinear, to open rifts in the continuous narration of a story," and he notes that although Cervantes's Don Quixote travels on a linear journey, he meets other characters who tell their own stories, thus allowing the reader to step outside the novel's linear framework (Kundera 1988, 74). Of course, although narrative digressions allow the reader to step aside from the unilinear progression of the *story* of Don Quixote's life, he or she is not able to step aside from the unilinear progression that is the *narrative* of the work of fiction *Don Quixote*. But the tension between these two sorts of unilinear progression can be aesthetically productive, not least in *An Outcast of the Islands*. In this novel we keep being reminded that while the reader of a novel must conventionally move from word to word, sentence to sentence, and chapter to chapter in sequential progression along a route that has *already* been written (it is after all *re*counted), the progressive living of a life does not involve movement along a predetermined sequence of events, but movement from choice to choice, a progression that is by no means predetermined or inevitable. As I have suggested, such a movement from choice to choice is far more like that involved in the *production* of grammatical utterances or the *writing* of a novel, where each successive choice constrains what may follow.

The reader is given a symbolic warning early on in the novel that Willems has not fully understood this difference.

> The billiard balls stood still as if listening also, under the vivid brilliance of the shaded oil lamps hung low over the cloth; while away in the shadows of the big room the Chinaman marker would lean wearily against the wall, the blank mask of his face looking pale under the mahogany marking-board; his eyelids dropped in the drowsy fatigue of late hours and in the

buzzing monotony of the unintelligible stream of words poured out by the white man. In a sudden pause of the talk the game would recommence with a sharp click and go on for a time in the flowing soft whirr and the subdued thuds as the balls rolled zig-zagging towards the inevitably successful cannon. (9)

Willems considers his own success to be as as inevitable as that of the path of the balls that he impels on their zigzag course, a devious trajectory that reflects his own confident pursuit of a detour from the "straight and narrow path." The parallel is underlined a page later: "How glorious! How good was life for those that were on the winning side! He had won the game of life; also the game of billiards" (10).

But Willems has forgotten at this point that he has stepped off the path ordained by the winning side of Europeans. And victory in games of chance is no more inevitable than is progression along what one imagines to be the path of one's existence.

A run of bad luck at cards, the failure of a small speculation undertaken on his own account, an unexpected demand for money from one or another member of the Da Souza family—and almost before he was well aware of it he was off the path of his peculiar honesty. It was such a faint and ill-defined track that it took him some time to find out how far he had strayed amongst the brambles of the dangerous wilderness he had been skirting for so many years, without any other guide than his own convenience and that doctrine of success which he had found for himself in the book of life—in those interesting chapters that the Devil has been permitted to write in it, to test the sharpness of men's eyesight and the steadfastness of their hearts. For one short, dark and solitary moment he was dismayed, but he had that courage that will not scale heights, yet will wade bravely through the mud—if there be no other road. (20)

Once again we have a bringing together of different sorts of unilinear progression: the path, the life, the book. But now the path is but a "faint and ill-defined track" that may lead into mud (or quagmires), and the book has chapters that are written not by Willems himself or by a friendly author but by the Devil. (Recall Conrad's assertion that Maupassant will not be led into "perdition" by turning away from the straight path of narrative.) If at the start of the novel Willems implicitly believes that he is destined to drop like a billiard ball into the pocket of victory, by the end of the novel "it seemed to him that he was peering into a sombre hollow, into a deep black hole full of decay and of whitened bones; into an immense and inevitable grave full of corruption where sooner or later he must, unavoidably, fall" (259). Rebecca Stott sees parallels between the fall of Willems and that of Kurtz, as the latter is observed and narrated by Marlow in *Heart of Darkness*. For Stott, Willems's progress mirrors that of Conrad's reader.

> [Willems] is led inexorably towards that "deep, black hole full of decay" into which he must inevitably fall. As Conrad's readers, this, too, is our fate: to follow the "capricious promise of the track" (the text), to move through the textual jungle (language itself) toward the deep black hole into which we and Marlow and Willems must all inevitably fall (the textual void). It is not just, then, that the prose describes the process of dissolution, but that the prose is continually dissolving and reconstituting *itself,* offering the reader glimpses of his/her destination and of a tantalising object toward which the text moves, and simultaneously dissolving that object and that centre. (Stott 1995, 133)

The argued parallel is an intriguing one; in both cases, we may note, the reader's confidence that he or she is observing a deserved fall from a safe distance is suddenly undercut by the suggestion that perhaps in some way the character who falls should be admired rather than pitied by the man who, like Marlow, only "peeped over the edge" (178). For Marlow, Kurtz's final cry "The horror! The horror!" represents "an affirmation, a moral victory" that causes Marlow to remain "loyal to Kurtz to the last, and even beyond" (179). In the earlier work, too, the reader's initial smugness about being unlike the doomed Willems is undercut by the sudden realization that this smugness ironically aligns us with, rather than distances us from, him.

Conrad's first two novels have often been dismissed as apprentice pieces that display little of the narrative originality and experimentation that are universally attributed to the works that were to follow them, starting with *The Nigger of the "Narcissus"* and *Heart of Darkness*. But *An Outcast of the Islands* is a more complex novel than such a judgment would suggest. Life-metaphors such as the sentence, the path or the river, or the narrative, all arrange and present the lived progression of a single human existence differently. A person can step off a path. It is possible to walk in either direction along a path or a road, but the current in a stream or a river (like the aging process) carries even a totally passive person in one direction (although it *is* possible to fight one's way upstream, and it is revealing that in *An Outcast of the Islands* the man who does so in a literal sense is Lingard). A narrative may contain a number of intersecting stories. If a story proceeds in stern chronological progression, a plot—especially if it is constructed by Joseph Conrad—need not. There may be a fork in a path, but written sentences and narratives cannot conventionally force a reader to choose between alternative ways forward.

Such variations between these differing forms of linear progression allow Conrad to point to unlike aspects of what I have termed "the lived progression of a single human existence." But they also allow the reader to use the actual formal structure of the narrative that he or she is reading—the novel *An Outcast of the Islands*—as an example of unilinear progression with which the unilinear progression of a life can be compared and contrasted. One of the effects of this strategy of making these patterns overt is that the reader has a sense of the ways in which living a life is both like and unlike the process of reading a book—especially with regard to issues of choice and moral responsibility. Life is *uni*linear in as much as one cannot live more than one life, and it is uni*linear* because we must go forward in time and cannot go backward. But it is not like reading a book because—for those of us who do *not* believe that the whole book of our life is written before we are born—while we are living, the "last page" has not yet been written. Indeed, as Conrad would have realized perhaps better than his readers, living a life has rather more in common with the process of writing a book than it has with the process of reading one. In Conrad's *Lord Jim*, published a few short years after *An Outcast of the Islands*, Marlow comments that "besides, the last word is not said—probably never shall be said. Are not our lives too short for that full utterance which through all our stammerings is of course our only and abiding intention?" (163). A novel has a beginning and an end, a life has a beginning and an end, but the last word *about* a person or a life is, paradoxically, never said. Moreover, in the case of *An Outcast of the Islands* the first words of the novel describe events that follow the last word of Conrad's next novel, while the last words of the novel describe events that occur prior to those with which Conrad's previously published novel begins. Here as elsewhere in his fiction we are reminded of the extent to which Conrad is what we can term an implicit narrative theorist in his fiction. And he is this, I would argue, right from the very start of his career as a novelist.

Works Cited

Bakhtin, M. M. *The Dialogic Imagination: Four Essays.* Edited by Michael Holquist, translated by Caryl Emerson and Michael Holquist. Austin: University of Texas Press, 1981.

Conrad, Joseph. *An Outcast of the Islands.* 1896. Edited by J. H. Stape and with notes by Hans van Marle. Oxford World's Classics Edition. Oxford: Oxford University Press, 2002.

———. *Heart of Darkness and Other Tales.* (*Heart of Darkness* 1899/1902.) Edited by Cedric Watts. Oxford World's Classics Edition. Oxford: Oxford University Press, 2002.

———. *Lord Jim.* 1900. Edited and with notes by Jacques Berthoud. Oxford World's Classics Edition. Oxford: Oxford University Press, 2002.

———. *Notes on Life and Letters.* 1904. Edited by J. H. Stape. Cambridge: Cambridge University Press, 2004.

Karl, Frederick R., and Laurence Davies. *The Collected Letters of Joseph Conrad. Volume 4, 1908–1911.* Cambridge: Cambridge University Press, 1990.

Kundera, Milan. *The Art of the Novel.* 1986 (French). Translated by Linda Asher. London: Faber, 1988.

Partridge, Eric. *Origins: A Short Etymological Diction of Modern English.* London: Book Club Associates, 1958.

Rabinowitz, Peter J. "They Shoot Tigers, Don't They? Path and Counterpoint in *The Long Goodbye.*" In James Phelan and Peter J Rabinowitz, eds., *A Companion to Narrative Theory.* Malden, MA, and Oxford: Blackwell, 2005. 181–91.

Stott, Rebecca. *The Fabrication of the Late-Victorian Femme Fatale: The Kiss of Death.* 1992. Houndmills: Macmillan, 1995.

Woolf, Leonard. *Beginning Again: An Autobiography of the Years 1911–1918.* London: Hogarth Press, 1964.

5

"She walked with measured steps"

Physical and Narrative Movement in *Heart of Darkness*

SUSAN JONES

It is a critical commonplace to refer to the literal and metaphorical resonances of Conrad's focus on travel throughout his fiction. The sea journeys described in *Lord Jim* or "Typhoon," the river expeditions of *Heart of Darkness* or "The End of the Tether," the shifts of location from land to sea in *Chance* initiate the psychological and epistemological journeys of these stories' protagonists. However, Conrad also draws attention to the localized movement phrases, gestures, and postures of individuals, complementing the geographical movements of the narrative with a sense of the physicality of characters' intimate actions (and nonactions) within the larger framework. Thus Jim's "leap" from the *Patna* offers a symbolic representation of the narrative's restless geographical and narratological leaps as it moves disjunctively but inexorably toward Jim's tragic demise in Patusan. Likewise, the sweeping geographical shift from Russia to Geneva in *Under Western Eyes* finds a more muted counterpart in the subtle modifications of Mrs. Haldin's posture. Seated in her armchair, gazing on the Rue des Philosophes, she registers, through her physical deterioration in Geneva, her perception of the truth of her son's death in Russia.

These examples illustrate Conrad's sensitivity to "body language," yet this feature of the fiction has often been overlooked. In this essay I shall explore this aspect of Conrad's work, using *Heart of Darkness,* his most famous exposition of the journey metaphor, as a test case.[1] Focusing on an analysis of the tale's ubiquitous attention to movement in both literal and metaphorical senses, I suggest ways in which movement and stillness, the use of active gestures and silent poses operate not just as isolated descriptive moments, but form part of a complex relationship between physical and narrative movement that contributes in significant ways to the author's predominantly skeptical mediation of the story.

In order to contextualize the narratological function of movement in *Heart of Darkness,* however, we need first to look closely at the language and structuring of the narrative to explore the ways in which physical movement occupies a constitutive role. To some extent Conrad's presentation of bodily movement in this text responds to contemporary philosophical discussions, where, for example, the body plays an important part in the aesthetics of figures such as Arthur Schopenhauer, Friedrich Nietzsche, or Stéphane Mallarmé. Reflecting in part this philosophical framework, Conrad harnessed the rhythmic and gestural properties of human action to his narrative strategy throughout the text of *Heart of Darkness,* astutely juxtaposing representations of movement and stasis in order to advance the skeptical tone of the narrative as a whole. The first section of the essay examines how he achieved this by creating a linguistic texture that privileged metaphors of movement and the human experience of embodiment, exploiting the metaphorical register to influence the narrative situation at the levels of the telling and the told throughout the tale.

The second section shows how Conrad further extended these qualities of the novella's discourse by developing structural and temporal links between movement phrases in the text, enabling his audience to recognize the relation between Marlow's literal and epistemological experience. This section calls for a reorientation of conventional readings of the novella's structure that place Marlow's meeting with Kurtz at the hollow "center" of the text.[2] Instead, I draw attention to another famous moment occurring at the "heart" of the story. Following his first encounter with the dying Kurtz at the Inner Station, Marlow describes his vision of a female figure running along the bank, her physical vitality offering a striking contrast with the emaciated body of Kurtz,

---

1. The Odyssean resonances of *Heart of Darkness* are well known. For a Dantean perspective, and a perspective on the "knitting women" as the Fates, see the article by Cleary and Thomas (1984).

2. Conrad's elliptical method in this novella has already provided narrative theorists with one of their most complex paradigms of dramatized storytelling (see, for example, Todorov 1978, 161–73; Brooks 1984, 238–63; Lothe 1989, 21–56; Hawthorn 1990, 171–202; Greaney 2002, 57–76).

which at this point has been reduced to "a voice." Rather than following exist-ing exegeses, I want to shift our perspective away from the meeting with Kurtz. I argue that Conrad's positioning of Marlow's vision of the African woman's "measured steps" (60) and atavistic gestures at the literal center of the tale constitutes the focus of a complex critique of the body and physical movement throughout the narrative.

I

The opening of *Heart of Darkness* immediately alerts us to the oppositions of movement and stasis that permeate the tale, as the frame narrator announces: "The *Nellie,* a cruising yawl, swung to her anchor without a flutter of the sails and was at rest. The flood had made, the wind was nearly calm, and being bound down the river the only thing for it was to come to and wait for the turn of the tide" (7). Conrad establishes the context of the tale as one that is not just about movement in a physical, psychological, or metaphorical sense, but one that is also constituted by movement and cessation of movement in its very syntactical and grammatical structures. In each sentence the dominant verbal tense is simple past, the dominant voice is active. Yet in each case the verb lacks the agent that typically accompanies the active voice, suggesting an unfinished or inconclusive action, only to be interrupted by the stative 'was,' which brings the rhythm of the sentence to a moment of poise or rest at the end, rather than to a definitive conclusion. An abundance of what George Lakoff and Mark Johnson term "image schema" metaphors occur here, denot-ing action strongly associated with physical experience: "swung to"; "at rest"; "the flood had made"; "being bound down the river."

Lakoff and Johnson's account of embodiment in language is useful in exploring Conrad's presentation of image schemata in this text (Lakoff and Johnson 1999, 6). They emphasize the prelinguistic experience that we meta-phorize in language in order to describe certain phenomena. Image schemata show how meaning emerges through embodiment, through our experience of certain actions, systemic processes, states within our bodies, often accom-panied by a directional preposition ("zoning out," "being laid back"). In an earlier work, Johnson uses the paradigm of "balance" to explore the way in which our cognitive processes convert prelinguistic physical experience (like learning to stand up) into metaphorical usage when we interpret "balance" in a painting:

When we look at a painting we have a complex metaphorical experience of visual weight and force. Weight is used metaphorically in the standard way—we structure and understand a domain of one kind (psychological/perceptual) in terms of structure projected from a domain of a different kind (gravitational/physical). What is unusual or unrecognized about this dimension of metaphorical activity is that it is an actual structuring operation *in our experience.* We may not consciously experience a metaphorical projection, but our experience of balance in the figure presupposes such a projection. (Johnson 1974, 80)

Such an example constitutes an individual's understanding of a phenomenon and thereby influences their acts of inference. The metaphors, or analogies, are in this case not merely convenient economies for expressing our knowledge; rather they *are* our knowledge and understanding of the particular phenomenon in question.

Conrad frequently introduced image schemata into the fiction of this period, especially when alluding to the movement of sailors on board ship, or the movement of the craft itself, whether at sea or on the river. In chapter 1 of *The Nigger of the "Narcissus",* the narrator tells us that the "carpenter had driven in the last wedge of the main-hatch battens" (3–4); in "The Lagoon," "the white man's canoe" was "advancing up stream" (27); in "The End of the Tether," "the *Sofala* would plough her way up-stream" (152). The use of image schemata is also prolific in *Heart of Darkness.* Yet in this text Conrad's method assumes an added significance insofar as these metaphors draw attention to prelinguistic physical experiences, something that Conrad seems intuitively to exploit in the larger narratological scheme of the tale, not only in its discussion of primitivism, but also in its structural relationship between the telling of the story and the told. As we read we may not initially be aware of the frequency of references to looking toward, stepping back, or giving in, as the language of both the frame narrator and Marlow implicitly metaphorizes the metaphysical or philosophical register of their narration in terms of physical action. This first paragraph establishes a narrative mood in which anticipation, reaching, forward motivation, the teleological thrust of the tale, is constantly frustrated, punctuated by moments of stillness, and of rest, or syncopated occasionally by sudden gestures and interpolations. Narrative interludes, where the representation of physical stillness "punctuates" the text, act as a guide to the reader in the manner of typographical punctuation, where the emphasis lies in the intake and exhalation of the breath during the reading process. But Conrad's frequent use of unexpected gesture, flashes of color or sound also suggests a form of "syncopation" in musical terms, where the representation of physical presence depends on an internal sense of rhythmic disruption, experienced by the reader as a visual dislocation. The juxtaposition of movement and stasis is symbolized temporally and spatially of course by the juxtaposition of the literal frame situation of the listeners on the boat and the situation of the story that Marlow recounts in narrative time, projecting his listeners back imaginatively in time and space.

Throughout the tale we are made implicitly aware of a relationship between the physical body's experience and its internalization. The familiar instance of Ian Watt's "delayed decoding" is only one example of Conrad's expression of perceptual reality, as he presents the phenomenological relationship of seeing and understanding (Watt 1979, 168–200). But Conrad's exploration of a range of physical experiences drives the metaphorical register of the text at the deepest level, contributing to his most skeptical treatment of language, paradoxically through his expression of a narrative structured in part by visions of movement and gesture. The most economic summary of the tale appears (through the use of image schemata) in terms of a choreographed moment, when Marlow confesses that he "had peeped over the edge" but stepped back from the abyss (69).

Conrad also presents the physical dimension of the tale through the rhythmic alternation of scenes of movement and stasis (syncopation in some cases, or perhaps what Genette would call "*effects* of rhythm" [1980, 88]). Movement and passage are frequently denoted throughout the text in an iterative mode suggesting repetition of an occasion, providing the prose with its rhythm, and, visually, the function of a back projection in film. For example, as Marlow describes his approach to Africa along the coast he first establishes the inexorable rhythm and ongoing inevitability of the journey with image schema metaphors. He talks of "watching a coast as it slips by," and how "we pounded along" in the boat (16). However, he signposts notable interruptions to this sense of physical continuity and flow. Using the adverbial phrase "now and then," he establishes the first in a series of habitual occasions: "Now and then a boat from the shore gave one a momentary contact with reality. It was paddled by African fellows. . . . They shouted, sang; their bodies streamed with perspiration; they had faces like grotesque masks—these chaps; but they had bone, muscle, a wild vitality, an intense energy of movement that was as natural and true as the surf along their coast" (17).

There is a striking ambiguity in the syntactical presentation of this scene. Marlow's account on one level appears to move from the iterative "now and then" to the singulative, "it was." But is it one boat that is glimpsed now and then, or is there a succession of similar boats, glimpsed one after another? The move to "it was" seems to involve the use of Genette's "pseudo-iterative," where, as Genette observed, "the "richness and precision of detail" of the description of each occasion in the series require a "willing suspension of disbelief" since "no reader can seriously believe they occur and reoccur in that manner, several times, without any variation" (Genette 1980, 121). By imbuing his use of the iterative, the series, with the quality of the singulative occasion, Marlow reinforces the physical description of the Africans. The temporal marker punctuates the scene of the "civilized" Marlow's passive observation on the boat with a vision of intense energy in the primitivism of the natives' movement. But by inserting the temporal ambiguity into the account, Conrad also extends the reader's awareness of Marlow's current position in the retelling of the tale. Conrad creates an interesting juxtaposition between Marlow's self-consciousness of his own faltering subject position (*his* is the place of unreality, not the paddle boat's), and the authenticity, "natural and true," of the natives' subjectivity. The force of Marlow's evocation of the natives' movement, within the told, implies that, yes, Marlow may have been partly aware of this distinction at the time, but that, now, sitting in the boat recounting the tale, the full impact of the physical "otherness" of the Africans, gathering force in the "singulative" expression of their action, has awakened in him, in the telling, his skepticism about the European subject.

The same effect occurs on another occasion, when the ongoing journey is characterized through the metaphorization of human experience: "the reaches opened up before us and closed behind, as if the forest had stepped leisurely across the water" (37). The adverb "suddenly" interrupts the teleological movement of the narrative: "But suddenly as we struggled round a bend there would be a glimpse of rush walls, of peaked grass-roofs, a burst of yells, a whirl of African limbs, a mass of hands clapping, of feet stamping, of bodies swaying, of eyes rolling under the droop of heavy and motionless foliage" (37). Again we are made aware of the immediacy of Marlow's experience, the force of the singulative "there would be" creating the effect of an unforgettable break in the movement of the journey. The use of the "pseudo-iterative" reinforces Marlow's recollections with the physical charge of each occasion, while simultaneously strengthening the sense of the effect on him of accumulated experience, which he expresses skeptically in the telling, with the benefit of temporal distance from the event.

Conrad uses these interludes to establish Marlow's particular ideological tone, mediating the seaman's experiences as a continuum of movement punctuated by discordant moments, startling visual interruptions or hiatuses where he is brought into contact with activities whose teleology bears no apparent relation to his own, yet whose impact on his own psychological journey is profound. Thus Conrad cultivates Marlow's sense of alienation and strangeness, at the same time questioning a Darwinian perspective of the Africans as he moves from an apprehension of their alterity toward his perception of sharing with them a common humanity. Marlow's empathy with the Africans arises not necessarily from dialogue with them, but through his observation of their movement: "The steamer toiled along slowly on the edge of a black and incomprehensible frenzy . . . this suspicion of their not being inhuman. It would come slowly to one. They howled and leaped and spun and made horrid faces, but what thrilled you was just the thought of their humanity—like yours—the thought of your remote kinship with this wild and passionate uproar" (37–38).

Yet again the use of the "pseudo-iterative," in conjunction with the experience of human embodiment suggested by the image schema metaphor, "The steamer toiled along," brings into play Marlow's sense of cultural shock contained in the seemingly singulative "They howled and leaped and spun." We could also argue that in his linguistic emphasis on "primitive" action and on human embodiment, Conrad's literary style here responds in part to contemporary anthropological and philosophical contexts, especially in Nietzsche's identification of the Dionysian in *The Birth of Tragedy* (1872), where Nietzsche associates the will of the unconscious, the life force, with the origins of tragedy in the Dionysian dithyramb—the hymn to the gods which constantly draws the individual back into the communal body of the chorus. Nietzsche gestures to the realm of the aesthetic when he associates the Dionysian force with "a symbolism of the body" ([1872] 2000, 26). Conrad's novella presents several examples of the Dionysian frenzy as Marlow talks of the Africans as "streams of human beings" (59); "the crowd of savages"; "that wedged mass of bodies" (66). Reflecting the communal impulse of the Dionysian, Marlow also expresses a pervasive turn-of-the-century anxiety generated by the Nietzschean vision of an energetic and unruly crowd: "all that wild mob took up the shout in a roaring chorus of articulated, rapid, breathless utterance" (66).[3]

On the other hand, Conrad's allusions to Schopenhauerian philosophy in this text tell us more about Marlow's skeptical position as narrator, which we apprehend both in the syntactical ambiguity of the retelling in the above examples and in the narrative frame, where Marlow sits on the boat recounting his story. Conrad is alert, throughout the text, to Schopenhauer's dominant idea of the will and critics have frequently alluded to echoes of *The World as Will and Representation* in Conrad's work.[4] Schopenhauer claims that as willing

---

3. See Carey's discussion of this phenomenon.

4. Schopenhauer's ideas became widely known in Europe from the 1850s onward (he published volume 1 of *Die Welt als Wille und Vorstellung* in 1818 and volume 2 in 1844). In his biography of Conrad, Frederick Karl frequently cites Schopenhauer as an important influence on the author, using Galsworthy's claim that Conrad read Schopenhauer with sympathy (1979, 362).

beings our nature leads us to suffering through insatiable desire, an argument strikingly illustrated in *Heart of Darkness* by Kurtz's corruption. Drawing on Buddhist and Hindu philosophy, Schopenhauer finds salvation from the cycle of 'willing' or desire in the denial of the will.[5] We may be reminded here that Marlow sits on the boat at the mouth of the Thames at the beginning of *Heart of Darkness* like "a Buddha preaching in European clothes and without a lotus-flower" (10). Conrad's gesturing to Schopenhauerian philosophy in the narrative situation is tinged with his characteristic skepticism, suggesting that Marlow's experiences have not gained him complete enlightenment. At the same time, Marlow has shown the restraint of the Schopenhauerian, someone who has suffered the knowledge of human desires but exhibited self-denial, stepping back from the abyss and confessing his tale.

But Schopenhauer also associates the action of the body with the will: "Every true act of his will is also at once and without exception a movement of his body" (2:130). Here Schopenhauer creates a problem, since the will constitutes desire and bodily needs leading to misery. He claims that you need to be in touch with the will but not to give in to it in order to reach a point of restraint, escaping the cycle of misery and desire. Schopenhauer's key to the will is provided by action, but our inner *awareness* of our own will manifesting itself in the body supposedly points us toward what exists beyond the realm of representations altogether. Thus he privileges the aesthetic, placing the creative artist, in relation to the aesthetic experience, in a state of will-lessness.

In some respects Conrad makes Marlow, in the telling of his tale, respond to Schopenhauer's account of the aesthetic. There is an increasing tension in Marlow's embrace, and simultaneous mistrust, of the physical body, in his representation of an originating will that is both "savage and superb" (60). The frenzied movement of the natives also fits with the Schopenhauerian association of perception with *intuition,* distinct from the *conceptual,* in the continuation of a Western philosophical emphasis on the mind/body split.

Conrad may have been familiar with *The World as Will and Representation* through the work of Eduard Brunetière, editor of the *Revue des Deux Mondes* and author of *Essais sur la littérature contemporaine* (1892). See also Pecora 1985.

5. See Schopenhauer 1969, 1:9, where he alludes to the Hindu veil of Maya. Marlow follows this theme when he observes, "as though a veil had been removed from my eyes, I made out deep in the tangled gloom, naked breasts, arms, legs, glaring eyes" (46). Schopenhauer's exploration of the dichotomy of subject and object in Book 1 is relevant to this discussion. He claims that the subject of experience can never be an object of experience. It is not identical with the person (since persons are constituted in part bodily, and bodies are objects of experience), nor is it identical with any part of the spatiotemporal, empirical world. From an objective standpoint there is only matter in time and space (this is true of oneself considered from an objective standpoint). Rather, partly borrowing from eastern philosophies, he offers a form of transcendentalism where "each of us finds himself as this subject" (1:5).

Schopenhauer's conflation of the will and the action of the body in a punctual moment is teased out throughout Marlow's narrative as he repeatedly emphasizes the immediacy of expression through the action of the body,[6] the naturalism of the physical movement of the natives given greater emphasis in the text through his use of the "pseudo-iterative." However, Conrad's text expresses ambivalence about the split between the intuitive body and the rational mind. Marlow speaks of the natives' actions as "an intense energy of movement that was as natural and true as the surf along the coast" (17), but he has nevertheless aestheticized their actions, both in the sense of positioning himself as voyeur in the told and in his aestheticizing practices in the telling. Moreover, Marlow admires Kurtz. His treatment of Kurtz's corruption is ambiguous, protecting the reputation of the remarkable man who lived in the discursive realm of concepts. Not only does he lie to the Intended on the topic of Kurtz's dying words (75), he excises from Kurtz's report on the "Suppression of Savage Customs" (70) the dead man's revealing postscript: "Exterminate all the brutes!" (51). In presenting Marlow's disillusionment, Conrad exploits in the relationship between his situation in the narrative frame and in the inner story a tension between Schopenhauer's theory of the will and his aesthetics, offering in Marlow's position a more skeptical relationship between aesthetics and ethics.

Most importantly for this discussion, the narrative situation is constructed in such a way that the skeptical relationship between aesthetics and ethics arises out of the very relationship of the telling and the told. Moreover, this latter relationship is constituted by a juxtaposition of movement and stasis that draws attention to Conrad's skeptical strategies throughout the tale. Marlow's retelling of the movements of the journey and of the natives' atavistic "frenzy" can be read against the image of his physical passivity, seated in the boat in the mouth of the Thames. But we also perceive Marlow's growing disillusionment, his distancing of himself from European values in his use of a language of physical experience, and the ambiguous interweaving of iterative and singulative expression to tell the tale. In short, Marlow's narrative style itself relies on syncopated rhythms of movement and stasis. Conrad's skeptical framework arises in part from a doubling effect of the physical oppositions of momentum and stillness in the narrative situation. Marlow's assertion of his physical presence, and his experience of physicality in the face of a breakdown of language (his narrative trails into a series of inconclusive dots), is repeated in the realms of both the telling and the told.

---

6. This resembles Isadora Duncan's theory of movement. As Mark Franko has observed, from Duncan's perspective there is no expressional *product* emanating from her body. Hers was a dance of feeling as embodied sensation, not of expressive reaction to sensation (1995, 1–17).

II

Against an ongoing rhythm of passage accompanying Marlow's slow perceptual dawning, Conrad posits a series of sudden interruptions, freeze-frame images, gestures that catch the reader by surprise. I now turn to one of the most evocative of these interruptions to show how Conrad uses the temporal and structural links between movement phrases to aid the readers' understanding of Marlow's experience. Shortly after his meeting with Kurtz, Marlow describes his vision of an African woman:

> . . . And from right to left along the lighted shore moved a wild and gorgeous apparition of a woman.
>
> She walked with measured steps, draped in striped and fringed cloths, treading the earth proudly, with a slight jingle and flash of barbarous ornaments. . . . She carried her head high, her hair was done in the shape of a helmet. . . . She was savage and superb, wild-eyed and magnificent. . . .
>
> She came abreast of the steamer, stood still and faced us. . . . She looked at us all as if her life had depended upon the unswerving steadiness of her glance. Suddenly she opened her bared arms and threw them up rigid above her head, as though in an uncontrollable desire to touch the sky. . . .
>
> She turned away slowly, walked on. . . . Once only her eyes gleamed back at us in the dusk of the thickets before she disappeared. . . . (60; the ellipses are mine)

Marlow's voyeuristic and erotically charged account of the African woman foregrounds her lavish attire, her physical prowess and atavistic responses, her embodiment of emotion in wild physical gestures, and the challenging return of her unnerving gaze. As with his descriptions of the Africans elsewhere in the text, Marlow reflects a contemporary aesthetics of movement that privileged the intuitive and the physically expressive. We could argue that the sudden upward thrust of the African woman's arms draws attention to the power and economy of gesture in Mallarmé's sense of the female dancer moving "with miraculous lunges and abbreviations" (62)[7] or that his admiration for her atavism offers a response to tensions arising in Schopenhauer's negative association of the will with the body or to Nietzsche's privileging of the Dionysian.

In fact, many diverse sources may be cited for the description of the African

---

7. See Mallarmé's description of the female dancer: "with miraculous lunges and abbreviations, writing with her body, she *suggests* things which the written work could express only in several paragraphs of dialogue or descriptive prose" ([1886] 1956, 62).

woman, including anthropological texts like Richard Burton's mid-nineteenth-century presentation of Amazonian dancers in West Africa.[8] Conrad's African woman reflects the atavistic energy of Burton's description in her rhythmic progress and bold gestures, and her 'helmet' of hair suggests the military prowess of the Amazons. But the undifferentiated primitivism of Conrad's description is hardly a distinctive anthropological account, attending, as Burton does, to the historicity and individuality of particular African dance traditions (Burton 1864, 47–48). Conrad's account is closer to the generalized presentation of Rousseau's "noble savage," or fictional accounts of exoticism, such as Flaubert's *Salammbô* (1862), Wilde's *Salomé* (1891), and various evocations of popular music-hall orientalism.[9] Moreover, for many feminist and postcolonial critics, Conrad's account intersects with an enduring rhetoric of exclusion depending for its success on the performative nature of the representation.[10]

However, if we momentarily set aside the negative implications of Conrad's representation of race and gender, I suggest that one important narratological function of the figure of the African woman has been overlooked in theoretical accounts of this tale's structure. This extraordinary moment is often referred to as "the image of the African woman" (presumed to be Kurtz's mistress). Yet by focusing on the notion of "image" and assuming a punctual, photographic framing of the body, we lose the significance of what Marlow in fact represents as a far more sustained movement phrase. The African woman strides along the bank; stops; changes direction and faces the men on the boat; thrusts her arms skyward; continues in her original trajectory; looks back. The even rhythm of her "measured steps" is syncopated by a wild upward gesture.

The operatic movement simultaneously fractures the reading process. Interrupting the narrative flow, it nevertheless synchronizes the actual time of story with reading time. Yet paradoxically the effect is to dehistoricize the textual moment. This atemporal effect accounts partly for the ease with which we may critique Conrad's method, as he solidifies the image of the African woman into a recognizable stereotype (Gilman 1985, 15–35).[11] Conventionalizing her

8. In *A Mission to Gelele* (1864) Burton describes how the female dancers of Dahome (now Bénin) "stamped, wriggled, kicked the dust with one foot, sang, shuffled and wrung their hands," the whole dance "ending in a *prestissimo* and very violent movement of the shoulders, hips, and loins" (10).

9. For Conrad's perception of music-hall exoticism see Karl 1979 (between 412 and 413), where he reproduces Conrad's pen-and-ink drawings "Woman with a Serpent" (1892–94) and "The Three Ballet Dancers" (1896).

10. For the early postcolonial discussion, see Achebe 1988, 1–13, based on a lecture of 1975, and also Watts's (1983) response. On the African woman, see Torgovnik 1990, 145–58; Mongia 1993, 135–50; Smith 1996, 16–84; Stone and Afzal-Khan 1997; Ogede 1999, 127–38.

11. The stereoype of the African woman occurs across a range of texts into the twentieth century, from Richard Burton's (quoted above) to David Garnett's novel, *The Sailor's Return*

subject position, Conrad nevertheless makes a political point in relation to an earlier episode. For the African woman's movement is in fact anticipated by another famous "image," in Marlow's apprehension of the chain gang:

> A slight clinking behind me made me turn my head. Six African men advanced in a file toiling up the path. They walked erect and slow, balancing small baskets full of earth on their heads, and the clink kept time with their footsteps. African rags were wound round their loins and the short ends behind waggled to and fro like tails. I could see every rib, the joints of their limbs were like knots in a rope, each had an iron collar on his neck and all were connected together with a chain whose bights swung between them, rhythmically clinking. (19)

In each case the use of silent gesture interrupts an even, rhythmic progress, freezing the image as if with a turn of the head or a "click of the shutter." But something else is going on. Marlow sets up the visual and aural image of the African woman with her jingling garments and fierce vitality, analeptically and ironically against the earlier image of physical degradation of the "clinking" chain gang. But the moment also points forward proleptically to the Intended's reaching out across the window during her interview with Marlow.

Jeremy Hawthorn has rightly emphasized Conrad's ironic use of parallelism in positing the African woman's role as a symbolic double for the Intended (Hawthorn, 185–92). When Marlow visits Kurtz's fiancée he observes her repetition of the African woman's gesture. As the boat leaves the Inner Station with the dying Kurtz aboard: "The barbarous and superb woman did not so much as flinch and stretched tragically her bare arms after us over the sombre and glittering river" (67). Likewise the Intended "put out her arms, as if after a retreating figure, stretching them black and with clasped hands across the fading and narrow sheen of the window." On this occasion Conrad explicitly refers to the chimeric repetition of the silent gesture: "a tragic and familiar Shade resembling in this gesture another one, tragic also and bedecked with powerless charms, stretching bare brown arms over the glitter of the infernal stream, the stream of darkness" (75).

These three moments, encapsulating the moving images of the chain gang, the African woman and the Intended, share a structural purpose in unifying the literal and epistemological aspects of Marlow's experience. In this context, Paul Ricoeur's well-known study of the relationship between time and

---

(1925), which drew on Burton's work, and G. B. Shaw's *Adventures of the African Woman in Her Search for God* (1932).

narrative offers a provocative framework for examining the phenomenological issues underpinning Conrad's representation of the moving body as a figure of the narrative. Where Conrad's language of embodiment throughout the text draws on prelinguistic physical experience, Ricoeur is useful in showing the ways in which our experience of the movement of time is nevertheless rooted in language itself. Leaving aside the extreme complexities of Ricoeur's theories, it is sufficient to say that he explores an interplay between Aristotle's account of "narrative" time in the *Poetics* and Augustine's analysis of time in the *Confessions*.[12] Ricoeur's thesis focuses on a strong relationship between the "discordant concordance" of both accounts (Ricoeur 1984, 42). He compares two sets of relationships: in Aristotle, that of the relationship of *muthos/mimesis*, and in Augustine, the relationship of *distentio/intentio*, opening up the possibility for an account of literary narrative that reflects our actual experience of time. Ricoeur observes that in Aristotle's insistence on the unity of the drama (*holos*) he nevertheless identifies both *muthos* and *mimesis* with activity. Ricoeur translates *muthos* as "emplotment," and, in its relation to *mimesis*, claims that "imitating or representing is a mimetic activity inasmuch as it produces something, namely the organization of events by emplotment" (34).[13] Ricoeur's most important statement here offers an interpretation of Aristotle's use of the term *mimesis*, not in the Platonic sense of a "redoubling of presence," but rather "the break that opens the space for fiction" (45).

However, Ricoeur reads Aristotle's idea of emplotment back through Augustine's remarks on time. For Augustine, earthly time (as distinct from eternity) can only be experienced in the "threefold present"—the past is experienced as an impression in the memory, the present as that of present things perceived, and the future as expectation. Crucial for Ricoeur is Augustine's account of *distentio animi*, the fact that the "impression is in the soul only as much as the mind acts, that is, expects, attends, remembers" (19). The emphasis falls on mental activity, and as Ricoeur puts it, Augustine uses the example of reciting a poem from memory in order to mark "the point at which the theory of distention is joined to that of the threefold present": Augustine's *distentio animi* (extension of the mind) offers a "'solution' to the aporia of the measurement of time" (19).[14] However, Ricoeur's most effective move is

---

12. See Ricoeur 1984, 32–37 for his harnessing of Aristotle's dramatic theory to a notion of narrative in general.

13. Note the distinction from Platonic mimesis, where "the metaphysical sense of mimesis . . . by which things imitate ideas, and works of art imitate things. Platonic mimesis thereby distances the work of art twice over from the ideal model which is its ultimate basis. Aristotle's mimesis has just a single space wherein it is unfolded—human making [*faire*], the arts of composition" (Ricoeur 1984, 34).

14. Ricoeur is referring to Book 11, paragraph 28:38 of *The Confessions*.

to view Augustine's theory in the light of Aristotle's silence about the relationship between temporal experience and poetic activity in the *Poetics*. Drawing attention to the emphasis on activity in both accounts, and on the creative, the *making* new by the effort of the mind, he shows the potential for reading Augustine's *distentio* in relation to the discordance or aporia inherent in narrative itself.

In relation to Ricoeur's account, Conrad's symbolic configurations of physical movement within the narrative movement unify, in an Aristotelian sense, the beginning, middle, and end of Marlow's tale. The movement phrases of the chain gang, the African woman, and the Intended, marked by a sudden gesture, a turn of the head, a move toward the window, offer descriptive pauses or discrete interludes that punctuate the journey narrative. But they also provide a chimeric overlaying, or Deleuzian repetition (Miller 1982, 5–6) symbolically synthesizing Marlow's journey of disillusionment. This structuring of the tale effectively metaphorizes the mental activity suggested by Augustine's *distentio*, which allows us to experience temporal reality by a movement forwards and backwards in the threefold present. Conrad's presentation of moments of physical gesture illustrate metaphorically the "discordant concordance" that Ricoeur associates with the activity of the mind in relation to the experience of time and its recreation in poetic or narrative activity. Marlow's aesthetic ordering of his recollection of these gestures emphasizes the temporal extension of the mind in the operations of memory, attentiveness of the present, and expectation of the future. The rhythm of the African woman's movement along the bank, syncopated by the effect of a sublime, silent gesture punctuating her progress, extends back toward his recollection of the chain gang, where the rhythmic clinking signifies monotony and degradation. Likewise, the African woman's tragic gesture of loss reaches forward to the future pathos of the Intended. Marlow marks the connection during his retelling of his interview with the Intended, when, in his reference to the gesture of the "tragic and familiar Shade" he uses the present participles, "resembling" and "stretching," suggesting the continuity of a memory reaching beyond the temporal limitations of the tale itself, toward the moment of future retelling on the boat.[15]

In this respect Conrad's introduction of these figures is supported by a language of movement that throughout the narrative turns our attention to the metaphorization of physical experience. These moments posit a rhythmic and gestural economy of phrasing, providing a narratological structure for Conrad's responses to a contemporary aesthetics of movement. While he draws on a Mallarméan admiration for the gesture's potential for economic expression,

---

15. In Conrad's work, the gesture is again repeated by Linda at the end of *Nostromo*.

he also turns to Schopenhauer's pessimistic account and Nietzsche's account of the Dionysian, both of which have helped to determine the direction of tragedy in a modernist context. For even as Marlow admires the "lunges and abbreviations" and the atavistic energy of the African woman, the liberated movement of her body is elided by the intervention of European "civilisation." Her rhythmic movement overlays the suffering of the chain gang, but she too suffers in losing Kurtz, her final gesture repeated by the Intended, confined as she is to the domestic spaces of the sepulchral city.

Returning to Ricoeur, we see that Conrad's manipulation of these textual moments illustrates a symbolic "refiguration of our temporal experience by this constructed time" (Ricoeur 1984, 34). However, an important aspect of Ricoeur's theory deals with the reception of the narrative, an issue that remains problematic in relation to the presence (actual in drama, imagined in fiction) of the physical body. In Ricoeur's theory the reader or spectator completes the meaning of the tale insofar as she/he reproduces imaginatively an individual interpretation of the narrated events in relation to her/his experience of time. Yet his account of the tale's embodiment in the reader largely elides the issue of imagining actual physical movement represented in the text.[16] This would require a further discussion of a phenomenology of movement itself, since movement possesses its own internal impulses and rhythmic configurations, its own internal narrative drive or, in Ricoeur's terms, poetic activity (65).[17] In *Heart of Darkness* Conrad seems to treat movement as always possessing certain properties of language.[18] The ghostly repetition of the rhythmic phrases and gestures of the African woman and the Intended provide a metaphoric aid to interpretation of Marlow's tale, and in this respect Conrad anticipates

16. Ricoeur alludes briefly to the symbolism of the physical body, but only insofar as its representations appear in narrative. The body "introduces a twofold relation of meaning into the gesture or the behavior whose interpretation it governs" (1984, 243 n.6). He draws on Clifford Geertz's notion of "thick description" (Geertz 1973, 207) stating that "the same gesture of raising one's arm, depending on the context may be understood as a way of greeting someone, of hailing a taxi, or of voting" (Ricoeur, 58). The African woman's upward gesture, however, is closer to a European symbolism of Romanticism in reaching for the sublime than to Geertz's anthropology (or Burton's account of Dahomean dance, which offers a vocabulary of movement belonging to an autonomous structure of indigenous traditions).

17. Maurice Merleau-Ponty, *The Phenomenology of Perception* (1945); Gaston Bachelard, *The Poetics of Space* (1958); discussions of Virginia Woolf's modernism in both Erich Auerbach's *Mimesis* (1946); space and narrative in Michel de Certeau (1984) and Ricoeur in a later volume of *Time and Narrative,* owe much to a phenomenological account of the physical experience of time and movement of the body.

18. Conrad often characterizes the women of his novels in terms of bodily movement and stillness: Aïssa's defiant gestures in *An Outcast of the Islands* (1896); Falk's lover, silent and statuesque throughout (1903); the women gliding between rooms of the Geneva apartment in *Under Western Eyes* (1911).

certain contemporary choreographic theories that have developed a semiotic understanding of dance.[19] And yet Marlow's appreciation of the power of movement as a nonverbal means of communication resonates throughout the text.

Conrad's attitude to the body, however, remains skeptical of its autonomy as a means of expression in itself, in the way that Mallarmé wished to treat the movement of the dancer. The Intended's unfinished gesture anticipates Marlow's skepticism about language, as his narrative, trailing into dots, mirrors her physical reaching beyond the parameters of the narrative, and points to the inadequacy of any verbal expression of his disillusionment. Nevertheless, Conrad has placed Marlow in the role of observer, controlling the realm of the aesthetic. I would argue that, as in both Schopenhauer's and Nietzsche's accounts, where the action of the body has been transferred to the objective domain of the controlling artist, Marlow at the last minute doubts the alternative potential for expression offered by the body. Marlow's evocation of these three symbolic moments forms a kinetic "triptych." Given his critique of language (and Western iconography) elsewhere in the novella, the 'natural' language of the body seems at first to offer him an alternative form of expression. Yet the vibrant movement of the African woman is finally absorbed into classical European drama as the gesture of a "tragic and familiar Shade." In presenting Marlow's disaffiliation from Europe and his discomfort in lying to the Intended at the close of *Heart of Darkness,* perhaps we sense Conrad's critique of Western European literary and visual traditions *and* his anxiety about that culture's tendency to confine the body to the realm of the aesthetic.

19. Kim Brandstrup, a living Danish choreographer who predominantly produces narrative dance pieces, often structures his work around a series of movement phrases in which the repetition of each phrase registers a slightly different accent or a modification of the initial sequence. The spectator's reading of the meaning of the dance is thus generated from within these moments of fracture of the repeated phrase.

Works Cited

Achebe, Chinua. "An Image of Africa: Racism in Conrad's *Heart of Darkness.*" In *Hopes and Impediments*. London: Heinemann, 1988.

Brooks, Peter. *Reading for the Plot: Design and Intention in Narrative*. Oxford: Clarendon Press, 1984.

Burton, Richard F. *A Mission to Gelele, King of Dahome*. Vol. I. London: Tinsley Brothers, 1864.

Carey, John. *The Intellectuals and the Masses: Pride and Prejudice among the Literary Intelligentsia, 1880–1939*. London: Faber, 1992.

Certeau, Michel de. *The Practice of Everyday Life*. Translated by Steven Rendall. Berkeley: University of California Press, 1984.

Cleary, Thomas R., and Terry G. Sherwood. "Women in Conrad's Ironical Epic: Virgil, Dante, and *Heart of Darkness.*" *Conradiana* 16.3 (1984): 183–94.

Conrad, Joseph. *The Nigger of the "Narcissus"* (1897). Edited by Jacques Berthoud. Oxford: Oxford University Press, 1984.

———. *Heart of Darkness* (1902). Edited by Robert Kimbrough. New York: Norton, 1988.

———. "The End of the Tether" (1902). In *Youth/ Heart of Darkness/ The End of the Tether*. Edited by John Lyon. Harmondsworth: Penguin, 1995.

———. "The Lagoon" (1896). In *"The Lagoon" and Other Stories*. Edited by William Atkinson. Oxford: Oxford University Press, 1997.

Franko, Mark. *Dancing Modernism/Performing Politics*. Bloomington: Indiana University Press, 1995.

Geertz, Clifford. *The Interpretation of Cultures: Selected Essays*. New York: Basic Books, 1973.

Genette, Gérard. *Narrative Discourse: An Essay in Method*. Translated by Jane E. Lewin. Ithaca, NY: Cornell University Press, 1980.

Gilman, Sander L. *Difference and Pathology: Stereotypes of Sexuality, Race, and Madness*. Ithaca, NY: Cornell University Press, 1985.

Greaney, Michael. *Conrad, Language, and Narrative*. Cambridge: Cambridge University Press, 2002.

Hawthorn, Jeremy. *Joseph Conrad: Narrative Technique and Ideological Commitment*. London: Edward Arnold, 1990.

Johnson, Mark. *The Body in the Mind: The Bodily Basis of Meaning, Imagination, and Reason*. Chicago: University of Chicago Press, 1974.

Karl, Frederick R. *Joseph Conrad: The Three Lives*. New York: Farrar, Straus, and Giroux, 1979.

Lakoff, George, and Mark Johnson. *Philosophy in the Flesh: The Embodied Mind and Its Challenge to Western Thought*. New York: Basic Books, 1999.

Lothe, Jakob. *Conrad's Narrative Method*. Oxford: Clarendon Press, 1989.

Mallarmé, Stéphane. "Ballets" (1886). In *Mallarmé: Selected Prose Poems, Essays, and Letters*. Translated by Bradford Cook. Baltimore: Johns Hopkins University Press, 1956.

Miller, J. Hillis. *Fiction and Repetition: Seven English Novels.* Cambridge, MA: Harvard University Press, 1982.

Mongia, Padmini. "Empire, Narrative, and the Feminine in *Lord Jim* and *Heart of Darkness.*" In *Contexts for Conrad,* edited by Keith Carabine, Owen Knowles, and Wiesław Krajka. Boulder, CO: East European Monographs, 1993.

Nietzsche, Friedrich. *The Birth of Tragedy* (1872). Translated by Douglas Smith. Oxford: Oxford University Press, 2000.

Ogede, Ode S. "Phantoms Mistaken for a Human Face: Race and the Construction of the African Woman's Identity in Joseph Conrad's *Heart of Darkness.*" In *The Foreign Woman in British Literature: Exotics, Aliens, and Outsider,* edited by Marilyn Demarest Button and Toni Reed. Westport, CT: Greenwood Press, 1999.

Pecora, Vincent. "*Heart of Darkness* and the Phenomenology of Voice." *English Literary History* 52 (1985): 993–1015.

Ricoeur, Paul. *Time and Narrative.* Vol. 1. Chicago: University of Chicago Press, 1984.

Schopenhauer, Arthur. *The World as Will and Representation.* Vol. 1. Translated by E. F. J. Payne. 2 vols. New York: Dover Publications, 1969.

Smith, Johanna M. "'Too Beautiful Altogether': Ideologies of Gender and Empire in *Heart of Darkness.*" In *Joseph Conrad,* edited by Ross C. Murfin. New York: Belford Books, 1996.

Stone, Carol, and Afzal-Khan, Fawzi. "Gender, Race and Narrative Structure: A Reappraisal of Joseph Conrad's *Heart of Darkness.*" *Conradiana* 29.3 (1997): 221–34.

Straus, Nina Pelikan. "The Exclusion of the Intended from Secret Sharing in Conrad's *Heart of Darkness.*" *Novel* 20.2 (1987): 123–37.

Todorov, Tzvetan. "Connaissance du vide: *Coeur des ténèbres.*" *Les Genres du discours.* Paris: Seuil, 1978.

Torgovnik, Marianna. *Gone Primitive: Savage Intellects, Modern Lives.* Chicago: University of Chicago Press, 1990.

Watt, Ian. *Conrad in the Nineteenth Century.* Berkeley: University of California Press, 1979.

Watts, Cedric. "'A Bloody Racist': About Achebe's View of Conrad." *Yearbook of English Studies* 13 (1983): 196–209.

6

Motion That Stands Still

The Conradian Flash of Insight

JOSIANE PACCAUD-HUGUET

> It's extraordinary how we go through life with eyes half shut, with dull ears, with
> dormant thoughts. . . . Nevertheless, there can be but few of us who had never
> known one of these rare moments of awakening when we see, hear, understand
> ever so much—everything—in a flash—before we fall back again into our agree-
> able somnolence. (*Lord Jim* [hereinafter *LJ*], 87–88)

This essay will explore the relation between such spots of insight into an often
undesirable truth and Conrad's "journey beyond nihilism toward a poetry of
reality" (Miller 1965, 1). It will consider Conrad's case as an illustration of
one of the most radical alterations brought by modernist writers to the art
of fiction. The "moment" is an accident which imposes a different tempo, a
jerky rhythm generating relations between motion and pause which modify
the significance of narrative progression. This exploration will also take us
beyond what is commonly called "literary impressionism" since the reality in
question contains its own kernel of darkness: its name in modern theory is
the Lacanian real for which the closest image would be "a grey and formless
mist, pulsing slowly as if with inchoate life . . . the presymbolic substance in its
abhorrent vitality" (Žižek 1991, 14). The flash makes a slash in the narrative
fabric "like a twist of lightning that admits the eye for an instant in the secret
convolutions of a cloud" (*LJ*, 74)—another thing of grey and formless mist.
And this slash is not without consequences for the economy of Conrad's narratives where the usual semblances of fiction—plot, setting, character—lose
consistency: the story presents itself less as an enigma to be solved than as

an opaque mystery. As we shall see in this essay, for the artist devoted to "the perfect blending of form and substance" (*The Nigger of the "Narcissus"* [hereinafter *TNN*], 146), this is the price to be paid for transmitting the memory of such points of contact with the "real thing" at the core of the modern moment.

Virginia Woolf detected in Conrad's character-narrator Charles Marlow the ability to experience what she also considered as the source of her own writing impulse: "He had a habit of opening his eyes suddenly and looking—at a rubbish heap, at a port, at a shop counter—and then complete in its burning ring of light *that thing is flashed bright* upon the mysterious background" (1984, 226; my emphasis). The burning ring sets into relief an object detached from its usual web of relations, as if the gap between subject and object were suddenly bridged. Concentrating on the early fiction, I will explore the narrative consequences of the impact of the thing beneath semblances which it is the privilege of a Kurtz or a Jim to encounter.[1]

The moment is *a thing of moment* to Conrad's art and the word can also be taken in its physical sense of momentum, an energy—a drive—whose variations inform three distinct narrative layers: first, the story where it marks the encounter with a disruptive cause which brings motion to a stop, affecting Jim and his likes with a *syndrome*, a variant of the Joycean paralysis of the will—a zero degree of energy in a suspended moment of awakening to the "spirit of perdition" which Marlow identifies as the source of Jim's predicament. Second, we shall see how Marlow's response to such an encounter affects his own narrative where the Conradian moment writes itself like a *symptom*, recognizable through an original treatment of the sublime, and the omnipresence of melancholy, related to a spectral gaze or voice effect; the last layer is that of *sinthom*, on the textual level of literary aesthetics and ethics. Neither the Lacanian symptom nor its later version, the sinthom,[2] are to be sought primarily on the level of the narrative content because of their constitutive opacity. As Slavoj Žižek explains in *Enjoy Your Symptom*, the Freudian symptom is a formation whereby the subject gets back in the form of a ciphered message the truth about some betrayed desire, the purpose of the cure being to decipher, then dissolve the symptom. It is through Joyce that Lacan begins to deal with the symptom as "a particular signifying formation which

---

1. In his *Epiphany in the Modern Novel*, Morris Beja reads *Lord Jim* as "a story developed by epiphany" (Beja 1971, 53) and much the same can be argued for "Youth" and *Heart of Darkness*.
2. Lacan's reference to the Greek spelling *sinthoma* in relation to Joyce is the occasion for a pun on Saint Thomas d'Aquin, the key reference of Joyce's aesthetics, on *sin* in the context of Catholic Ireland and the father's "sin," etc.

confers on the subject its very ontological consistency, enabling it to structure its basic, constitutive relationship to enjoyment (*jouissance*) [. . .]" (Žižek 2001, 155). The passage from symptom to *sinthom*, a language formation loaded with affective intensities is a question of the creative use which the subject, in particular the artist, can make of the symptom: this time, the energy is not blocked—on the contrary, it is liberated and becomes as it were radioactive. Žižek takes the example of the stains that "are" the yellow sky in Van Gogh, or the water or grass in Munch: their "uncanny massiveness" pertains to a kind of intermediate spectral domain, a "spiritual corporeality" radiating jouissance, *enjoy-meant* (Žižek 2004, 199). Such traces of affective intensities in the work's texture also designate the limit of interpretation. It is worth quoting another example from Eisenstein's *Ivan the Terrible* where the motif of the thunderous explosion of rage

> assumes different guises, from the thunderstorm itself to the explosions of uncontrolled fury. Although it may at first appear to be an expression of Ivan's psyche, its sound detaches itself from Ivan and starts to float around, passing from one to another person or to a state not attributable to any diegetic person. This motif should be interpreted not as an allegory with a fixed "deeper meaning" but as a pure "mechanic" intensity beyond meaning . . . such a motif even seems to have no meaning at all, instead just floating as a provocation, as a challenge to find the meaning that could tame its sheer provocative power. (2004, 5)

Eisenstein called this process "naked transfer." As we shall see, there are analogies to be drawn with Conrad's "Kurtz the Terrible," with the ways in which the "thunderous explosion" of his last cry produces waves which, if they resist interpretation, do not lack provocative power.[3]

We shall also see what "sinthomatic" use Conrad can make of the "inspiring secret" of his fiction through a creative use of repetition, by grouping characters around the figures of Jim or Kurtz, and above all by exploiting the acoustic and graphic aspects of language. All these elements are already part of the method exposed in the Preface to *The Nigger of the "Narcissus"*, to which we shall now turn.

---

3. "We are dealing here with the level of material signs that resists meaning and establishes connections not grounded in narrative symbolic structures: they just relate in a kind of pre-symbolic cross-resonance. They are not signifiers, neither the famous Hitchcockian stains but elements of what, a decade or two ago, one would have called cinematic writing, écriture" (Žižek 2001, 199).

A Passionate Preface

Ian Watt reads the Preface as a rather anomalous contribution to the criticism of fiction which "says nothing about such hallowed matters as plot or character" (Watt 1981, 85) but a lot about what Conrad calls "temperament": "Fiction—if it at all aspires to be art—appeals to temperament. . . . [T]he artistic aim when expressing itself in written words must also make its appeal through the senses, if its high desire is to reach the secret spring of responsive emotions" (*TNN*, 146)

We know that Conrad wrote the Preface just after reading Walter Pater's *Marius the Epicurean,* an important work in the history of epiphany (Beja 1971, 39). Conrad's emphasis on the present moment of intensity, however, aims less at Epicurean enjoyment than at the transmission of a whole range of affects: the artist's appeal is not to the senses, but *through* the senses. The question for him is to present the fragment's vibration, color or form, to "disclose its inspiring secret," so that "at last the presented vision of regret or pity, of terror or mirth, shall awaken in the hearts of the beholders that feeling of unavoidable solidarity" (*TNN*, 147).

It is indeed possible to read the Preface against the background of what Žižek calls the "authentic twentieth-century passion for penetrating the Real Thing (ultimately, the destructive Void) through the cobweb of semblances which constitutes our reality" (2002, 12). This passion is a response both to nineteenth-century utopian or positivist projects for the future and to the major epistemic break which opened the twentieth century, laying bare the inconsistency of the divine or socially symbolic Other—the loss of transcendence.[4] Conrad's own writing is contemporary with the birth of modern physics out of abstract mathematics, with the rise of what Žižek, in a recent book on Gilles Deleuze, calls a new "transcendental empiricism" whose field is "an impersonal pre-reflexive consciousness, a qualitative duration of consciousness without self" (2004, 4).[5] The least that can be said is that Conrad's

4. I am referring here to the Lacanian distinction between the other with a small o (my fellow being in the social mirror, the stranger who is like me but not me, who has a physical presence and whom I meet in social intercourse) and the Other with a capital O, an invisible presence which functions exclusively at a symbolic or imaginary level. I cannot touch it—it is the place of radical alterity whose equivalent in the realm of language is the unconscious: no one has access to it, no one has ever seen it, and yet some say that it is the source and master of the subject's desire. Any human being may be construed as a figure (imaginary) of this Other, like Big Brother, or Big Mother who, as is well known, is watching us. All forms of deities—including totalitarian ones—can be candidates to the place of the Other and may compete to fill that position of unlimited power over the destinies of human beings. But as soon as the Other assumes a human shape, we enter the realm of paranoïa and violent power relations.

5. "In contrast to the standard notion of the transcendental as the formal conceptual

122   PART II: CHAPTER 6

conception of art in the Preface is also physical: it is an attempt to find "in the aspects of matter and in the facts of life, what of each is fundamental, what is enduring and essential—their one illuminating and convincing quality" (*TNN*, 146). When he speaks elsewhere of "waves whose varied vibrations are at the bottom of all states of consciousness," composed of the same matter, "that thing of inconceivable tenuity" giving birth to "our sensations—then emotions—then thought" (*The Collected Letters of Joseph Conrad* [hereinafter *CLJC*] 2:94–95), we are not very far from the empiricism of quantum theory which treats the real as a set of virtual possibilities out of which one reality is actualized:

> What matters to Deleuze is not virtual reality but the reality of the virtual (which, in Lacanian terms, is the Real) [. . .] as such, for its real effects and consequences. [. . .] Perhaps, the ontological difference between the Virtual and the Actual is best captured by the shift in the way quantum physics conceives of the relationship between particles and their interactions: in an initial moment it appears as if first (ontologically, at least) there are particles interacting in the mode of waves, oscillations and so forth; then, in a second moment we are forced to enact a radical shift of perspective—the primordial ontological fact are the waves themselves (trajectories, oscillations), and particles are nothing but the nodal points in which different waves intersect. (Žižek 2004, 3)

In this sense the Deleuzian field of proto-reality (Conrad's darkness) is infinitely richer than reality: "the proper transcendental space is the virtual space of the multiple singular potentialities, of 'pure' impersonal singular gestures, affects and perceptions" (19–20).

This connection sheds an interesting light on the process of repetition: "what repetition repeats is not the way the past 'effectively was' but the virtuality inherent to the past and betrayed by its past actualization" (12). This could be a way of looking at Conrad's narrative economy based on the figure of the leap, the impulsive gesture whose diegetic prototype is Jim's series of leaps in watery or muddy substance, marking the point where the Actual and the Virtual meet. In short, to use the Lacanian coinage, the Real (the Deleuzian Virtual) is not external but *extimate* to reality. The Conradian moment similarly marks a narrative leap in the extimate, opaque substance of language out

---

network that structures the rich flow of empirical data, the Deleuzian 'transcendental' [. . .] is the infinite potential field of virtualities out of which reality is actualized. The term 'transcendental' is used here in the strict philosophical sense of the a priori conditions of possibility of our experience of constituted reality" (Žižek 2004, 4–5).

of which we may awaken to a new reality: "All creative art," Conrad observes, "is evocation of the unseen . . . the most insignificant tides of reality" (*Notes on Life and Letters*, 13) which is "fluid-multiple-open"; it is only afterward that conscious perception reduces "this spectral, preontological multiplicity to one ontologically, fully constituted, reality" (2004, 3, n.2). Hence, I would argue, Conrad's insistence on the fact that the history of his books is a question of "fluid," "temperamental" grouping "which shifts and [of] the changing lights giving varied effects of perspective" (letter to Richard Curle, 14 July 1923).

The modern passion for the real thing, then, privileges the singular gesture, affect, perception over the constructed image. Yet, Ian Watt suggests, if Conrad was convinced that everything began with sense impressions, he also had "to avoid reducing writing to a simple circuit which merely transferred the author's immediate sensory impression to the reader, as if the work were a mere photograph being developed in words and handed over to the recipient" (Watt 1981, 146). What the Preface makes clear is that narrative transmission is less a matter of photographic duplication than of a physical *action* of the word with its real effects and consequences, where ethics is necessarily involved. Conrad is quite clear as to the kind of waves of *enjoy-meant* he meant to produce—"a sort of lurid light" for *Lord Jim* (*CLJC* 2:302) and "a sinister resonance, a tonality . . . a continued vibration that . . . would hang in the air and dwell on the ear after the last note had been struck" for *Heart of Darkness*.[6]

Why "sombre" or "lurid"? Because unless contained/constrained through the art of narrative, the passion for the real is not good news for reality, it is attuned less to the logic of desire than to an economy of enjoyment: its name in Walter Pater's day was hedonism which became later in the twentieth century an economic doctrine privileging the maximum of satisfaction with the minimum of pain, laying emphasis on the object produced rather than on its origin in labor. Conrad already hints at this collusion when he associates Kurtz's reified being with the visual enjoyment of his possessions:

> The wilderness had patted him on the head, and, behold, it was like a ball—an ivory ball; it had caressed him, and—lo!—he had withered; it had taken him, loved him, embraced him, got into his veins, consumed his flesh. . . . He was its spoiled and pampered *favourite*. *Ivory?* I should think so. Heaps of it, stacks of it. . . . We filled the steamboat with it, and had to pile a lot on the deck. Thus he could see and enjoy as long as he could see,

6. Conrad, Author's Note to the 1917 edition of *Youth, Heart of Darkness and the End of the Tether* (1974), xxxix.

because the appreciation of this favour had remained with him to the last.
(*Heart of Darkness*, 205; my emphasis)

The metaleptic shift in diegetic levels[7] here opens a hole in the narrative fabric: in a brief flash our attention shifts from the story line to a resonance, a sound wave which, if you open your ears like Marlow, suggests a link between the passionate embrace of the real (Kurtz being the "fa*vourite*" of the wilderness) and economic possession ("*ivory*"). Marlow is the sounding board and the barrier pitched against Kurtz's Christian passion without a God with its undertones of enjoyment in destruction, since "the Real in its extreme violence [is] the price to be paid for peeling off the deceptive layers of reality" (Žižek 2002, 9).

The writer's task will be to *temper* its deadly impulses by a kind of sublimation without an ideal, and I would suggest that the Preface's reference to the word "temperament" in the original sense of a subject's response to "sensory, emotional, intellectual and aesthetic experience" (Watt 1981, 82) is surely not accidental. The Conradian moment, like Rimbaud's *Illuminations*, conveys the throb of the passion for the real into sensory, secular illumination which means to awaken us from our everyday ideological universe.

The Paralyzing Syndrome

The roots of the moment go back to Romanticism, in particular those "spots of time" which Wordsworth situates at the core of poetic experience, when the subject, led by Nature's appeal, stands on the sublime limit close to the Real, to the Kantian Thing-in-itself, like the "huge peak, black and huge" which is the visual blind spot in the episode of the stolen boat (Wordsworth 1960, I, 1:357–400). In Romantic experience, however, Nature is still the poet's Other. The Thing materializes into some sort of supernatural monster whose grim shape seems to pursue the trespasser "with purpose of its own / And measured motion like a living thing." Its presence will continue to nourish the poet's imagination with "huge and mighty forms, that do not live / Like living men" (378–400). Nothing of the kind happens in the modernist spot of time where the experience of the extimate Real does not nourish any phantasmatic world: Conrad's Author's Note to *The Shadow-Line* is quite explicit:

7. Gérard Genette defines a metalepsis as the transgression of diegetic levels, which seems to be the case here: we leap from the most deeply embedded diegetic level (Kurtz in Africa, with its own temporality) to the internal narrative frame constituted by Marlow and his audience on the *Nellie* (present tense), a frame itself framed by the second external frame (the frame narrator) (Genette 1980, 234–35).

This story . . . was not intented to touch on the supernatural. Yet more than one critic has been inclined to take it in that way, seeing in it an attempt on my part to give it the fullest scope to my imagination by taking it beyond the confines of the world of the living, suffering humanity. But as a matter of fact my imagination is not made of stuff so elastic as all that. . . . [A]ll my moral and intellectual being is penetrated by an invincible conviction that whatever falls under the dominion of our senses must be in nature and, however exceptional, cannot differ in its essence from all the other effects of the visible and tangible world of which we are a self-conscious part. The world of the living contains enough marvels and mysteries as it is; marvels and mysteries acting upon our emotions and intelligence in ways so inexplicable that it would almost justify the conception of life as an enchanted state. (*The Shadow-Line* [hereinafter *TSL*], xxxvii)

In other words, the modern experience is a traversing of fantasy which lays bare something already latent in the phrase "spot of time" evoking *stasis* in time and space, a person's *symptomatic* soft spot which is like a *blot* in the field of the visible.

Just like the vanishing point around which the perspective of an image is drawn, it is the ineradicable presence of that blind spot, like the archive of a void, that constitutes a given reality: Lacan has given to this unsubjectivized visual point the name of the object-gaze, a source of anxiety. The Conradian tour de force will be to make us see such blots otherwise since we tend to forget them when we are immersed in actual reality. The spot of time marks the point of encounter with the Real and the subsequent collapse of one's Ideal image. Does not Conrad declare that "the effect of a mental or moral shock on a common mind . . . is quite a legitimate subject for study and description" (*TSL*, xxxviii)? This, precisely, is the subject of narratives like *Heart of Darkness* and *Lord Jim*. The least that can be said is that not just anyone is able to bear the violence of the shock. Is not Captain Brierly's leap on some "exact spot in the midst of waters" the symptom of his inability to face "one of those trifles that awaken ideas" (*LJ*, 39)? Jim's case has touched a soft spot in Brierly's history, so far veiled by a decorum of semblances. The true hero is Jim, because of his ability to hold up against that "thing of mystery and terror" (*LJ*, 35); and Marlow tells us that it is the presence of the "soft spot, the place of decay" permeated with malignant enjoyment that urges him to attend the inquiry *thing:*[8] the stigmatizing soft spot, therefore, is the true kernel of the narrative web.

---

8. "'What kind of thing, you ask? Why, the inquiry thing, the yellow-dog thing [. . .] the kind of thing that by devious, unexpected, truly diabolical ways causes me to run up against men with soft spots, with hard spots, with hidden plague spots, by Jove! and loosens their tongues at the sight of me for their infernal confidences'" (25).

Marlow himself often stands at the visual pressure point which modifies the perception of the symbolic fabric in which he is enmeshed. One of the passages which drew Virginia Woolf's attention is his awakening in the Eastern port of "Youth":

> when I opened my eyes again the silence was as complete as though it had never been broken. I was lying in a flood of light, and the sky had never looked so far, so high, before. I opened my eyes and lay before moving. . . . And then I saw the men of the East—they were looking at me. . . . They stared down at the boats, at the sleeping men who at night had come to them from the sea . . . the three boats with the tired men from the West sleeping, unconscious of the land and the people and of the violence of sunshine. . . . The East looked at them without a sound. ("Youth" [hereinafter *Y*], 130–31)

Such a suspended moment is situated at the exact point where two virtual waves clash, where "reality" previous to its perception is still "fluid-multiple-open," before conscious perception. The sleeping Westerner awakens to a silent stare which is the vanishing point of his own reality; but he equally makes a blot in the landscape of the East who looks at him. What is remarkable is that East and West in turn occupy that blank which materializes the gaze *qua* object. This scene of origins, revisited through shifting angles, exposes the violence of colonial history and the *relativity* of our symbolic fabric.

The decisive criterion for such epiphanies is "some cruel, little, awful catastrophe" (*LJ*, 193): a word, a gesture brings forth the *blot* that spoils the idyllic vision of oneself or the world. Marlow's predecessor in "Karain" is impressed by the eponymous "hero"'s power "to awaken an absurd expectation of something heroic going to take place." But the Malay chief's face soon betrays fear at

> a shadow, a nothing, unconquerable and immortal, that preys upon life. . . . His chest expanded time after time, as if it could not contain the beating of his heart. For a moment he had the power of the possessed—the power to awaken in the beholders wonder, pain, pity, and a fearful near sense of things invisible, of things dark and mute, that surround the loneliness of mankind. (*Tales of Unrest* [hereinafter *TU*], 61)

The resonances with the Preface suggest that Karain incarnates a question of poetics which is actually the pulsing heart, the darkly illuminating kernel of Conrad's narratives. The "mysterious cause" (*TU*, 57) which makes Karain appear "enigmatical and touching" is a faceless, silent voice driving him to "kill with a sure shot" until he comes on board, asking for some amulet that will block the drive—"Have I not killed enough?" (*TU*, 77). Does not the figure of the Western narrator anticipate Marlow, the one touched by the word of those who have been in touch with this shadow, this nothing? If Jim and Kurtz affect Marlow, this is because they too have gone far in peeling off the layers of reality toward the destructive void.

As in the Joycean epiphany, a trivial phrase throws the masks to the ground, like the French Lieutenant's "Mon Dieu! how the time passes!" (*LJ*, 88). What does Marlow then see? He sees a naked human being who is like a leftover of the symbolic fiction which his uniform is supposed to represent. Or it will be the famous "Look at that wretched cur!" which strips Jim naked in the public gaze. Or it can be a woman's word, for example, Jewel's (*LJ*, 186). And if Marlow incarnates the symbolic function of language to order experience, the "feminine" knowledge, a sense of "that blight of futility that lies in men's speech and makes a conversation a thing of empty sounds" (*LJ*, 91) still remains. It is also quite clear that, for Conrad, the encounter with the vanishing point where the protective film of semblances fades is actually where the experience of writing begins: "One goes through it, and there's nothing to show at the end. Nothing! Nothing! Nothing!" (*CLJC* 2:205). But this nothing is not the Sartrean void, it gives body "to some elementary matrix of jouissance" which is our common (b)lot.[9]

Why, then, should Marlow declare himself loyal to what he calls a "moral victory" in Kurtz's own deathbed cry (*Heart of Darkness* [hereinafter *HD*], 241)? What kind of victory is this? It may be that Marlow, who has also been in touch with "the unseen presence of victorious corruption" (*HD*, 228), sees the brand of heroism in Kurtz's acceptance of his passion. It is clear that Kurtz is a good candidate for "enjoy-meant" at its purest: he rejoins the order of being and loses his place in the symbolic order, which is the reverse of the humanizing process of language whereby we lose our being and gain a place in the symbolic. Marlow is quite aware that he is "striving after something altogether without a substance" (*HD*, 203), a thing of nothing really: a blank silence and a vacant eye at the core of reality. In this sense Kurtz's cry is like a *vocal* anamorphotic blot, the Deleuzian spectral Event loaded with affect, materializing the truth of jouissance.

Jim is less "authentic" in his destructive passion[10] but there is in him some-

9. "In contrast to symptom which is a cipher of some repressed meaning, sinthom has no determinate meaning: it just gives body, in its repetitive pattern, to some elementary matrix of jouissance, of excessive enjoyment. Although sinthoms do not have sense, they do radiate jouissance, enjoy-meant" (Žižek 2001, 199).

10. As Slavoj Žižek notes, "authenticity resides in the act of violent transgression, from the Lacanian Real—the thing Antigone confronts when she violates the order of the city—to the Bataillean excess" (Žižek 2000, 6).

thing of Antigone's drive toward perdition. One of the early occurrences of the word *spot* in the novel is revealing. Jim tells that once on the lifeboat, he wanted to go back to *see* the spot of the *Patna*'s supposed wreckage—in other words . . . nothing—that is, the spot where something which might have happened actually did not happen.[11] It is therefore as if Jim meant to *repeat* the traumatic encounter with "that thing" during the *Patna* episode: "something invisible, a directing spirit of perdition that dwelt within, like a malevolent soul in a detestable body" (*LJ*, 23).

The point is of course that Jim also surrendered to that spirit within, that *extimate* kernel. It is no real surprise therefore if after his own symbolic beheading, the cancellation of his certificate, his next step takes him to Patusan, the land without past or future, the "very thing" he wants. And yet out there, his own heroism consists in trying to save the symbolic fiction, to "fight this thing down" (94): not to let himself be absorbed by the blind spot—hence his sublime position.

Melancholy as Symptom: Gaze and Voice as Love Objects

If we look for the particular signifying formation enabling the Conradian narrative to structure its relationship to enjoyment, we shall find it in the threshold device called Marlow. It is through him that Conrad produces a tale both horrible and beautiful, able to *block* and to *communicate* something of "the haunting terror, the infinite passion," to convey "the abiding memory of the sublime spectacle" (*A Personal Record*, 92).

In *Lord Jim*, Patusan is of course the blind spot on the map, the projection space for Western fantasy and the site for Jim's most ironical last "epiphany." But before that, there is the decaying ship, an important Conradian *topos* where the extimate real undermines the ideal from without *and* within. Does not Marlow's true adventure in "Youth" already consist in trying to keep "that old thing," the *Judaea* (*Y*, 110), afloat by pumping water out, then in, until the ship's explosion in the black Eastern night? The *Judaea* foreshadows the *Patna* (a near anagram of Patusan) half sunk by the waves of pilgrims loaded for commercial imperatives absolutely indifferent to religious ideals. What this lack of transcendence reveals is that the modern sublime does not pertain to elevated ideas, it is the effect of the passion for the real which reveals a central vacuity.

---

11. "Why back to the very spot, to see," Marlow wonders. "It was one of those bizarre and exciting glimpses through the fog . . . an extraordinary disclosure" (*LJ*, 71).

When is Jim sublime in Marlow's eyes, then? He is less sublime when he gives himself to his notorious "ability in the abstract" than when he appears bathed in an *unnatural* (not supernatural) light which signals the contiguity of the void, the locus of the object-gaze, with the spectacle of the world: "At the moment of greatest brilliance the darkness leaped back with a culminating crash, and he vanished before my dazzled eyes as though he had been blown to atoms" (*LJ,* 107). At other times he is a spot of white light, "a tiny white speck, that seemed to catch all the light left in a darkened world" (199): no matter whether black or white, Jim is Marlow's true auratic object, located at the liminal point of visual sensation— "an object whose positive body is just an embodiment of Nothing . . . an object which, by its very inadequacy, 'gives body' to the absolute negativity of the Idea" (Žižek 2002, 206). He is sublime not in himself, but because he occupies a position which the halo around him makes visible: "He appealed to all sides at once—to the side turned perpetually to the light of day, and to that side of us which, like the other hemisphere of the moon, exists stealthily in perpetual darkness, with only a fearful ashy light falling at times on the edge" (*LJ,* 59). It is Marlow's ability to be affected by "that side of us" that designates him as a partner to Jim, or Kurtz: with modernity, we enter the area of the Lacanian symptom which is the most real part, the true secret agent of our lives.

The consequences of Jim's drama will be negotiated in Stein's house, another place of darkness and glimmers hovering in the Lacanian *entre-deux-morts,* where human forms are seen "for a moment stealing silently across the depths of a crystalline void" (*LJ,* 130). Marlow comes asking for "a cure" for his protégé, "a case" (130)—and is it really surprising to see the language of psychoanalysis emerge in those pages? The entymologist has his own way of dealing with beautiful specimens: he puts them in glass cases. But this is not what Marlow wants for his own human case: he wants to convey the palpitating throb of the thing itself *through* his narrative. Viewed from the perspective of the oppositions set up by the Preface to *The Nigger of the "Narcissus",* Stein is on the side of science, whereas Marlow stands on the side of art: they do not serve the same version of truth. And it is Marlow's impression of being "the last of mankind," delivered to "a strange and melancholy illusion," that urges him to hand on his story.

There are many occasions in Conrad's fiction when a character suddenly discovers a vacuity in the crystal of the Other's eye, often in relation to the *not-all* of femininity which relativizes the "male" narrative. The visual field of Patusan is dominated by a gaze without a face, "the melancholy figure of a woman": a vanishing point which defies "the ordinary standpoint" (*LJ,* 165), another anamorphotic blot in which Marlow sees "the significant fact" of Jim's journey. Over Jewel's head looms the Eastern bride which is no other than a metaphor for death, the true cause of his desire (165). The care which Jim takes of the fence around the mother's grave, the place of "feminine sublimities," marks out his exact position at the beck and call of the Thing against which Jewel, the living woman, rebels (187). Even though Jim ends up rejoining, like Kurtz, the petrified forest of enjoyment, he remains in Marlow's memory the auratic object in which there is something more than himself since he stands against, in all the senses of that word, "*this thing*" of darkness.

Karain, the matrix of many of Conrad's characters, is also under the spell of a seductive maternal ghost and tongue, the invisible and inaudible "she" of his dreams (*TU*, 69) who has more power over him than the law of his community. After the shot which saves Pata Matara's sister from the knife of revenge which nowadays would be called a crime of honor, Karain is carried into her presence but she says that she has never seen him before (73). His own spot of time is a traversing of fantasy which reveals the horror of his gesture: he has killed his own brother for the sake of a ghost behind a living woman's head—exactly like the figure looming above Jewel's head. This moment of dispossession gives the exact formula of melancholy which is the encounter of that blank in the love object's gaze: "there is nothing, no reflection of my own image in the pool of her eyes, therefore I am nothing." The encounter with this nothing is the primal scene of all Conrad's writing to come:[12] *Heart of Darkness* is structured around a black epiphany foreshadowed by the "inscrutable intention" of the "feminine" wilderness (*HD*, 185), followed by the encounter of the "vacant glassiness" in the dying helmsman's "lustrous and inquiring glance" (*HD*, 202), then by Kurtz's deathbed epiphany. What is crucial here is that another spectral event accompanies the gaze: a nearly inaudible voice effect, "a cry that was no more than a breath" (*HD*, 239).

There are many enigmatic, unsubjectivized cries or calls in Conrad's work. The first thing greeting Marlow in the silence of the Eastern port in *Youth* is a faceless Western voice cursing violently:

> It began calling me "Pig!," and from that went crescendo into unmention-
> able adjectives—in English. The man up there raged aloud in two lan-
> guages, and with a sincerity in his fury that almost convinced me I had, in
> some way, sinned against the harmony of the universe. (*Y*, 129)

Marlow, one among a whole succession of conquerors, has indeed so sinned. Why is it crucial here that the voice should be floating like an organ without a

---

12. Morris Beja sees the short moment of Jim's "last proud and unflinching glance" at the Eastern bride (*LJ*, 246) as the novel's climactic epiphany (Beja 1971, 53).

body? It is crucial because the charge which the narrative whispers *sotto voce* cannot be openly endorsed by the diegetic Marlow. It is this objective quality of voice which is most likely to convey some sort of revelation—"*objective*" simply means that the emphasis is on material presence: in other words, on the signifier's real, opaque *substance* as opposed to the realities words can depict. In short, the literary sinthom and its radiating power are related to the manifestation of the Lacanian object-voice.

Indeed, the more detached from subject (whether addresser or addressee), the closer to the status of reified message detached from sender and addressee, the more likely the voice will be to carry its blind flash of knowledge—thus illustrating the definition of the unconscious as a blank that cannot be endorsed in the subject's history or by the text's authority. Does not Jim leap in answer to a call from the lifeboat in the dark addressed not to him but to George, the sailor who has just died of a stroke on the *Patna*'s deck? The anonymous call designates Jim's true place as that of a living dead, just as in the *wretched cur* episode where a street voice stretches at him, threatening his ideal self-image ("Look at that wretched cur!" *LJ*, 47). The voice deserves the quality of object because its sender and addressee—someone in the street, Marlow, Jim, the yellow dog?—are undetermined: this is the moment when the spoken chain vibrates with *virtual* waves of interpretations.

In the economy of Conrad's early narratives, Marlow is the device invented for registering the shock of the encounter with the glassy gaze or the blank voice. And it is in response to a speechless bond that he becomes "a helper" (*LJ*, 59) to the symptom incarnated by Jim or Kurtz: by lending his ear, his voice, and his words to the mysterious cause which has touched him, he makes the passage from paralyzing symptom to creative sinthom possible.

"Sinthomatic" Radiations

Recordings, transmission, network: the words sum up the construction of the text's very special memory. After the first moment of recording, the vocal/visual spot of inert substance continues to radiate, not so much as a poetic translation of quantum theory than as one of the first narrative enactments of sinthom: Conrad, "one of the first novelists to articulate an affective view of aesthetic experience" (Beja 1971, 52), is remarkable for the proliferation of such traces of affective intensities in his work. There is always a "flash of darkness" that *spoils* the picture, even in an early production like "Karain": "a torrent wound about like a dropped black thread . . . a sudden cry on the shore sounded plaintive in the distance. . . . A puff of breeze made a flash of darkness on the smooth water, touched our faces, and became forgotten. . . . The sun blazed down into a shadowless hollow of colours and stillness" (*TU*, 40). Like Karain's *spot* of land, "a marvellous thing of darkness and glimmers" (53), the Conradian tale will remain faithful to the cry, the hollow, the darkness. The encounter of the vacant glassiness, however, cannot be wholly absorbed by the blot: there is a remainder which can be conveyed only by the acoustic and graphic properties of language, a certain repetitive use of presymbolic, meaningless vocal fragments, little jolts of enjoyment which Lacan calls *lalangue,* the child's little language:[13] their pictorial equivalent would be the concentric lines swelling through the substance of the sky around the mouth of darkness in Munch's *Scream.*

If we ask ourselves who screams "The horror!" in *Heart of Darkness,* the first answer is, of course, Kurtz. And yet nothing prevents us from supposing that the cry might also be Marlow's, in the retrospective *souvenir* of the moment when the veil also fell for him (etymologically, *sous-venir* is what comes from under). To put this in another way, if we treat the meaningless cry as a *detached object,* it begins to operate like a broken phrase floating throuth the novel's texture, breaking through the cottonwool of another spectral house much later: "It was a moment of triumph for the wilderness, an invading and vengeful rush which, it seemed to me, I would have to keep back alone for the salvation of another soul . . . those broken phrases came back to me, were heard again in their ominous and terrifying simplicity" (*HD*, 245). If Marlow tries to keep back the vengeful rush for the sake of the Intended, his ethical task as narrator will be to transmit/convey the impact. "The horror!" truly works as the *hypogram* of his narrative, the metonymic fragment from the "*original Kurtz*" (*HD*, 207) running along the narrative web, through the dissemination of the *hor-ror* into vocal débris that tickle the ear disagreeably: the impersonal effect comes off as the sinthomatic realization of the "voices . . . the dying vibration of one immense jabber, silly, atrocious, sordid, savage, or simply mean, without any kind of sense" which haunts Marlow (205).[14]

In *Lord Jim* the resonances are more visual. The dissolution of reality is

---

13. "The initial move of a human being is not thought, reflexive distance, but the 'fetishization' of a partial moment into an autonomous goal: the elevation of pleasure into jouissance—a deadly excess of enjoyment as the goal-in-itself—e.g. a vulgar tune that inexplicably pursues us. . . . Is such an intrusive sinthom, a figment of obscene enjoyment spreading like a virus, really at the same level as, say, an intellectually stimulating theoretical insight that haunts us? Could it be maintained that such intrusive sinthomes provide the reo-level, the elementary matrix of memes? . . . This babble provides 'anchors of familiarity,' knots of potential meaning identified, recognized as 'the same,' independently of their actual meaning. . . . [T]his babble has to be devoid of meaning proper: first, signifiers have to be crystallized as identifiable entities; it is only then that they acquire a propoer meaning. And is this babble not what Lacan called lalangue (llanguage), preceding the articulated language: the succession of Ones, signifiers of jouis-sense ('enjoy-meant')" (Žižek 1992, 143).

14. On this question see Josiane Paccaud-Huguet 2004, 167–84.

often rendered by the aesthetics of the grotesque—the image trembles, the proportions of the body change, something ob-scene, off-stage threatens to break through as if under the thrust of a wave carrying the force of decay. Jim went through a first revealing moment on the *Patna*, at the sight of his skipper's eye "staring stupid and glassy," of his voice "harsh and dead, resembling the rasping sound of a wood-file on the edge of a plank" (*LJ*, 17). Later on Marlow has another glimpse of the man's gaze, of his mouth about to utter a wordless scream as he embarks on a gharry:

> The little machine shook and rocked tumultuously, and [. . .] the whole burrowing effort of that gaudy and sordid mass, troubled one's sense of probability with a droll and fearsome effect, like one of those grotesque and distinct visions that scare and fascinate one in a fever. He disappeared. I half expected the roof to split in two, the little box on wheels to burst open in the manner of a ripe cotton-pod—but it only sank with a click of flattened springs. (*LJ*, 32)

Marlow's troubled "sense of probability" signals the insistence and the return of a virtual wave: the repetition of words like *jerk, terror, rock tumultuously, sank* recall the *Patna* episode, the blind spot around which the kaleidoscopic narrative revolves: did not Jim also expect the sinking of the *Patna* which did not take place?

Jim is also, of course, the visual blind spot and the mystery which resists, insists, and propagates its waves of mist on Conrad's cloudy narrative. The bright picture of Patusan and its people exists in Marlow's memory, but, he says, "the figure round which all these are grouped—that one lives, and I am not certain of him" (*LJ*, 196). However unconventional and temperamental, the word *grouped* is crucial to Conrad's narrative constructions. Not only does the static figure in the center remain but its opaque darkness fuels the narrative economy: Marlow will side with the uncertainty, the throbbing presence at the core of the suspended image, he will not give in as to his desire to hand over "its very existence, its reality—the truth disclosed in a moment of illusion" (*LJ*, 192), through his grouping of characters around Jim's figure. And if, as Slavoj Žižek reminds us, "we should be able to discern, in what we experience as fiction, the hard kernel of the real which we are able to sustain only if we fictionalize it" (Žižek 2004, 19), is this not exactly what Conrad does?

The "stress and passion within the core of each convincing moment" (*TNN*, 147), then, are the dark spot which fuels the narratives of both *Heart of Darkness* and *Lord Jim*. This sheds another light on the famous metaphor of Marlow's narrative as an empty kernel surrounded by a misty halo made visible by "the spectral illumination of moonshine" (*HD*, 138): does not

Conrad record here the structuring importance of the black epiphany? The thing will be to create the glow bringing out the particles of matter suspended in the halo, the "nodal points in which different waves intersect" at the intersection of the Deleuzian Virtual with Actual reality. Are not Conrad's stories produced by contact with "the most insignificant tides of reality," next to the pulsating substance of the real? Discussing the connotations of the word *see* in the Preface, Ian Watt notes that it may include the perception of "the spiritual truths, as in 'a seer'" (83). And in order to be a seer, one has to have a fine ear. Conrad's narrators are less *voyeur* than *voyant,* and their affinity with the concrete substance of words is clearly preferable to Jim's disastrous "ability in the abstract."

How, then, can *words* possibly send out flashes on the threshold of meaning? It is a question of presentation.[15] Edward Said has underscored the importance of the text as *produced thing* (Said 1984, 93), of the eerie power of the Conradian word-*object:* "minimal but hauntingly reverberating phrases like 'the horror' or 'material interests': these work as a sort of *still point,* a verbal center glossed by the narrative and on which our attention turns and returns" (96; my emphasis). Just like Jim, the Conradian word is a still point, both dark and luminous, radiating with unexpected flashes against the "broad gulf that neither eye nor voice could span" (*LJ,* 202). Conrad also liked to portray himself as a worker extracting his material from the pitch dark of a mine where the Other of ideals does not exist but where you may exploit the material properties of coal or diamond: "I've tried to write with dignity, not out of regard for myself, but for the sake of the spectacle. . . . Thus I've been called a heartless wretch of a man without ideals and a poseur of brutality . . . I have been quarrying my English out of a black night, working like a coalminer in his pit" (*CLJC* 4:113–14). How can writing raise the ideals to the dignity of . . . no-thing? How does one make visible/audible that nothing loaded with spoils of enjoyment?

From the point of view of the modern sublime, the countless *un-, in-, -less, dis-* affixes, more prominent in *Lord Jim* and *Heart of Darkness* than anywhere else, constitute the linguistic spot where the real contaminates representation: they are metonyms of the darkness which bites into the outer edge of the word: a textual realization of the insistence of the real through the agency of the letter. Likewise, common words and phrases like *"one of us"* are lifted from their trivial usage to shine against a central vacuity. In short,

---

15. A question central to Conrad's ethics of writing: "the whole of the truth lies in the presentation . . . the only morality of art apart from subject . . . no word is adequate. The imagination of the reader should be left free to arouse his feeling" (*CLJC* 1, 200).

what used to be a sign in a symbolic system is turned into a thing-word: "a sign designates positive properties of the object, whereas a word captures, encircles, precisely the elusive *je ne sais quoi* beyond the properties. [It] opens up the sublime, 'ineffable' dimension and thus makes a Thing out of an object" (Žižek 2002, 170). If Conrad's words bear comparison with gems, it is of course not because they are precious but because they are possessed of a physical quality: they have incorporated something of the crystalline void and, once raised before the reader's eye, their translucent substance shines forth exactly like Jim against the real, communicating sinthomatically something of the "infernal alloy" which is also kept at bay. The *verbal* illumination operates like "matches struck unexpectedly in the dark" (Woolf 1994, 175) and alters the narrative network, in particular its *distribution of symbolic places,* both for characters and for the reader: what does this "one of us" ultimately mean, unless every man's ability to make a jump in the dark at the call of a maddening voice?

We can now return to another broken phrase included in the massive proleptic digression set off by Marlow's account of the killing of the helmsman in *Heart of Darkness:* [16] I am referring to the little note at the bottom of Kurtz's report which "blazed at you, luminous and terrifying, like a flash of lightning in a serene sky: 'Exterminate all the brutes!'" (*HD,* 208). Who are the brutes? Who should exterminate whom? Is it Kurtz whom the white manager dreams to get rid of? The vocal object strikes the reader's ear, recalling some disturbing truth about the death wish. After all, is not the Western narrator listening to Karain pursued by the detached phrase "Kill with a sure shot!" also a gunrunner? "I left him calling on the edge of black water. . . . [. . .] I swam . . . he called out after me . . . I swam . . ." ". . . Left whom? Who called? We did not know. We could not understand" ("Karain," 58). It is precisely when you cannot understand that you are most likely to awaken in surprise.

Does not Conrad prefer "a flash of light into a dark cavern," and "such knowledge as comes of a short vision—the best kind of knowledge because most akin to a revelation" (*CLJC* 1:342)? His care for transmission—in the Preface's own words, "to make you hear, to make you see . . . to make you *feel*" (*TNN,* 147; my emphasis)—opens new perspectives to narrative theory if, in the process of analyzing texts, we accept to take into account the dimension

16. As noted by Diana Knight, "a spectacular disturbance of narrative order ranges back beyond the starting point of the story to Kurtz's education, and forward through stacks of ivory, through extracts of his pamphlet (including its P.S.), through midnight dances and unspeakable rites, right up to the chronological end-point of his narrative—the visit to the Intended" (1991, 19).

of the sinthom which, it has been the argument of this essay, constitutes the actual Conradian voiceprint: a creative response to the presence of the real at the core of fictional reality, which can be apprehended through attention to any device likely to create a radioactive blot in the picture—repetition, transgressions in discursive levels, disturbances in temporality (like analepses and prolepses) hindering the progress toward meaning.

Works Cited

Beja, Morris. *Epiphany in the Modern Novel*. Seattle: University of Washington Press, 1971.

Conrad, Joseph. *The Collected Letters of Joseph Conrad*. Edited by Frederick R. Karl and Laurence Davies. Cambridge: Cambridge University Press, Vol. 1 (1861–1897), Vol. 2 (1898–1902), and Vol. 4 (1911).

———. *Youth, Heart of Darkness and The End of the Tether*. London: J. M. Dent, 1974.

———. *Tales of Unrest* (1898). London: Penguin Books, 1977.

———. *The Shadow-Line*. Edited with an introduction by Jeremy Hawthorn. Oxford: Oxford University Press, 1985.

———. *The Nigger of the "Narcissus."* Edited by Robert Kimbrough. 2nd ed. New York: Norton, 1986.

———. *Heart of Darkness and Other Tales*. Edited with an introduction by Cedric Watts. Oxford: Oxford University Press, World's Classics, 1990 (updated 1996).

———. *Lord Jim*. Edited by Tom Moser. 2nd ed. New York: Norton, 1996.

———. *Under Western Eyes*. Edited with an introduction by Jeremy Hawthorn. Oxford: Oxford University Press, 2003.

———. *Notes on Life and Letters*. Edited by J. H. Stape. Cambridge: Cambridge University Press, 2004.

Genette, Gérard. *Narrative Discourse: An Essay in Method*. Translated by Jane E. Lewin. Ithaca, NY: Cornell University Press, 1980.

Knight, Diana. "Joseph Conrad: Heart of Darkness." In *Literary Theory at Work: Three Texts*, edited by Douglas Tallack. London: Batsford, 1991.

Miller, J. Hillis. *Poets of Reality: Six Twentieth-Century Writers*. Cambridge, MA: Harvard University Press, 1965.

Najder, Zdzisław. *Conrad under Familial Eyes*. Cambridge: Cambridge University Press, 1983.

Paccaud-Huguet, Josiane. "The Remains of Kurtz's Day." *Conradiana* 36 (Fall 2004): 167–84.

Said, Edward. "Conrad: the Presentation of Narrative." In *The World, the Text, and the Critic*. London: Faber and Faber, 1984.

Watt, Ian. *Conrad in the Nineteenth Century*. Berkeley: University of California Press, 1981.

Woolf, Virginia. "Joseph Conrad." In *The Common Reader*. London: Hogarth Press, 1984.

———. *To the Lighthouse*. 1927. London: Flamingo Modern Classics, 1994.

Wordsworth, William. *The Prelude*. Book 1. Edited by Ernest de Selincourt. Oxford: Oxford University Press, 1960.

Žižek, Slavoj. *Looking Awry*. Cambridge, MA: MIT Press, 1991.

———. *Enjoy Your Symptom*. London: Verso, 2001.

———. *Welcome to the Desert of the Real*. London: Verso, 2002.

———. *Organs without Bodies: On Deleuze and Consequences*. London: Routledge, 2004.

III

History

7

The Nigger of the "Narcissus"

History, Narrative, and Nationalism

ALLAN H. SIMMONS

The Nigger of the "Narcissus" takes its place alongside other literary myths of national character, such as Hardy's bucolic image of England, Kipling's imperial vision, and the hymn to manhood-as-martial-ardor delivered by Shakespeare's Henry V before the Battle of Agincourt. Speaking to the mustered "happy few," Henry appeals to what Conrad calls "the permanence of memory" (*Notes on Life and Letters*, 16): his hopelessly outnumbered soldiers will be remembered by "gentlemen in England, now abed" (4:3). In the first chapter of the novella, the narrator identifies his implied readers as "the few," those who will remember: "The sea and the earth are unfaithful to their children: a truth, a faith, a generation of men goes—and is forgotten, and it does not matter! Except, perhaps, to the few of those who believed the truth, confessed the faith—or loved the men" (25). Aristocrats and yeomen alike are included in Henry's "band of brothers"; at the end of the novella the first-person narrator's "brothers" are the crew: "As good a crowd as ever fisted with wild cries the beating canvas of a heavy foresail; or tossing aloft, invisible in the night, gave back yell for yell to a westerly gale" (173).

This essay will argue that the narrative of *The Nigger of the "Narcissus"* offers a maritime myth of national identity. First, I shall place *The Nigger of the "Narcissus"* within a historical frame, looking particularly at the history of its composition and its moment of reception. Second, I shall consider the work's narrative techniques, especially its obsession with symmetrical patterning, to argue for its self-conscious artistry. And, third, I shall draw on these two strands to argue that the novella contributes to a sense of national self-fashioning, focused on the sea. My object in linking these three areas is to show that, at the levels of composition, narrative technique, and the fashioning of a nationalist ideology, *The Nigger of the "Narcissus"* demonstrates the self-styled "homo duplex" Conrad's inclusive and conflicted approach to tensions and oppositions.

History

The Nigger of the "Narcissus" was published in 1897, Queen Victoria's Diamond Jubilee year, and a moment when notions of "Englishness" were undergoing important revision. The Women's Suffrage movement and the formation of the Labour Party in 1896, at home, had their counterpart in challenges and setbacks to Empire abroad. For instance, 1896 had seen the Jameson raiders repulsed by the Boers in South Africa—and the first major defeat of a white colonizing power when the Italians were defeated by the Abyssinians at Adowa. This is not to say that Empire was on its last legs: what Kipling termed "the white man's burden" still provided a mainstay of the British economy and, as the Battle of Omdurman in 1898 demonstrated, its defense was ruthless. But other voices were being heard, too.

The example of Kipling himself is a case in point, for while his standing as the poet of Empire is deserved, he is far more nuanced than this allows. Written for Victoria's Diamond Jubilee, his hymn "Recessional" warns Britons against pride in their inevitably transient empire. Similarly, his invitation to "take up" the "burden" of colonialism is directed abroad, to the United States (in the Philippines). The Jubilee celebrations were, of course, imperial in pageant and ceremonial: colonial premiers and troops paraded in the procession, and Elgar marked the year with his *Imperial March*. As David Cannadine argues, the late-Victorian and Edwardian eras saw "the heyday of 'invented tradition,' a time when old ceremonials were staged with an expertise and appeal which had been lacking before, and when new rituals were self-consciously invented to accentuate this development" (1992, 108). A paradox ensues, however, as Cannadine traces the emphasis upon ceremonial in this period to the waning power of monarchy, in the face of a growing, politically conscious electorate: "as the real power of the monarchy waned, the way was open for it to become the centre of grand ceremonial . . . made possible because of growing royal *weakness*" (1992, 121; emphasis in original). Thus historicized, the inverse relationship between power and popularity inflects the 1897 Diamond Jubilee celebrations with equivocalness.

William Gladstone's decision to espouse the cause of Home Rule for Ireland split the Liberal Party in 1886 and resulted in twenty years of virtually uninterrupted Conservative rule sustained by an anti-Gladstone, anti–Home Rule alliance. Empire, *the* fact of contemporary British life, was the currency of political debate and Gladstonian liberalism was perceived as anti-imperial. In a letter to W. E. Henley, of 3 January 1893, Rudyard Kipling noted with mock annoyance that his daughter, Josephine, had been born on 29 December, Gladstone's birthday, adding that if she had been a boy he would have disposed of her "lest she also should disgrace the Empire" (in Lycett 1999, 256). By contrast, the Conservatives were the party of Empire. Benjamin Disraeli enhanced this through, among other things, the purchase of shares in the Suez Canal, gaining a controlling interest for Britain, in 1875, and proclaiming Queen Victoria "Empress of India" the following year.

But imperial might and method was also being questioned. In the face of the statistics at Omdurman, forty-seven British casualties against ten thousand Mahdists, Belloc's jibe seems heartless: "Whatever happens, we have got / The Maxim Gun, and they have not" ("The Modern Traveller"). A year later Conrad rightly predicted that the Boer War would become "repugnant to the nation" and offensive to "*reasonable English ideals*" (*CLJC* 2: 211; emphasis in original). And 1899, of course, also saw the publication of "The Heart of Darkness" in *Blackwood's Magazine.* By the end of the nineteenth century, the narrative of Empire had become irresistibly dialogic.

In March 1896, Conrad wrote to Edward Garnett: "You have driven home the conviction and I *shall* write the sea-story" (*CLJC* 1:268). But the "sea-story" he commenced was what would become *The Rescue,* the final novel in his Lingard trilogy-in-reverse. In the same month, Conrad married Jessie George and the couple departed for a six-month honeymoon in Brittany during which work on "The Rescuer," as it was then titled, was suspended while Conrad turned his hand to writing short stories for the more lucrative and burgeoning magazine market. Three of the five stories that comprise *Tales of Unrest* (1898) were written in Brittany, where *The Nigger of the "Narcissus"* was also begun, intended as "one of the short stories" for the collection (*CLJC* 1:319). Instead, it grew to novella length and was published in the *New Review* between August and December 1897, with the "Preface" following the December installment.

The Nigger of the "Narcissus" offers a blatantly different kind of "sea story" from that contained in *The Rescue.* In it, Conrad rethinks the subject of the sea, wresting it from mimetic backdrop to active and determining foreground. The creative keys to unlocking this trove of past experiences include his recent reading of another writer of the sea, Louis Becke. Conrad's letters to T. Fisher Unwin of August 1896 record that he has reread *Reef and Palm*, which he admires—envies—for Becke's "perfect unselfishness" in telling his stories (*The Collected Letters of Joseph Conrad* (hereinafter *CLJC* 1:298), and has read *First Fleet Family,* sent to him by Unwin and which, he claims, "speaks of life—but it has no more life in it than a catalogue" (*CLJC* 1:302). In its narration and scope *The Nigger of the "Narcissus"* can be seen to respond to both of these issues. An obvious, further source of inspiration came from Brittany itself. To Unwin he professed himself "exhilarated by the view of the wild coast, of the great sands and of the blue and immense sea."[1] From the perspectives of biography and psychology, rather than literature, this tale of the sea is also about the experience of foreignness. Begun on honeymoon in France, composition of *The Nigger of the "Narcissus"* was attended by Jessie's experience as the Englishwoman abroad for the first time and by Conrad's confrontation with France, the land of his second language.

Recent critics, including Willy (1985) and McDonald (1996), have examined the novella's publication in W. E. Henley's *New Review* as an expression of Conrad's self-fashioning at this stage of his career. The argument runs that the patriotism and antiliberal sentiment in *The Nigger of the "Narcissus"* were designed to appeal to Henley's Toryism and the *New Review*'s masculine, imperial tenor.[2] In addition to overlapping with Henry James's *What Maisie Knew,* serialization in the *New Review* meant that *The Nigger of the "Narcissus"* rubbed shoulders with pieces entitled "The Art of Cricket" or "William Blackwood and His Men," a review of Mrs. Oliphant's *William Blackwood and His Sons* (1897);[3] Nicholson's portraits of Kipling and Rhodes; and C. de Thierry's three-part essay, "Imperialism."

1. Letter dated 9 April 1896; *CLJC* 9. Sea-references dominate Conrad's honeymoon-letters: he describes his situation as "on as rocky and barren [an] island as the heart of (right thinking) man would wish to have," the coast as "rocky, sandy, wild and full of mournful expressiveness," and himself as "looking at the sea" (*CLJC* 1:272, 274, 275). When Garnett contracted typhoid, Conrad invited him to Brittany to recuperate: "This sea air here is quite tonic" (*CLJC* 1:277).

2. Conrad's association with the magazine began indirectly. H. G. Wells, to whose anonymous review of *An Outcast of the Islands* Conrad responded with an appreciative letter (*CLJC* 1:278–79), was, for a time, a member of the group of writers known as "Henley's young men" or the "Henley Regatta" (*CLJC* 1:281 n. 4).

3. "Karain: A Memory" appeared in *Maga's* November 1897 issue, beginning Conrad's association with *Blackwood's,* one that lasted until the publication of "The End of the Tether" in 1902. In his review of Mrs. Oliphant's book, J. H. Millar stresses the "robust stamp" of Blackwood's Toryism and claims that she "is quite within the mark in pointing out how *Maga* has evoked in her contributors much the same feeling of proud and devoted attachment as that with which sailors regard their ship" (1897, 654).

After *Almayer's Folly* and *An Outcast of the Islands, The Nigger of the "Narcissus"* certainly signaled a new, identifiably "English" note in Conrad's writing. The *Narcissus* is sailing "home" to England. Even Donkin boasts that he is "an Englishman" (12). Furthermore, after Conrad's earlier use of epigraphs from Amiel and Calderón, the epigraph is now provided by an Englishman: diarist and chronicler Samuel Pepys. Stylistically, Conrad attempts to distinguish regional and national types—the bo'sun is a "West-country man" (79); "Taffy" Davies is Welsh—and to ventriloquize accents, at times with confusing results: "Belfast" Craik, an "Irish beggar" (80) to James Wait, is now Irish, now cockney, and now Scot on the transliterated aural evidence. The officers in the *Narcissus* are British, the crew is international. All, however, are serving in the British Merchant Service, under the Red Ensign. In "Imperialism," de Thierry claimed that, "by means of the Navy and Mercantile Marine, England unites a world" (1897, 316). Published in the Jubilee year, Conrad's novella implicitly queries what nationality is. After all, the "home" to which she sails is presumably not home to Hansen or Wamibo.

In his iconographic representation of crew life Conrad achieved his intention "to do for seamen what Millet . . . has done for peasants" (*CLJC* 1:431). The result is a poetics of the everyday that, by dignifying the lives of ordinary sailors, "the humble, the obscure, the sinful, the erring" (*CLJC* 1:355), offers both eulogy and chronicle, for whatever else it is *The Nigger of the "Narcissus"* is a celebration of the British Merchant Marine, the workhorse of the British Empire—whose scope included James Wait's birthplace, the St. Kitts islands in the British West Indies. This historical fact gives an added inflection to Wait's claim to "belong to the ship" (18).

But despite such evident and national realignment of his subject matter, I do not find compelling the evidence that Conrad was attracted to Henley's view of England when composing *The Nigger of the "Narcissus."* In Garnett's words: "Conrad wrote from necessity" (1934, 14), and as his output in Brittany suggests, he recognized the financial responsibility placed upon him by his recent marriage. Simply put, the author's financial circumstances surrounding the novella's publication are these: wanting better terms than Unwin was offering, on Garnett's advice Conrad turned to the *New Review* as an outlet for his new tale. In October 1896, he informed Unwin: "I would like to try *W. Henley* with my '*Nigger*'—not so much for my own sake as to have a respectable shrine for the memory of the men with whom I have, through many hard years lived and worked" (*CLJC* 1:308–9).[4] A week later, Conrad informed Garnett, who was by then steering the novella's public fortunes: "I shall try to place it for

---

4. Does one detect a turn of the screw, perhaps, in the reference to one publisher that another's pages offer a "respectable shrine"?

serial publication with Henley *or elsewhere*" (*CLJC* 1:310; emphasis added). Against this one needs to set Conrad's evident delight in being taken up by Henley: "Now I have conquered Henley I ain't 'fraid of the divvle himself" (*CLJC* 1:323), he wrote to Garnett in December 1896.

Attached to the manuscript of *The Nigger of the "Narcissus"*, now housed in the library of the Rosenbach Foundation in Philadelphia, is a note in Conrad's hand that includes the following dating: "Begun in 1896 June. Finished in 1897 Febry." If this dating is correct, he began the novella halfway through his honeymoon in Brittany. It follows that, by the time Henley is mentioned—in October—Conrad was halfway through the period of composition. Although one needs to be wary of the tones adopted for different addressees in private correspondence, Conrad's letters of the period repeatedly place his financial anxieties above the prestige of the publishing house. To Fisher Unwin he writes: "I must live. I don't care much where I appear since the acceptance of such stories is not based upon their artistic worth. It is probably right that it should be so. But in that case there is no particular gratification in being accepted *here* rather than *there*" and "I can't afford to work for less than ten pence per hour" (*CLJC* 1:293, 308); and to Garnett: "I do not want to leave him [F.U.] if he gives me enough to live on. If cornered I would try to escape of course. It's simply a matter of 'to be or not to be'" (*CLJC* 1:306).

I suggest that Conrad's ideological vision of England and Englishness, as expressed in *The Nigger of the "Narcissus"*, is discordant with what Watts calls Henley's "virile imperialism" (1989, 68). The author of poems like "What Can I Do for Thee, England, My England" and such collections as *For England's Sake* (1900), William Ernest Henley (1849–1903) was Scottish, though London-based. *Lyra Heroica: A Book of Verse for Boys*, edited by Henley, was published in 1892 and quickly became standard fare in British classrooms with its poetic rendering of patriotic deeds and masculine prowess. Henley's most famous poem, "Invictus" (1888), includes the ultraconservative apostrophe to individualism: "I am the master of my fate: / I am the captain of my soul."[5] Despite the narrative's fluctuating focus of perception, which contains formal echoes of the clash between social organization and individualism, this is obviously not the vision of Conrad's tale of the forecastle. Slight discrepancies between

---

5. This widely anthologized piece has recently been quoted by both the Atlanta Olympic Games bomber, Eric Rudolph, and the Oklahoma City bomber, Timothy McVeigh, in their respective "explanations" of their actions. Oscar Wilde also turned to "Invictus" in his prison cell, in the early months of 1897, but only to detach himself from its message of invincibility. Instead, he told Lord Alfred Douglas in the letter since called *De Profundis:* "I was no longer the captain of my soul" (Hyde 1982, 437). Henley had published Charles Whibley's virulent review of *The Picture of Dorian Gray* in the *Scots Observer* of 5 July 1890.

the serial and book versions of *The Nigger of the "Narcissus"*—for instance, in the paean to England as "[a] ship mother of fleets and nations!" (163)—have been discussed by Cedric Watts, who distinguishes between the *New Review*'s "persuasively deliberate and controlled" tone and that of the first English edition: "excitedly rhetorical" (1989, 72). Even here, though, the inference that Conrad is under the influence of Henley should be resisted: the "excited" ideal vision of England only increases the discrepancy with the all too real vision that succeeds as the *Narcissus* sails up the Thames. In other words, the rhetorical style facilitates disillusion.

Narrative Technique and Style

Generally perceived to be the author's early artistic credo, the "Preface" to *The Nigger of the "Narcissus"* has attracted almost as much critical attention from Conrad scholars as the novella itself. In it, Conrad's attempt to explain how the artist "endows passing events with their true meaning" (xli) leads to the famous formulation: "My task . . . is, by the power of the written word, to make you hear, to make you feel—it is, before all, to make you *see!*" (xlii). Thus what he calls the "moment of vision" (xliv) that the successful artist communicates is formulated in terms of a progression in which sensory perception leads, by way of affective conviction, to mental insight.[6] This process has a direct bearing upon the theme of community in the novella for, Conrad claims, the artist appeals to "the subtle but invincible conviction of solidarity that knits together the loneliness of innumerable hearts" (xl), and, as Berthoud notes, "if there is a necessary connection between 'visionary truth' and 'human solidarity' it is because the latter is the test of the former" (1992, 181). My examination of the narrative will necessarily extend to the cadences and rhythms whereby the reader is invited to "hear" and "feel" as a prelude to "seeing."

In its repeated recourse to symmetry, iconography, and framing, the narrative of *The Nigger of the "Narcissus"* has affinities with the techniques of nineteenth-century narrative painting.[7] In the hands of the Pre-Raphaelites this genre of painting, which sets a scene to tell a story, acquired a distinctly social conscience. So, for example, Madox Brown's portrait of the dignity of manual labor, entitled *Work* (1862–65), also serves as a comment upon the idle rich and social ills.[8] Structurally, the southbound progress of the *Narcissus* in

---

6. See Berthoud 1992 for a full discussion of this.

7. See Simmons 1997, xxv–xxx.

8. The *New York Times Review of Books and Art* of 21 May 1898 described *The Nigger of the "Narcissus"* as "a pre-Raphaelite picture of actual life in the Forecastle" (344).

the Indian Ocean is balanced by her northbound progress in the Atlantic; the
two storm scenes, meteorological and social, afford contrasted visions of the
crew's solidarity; and, framing the voyage itself, the muster in the first chapter
is symmetrically complemented by the paying-off and dispersal of the crew in
the last.[9] Within this arrangement, a host of pictorial images acquire symbolic
weight: Singleton is portrayed, standing like a caryatid in the forecastle door-
way, "with his face to the light and his back to the darkness" (24), and James
Wait as "a black idol" in "a silver shrine" (105). In a letter to Helen Watson,
Conrad writes: "Candidly, I think it has certain qualities of art that make it
a thing apart. I tried to get through the veil of details at the essence of life"
(*CLJC* 1:334).

The variable perspective from which the narrative is presented serves the
parallel with the visual arts. Not only is the shift from third-person narration at the beginning to first-person narration at the end symptomatic of the
trajectory of Modernism in its surrender of omniscience, but the fluctuating
focus of perception, which includes omniscience, (paradoxically) qualified
omniscience, first-person plural, and first-person singular—together with the
use of free indirect discourse—also has obvious consequences for narrative
distance and narrative authority as the reader is encouraged to "see" the voyage
from within and without, felt and reflected experience, isolated incident and
the broader canvas in and against which it acquires meaning.

The Nigger of the "Narcissus" ushered in the period of Conrad's most sustained creative interest in the merchant service: it was followed by the early
Marlow-trilogy and "Typhoon." But by the time of its publication in 1897,
steamships like the *Nan-Shan* had already stolen the seas from sailing ships.
As Wilson claims: "Technology is the vital fact in the imperial story" (2002,
493)—and Conrad described himself as "the last seaman of a sailing vessel"
(*CLJC* 3:89). Historicized, the novella's paean to the era of sail thus offers one
in a series of contrasts or binary oppositions that pattern the narrative. Others
include land and sea values, the weight of inherited tradition and the irresistible claims of the present, marine romance and economic realism, and low
subject matter and high art. I shall argue that the coexistence of such "irrec-
oncilable antagonisms" (*CLJC* 2:348) yields the mythical dimension of *The*

9. I am grateful to Jeremy Hawthorn for pointing out the contrasting structural arrangements
of *The Nigger of the "Narcissus"* and *The Shadow-Line* (1917). The later novel opens with the
narrator leaving his ship mid-voyage and ends with him preparing to set sail the following day.
Moreover, the previous captain dies mid-voyage and Ransome leaves the ship mid-voyage at
the end of the novella—just as the young captain does at the beginning. In contrast, the near
equivalence of voyage and narrative in *The Nigger of the "Narcissus"* suggests a more optimistic
view of the power of journeys and fictions to subsume human differences into a common pattern
than do the varied trajectories of different characters in *The Shadow-Line.*

Nigger of the "Narcissus" and by extension the vision of England that is composed of both the inherited privileges of class that ensure that Mr. Creighton rather than Mr. Baker will "get on" in the service, being "quite a gentleman" (167), *and* the necessary if necessarily subversive clamour for "the right of labour to live" (172).

The structural elegance of the tale is complemented by the microcosmic narrative detail of which paired descriptors and phrases are a noticeable feature. (The following list is not meant to be exhaustive but rather to reveal the widespread nature of this feature.) Singleton is "a lonely relic of a devoured and forgotten generation" (24); his contemporaries were "strong, as those are strong who know neither doubts nor hopes. They had been impatient and enduring, turbulent and devoted, unruly and faithful" (25); "the slim, long hull" of the *Narcissus* moves beneath "loose upper canvas" blowing in "soft round contours, resembling small white clouds" (27); her passage is "lonely and swift like a small planet" (29); sailors' lives are "busy and insignificant" (31); during the storm they are "obstinate and exhausted . . . vacant and dreamy" (77); the rescued Wait's lower lip hangs down "enormous and heavy," his rescuers are "bothered and dismayed," and totter with "concealing and absurd gestures" (71); following the storm, "Our little world went on its curved and unswerving path carrying a discontented and aspiring population" (103); Podmore views himself as "meritorious and pure" (83); when he visits Wait, the cabin contains "an immensity of fear and pain; an atmosphere of shrieks and moans; prayers vociferated like blasphemies and whispered curses" (117); addressing the crew, Allistoun's movements are "unexpected and sudden," his tone to Donkin "short, sharp" (135); Wait is "black and deathlike . . . appealing and impudent" (122–23); dying, his face is "strange" and "unknown," "a fantastic and grimacing mask of despair and fury" (151); the sea reveals "the wisdom hidden in all the errors, the certitude that lurks in doubts, the realm of safety and peace beyond the frontiers of sorrow and fear" (138).[10]

I am not suggesting that such pairing is the only characteristics of the narrative. *The Nigger of the "Narcissus"* is also stylistically marked by what we might call the "generative sentence-construction" that is a hallmark of Conrad's style in, say, *An Outcast of the Islands,* where descriptive phrases and clauses proliferate, breeding further phrases and clauses. But here such expansion, often designed to convey scale or grandeur, tends to incorporate or extend to the pattern I have identified. Thus, during the storm: "Never before

---

10. In a letter of 30 December 1897, Constance Garnett thanked Conrad for transporting her to "a new world" in *The Nigger of the "Narcissus",* observing: "Your use of adjectives–so chosen, & fastidious—often ironical—reminds me again & again of Tourgenev's [*sic*] manner" (Stape and Knowles 1996, 29).

had the gale seemed to us more furious, the sea more mad, the sunshine more merciless and mocking, the position of the ship more hopeless and appalling" (70–71); and "[t]hrough the clear sunshine, over the flashing turmoil and uproar of the seas, the ship ran blindly, dishevelled and headlong, as if fleeing for her life; and on the poop we spun, we tottered about, distracted and noisy. We all spoke at once in a thin babble; we had the aspect of invalids and the gestures of maniacs" (88).

Bearing out the appeal in the "Preface" to the "perfect blending of form and substance" (xli), this pattern of paired descriptors replicates at the level of grammar the rhythms that structure the lives of the sailors—as seen in their division into starboard and port watches, for instance, and such claims as: "They must without pause justify their life to the eternal pity that commands toil to be hard and unceasing, from sunrise to sunset, from sunset to sunrise" (90). The narrative emphasizes the nature of seaboard life as cyclical when comparing the *Narcissus* to the seasons: in the morning she has "an aspect of sumptuous freshness, like the spring-time of the earth" (132); while "[o]n clear evenings the silent ship . . . took on a false aspect of passionless repose resembling the winter of the earth" (145).

But while the synthesis of form and substance attests to the self-conscious artistry of the narrative, the appeal to aesthetics that it illustrates has a crucial bearing upon the ultimate meaning of the tale. Consider this set of pairings: Allistoun reproves errors "in a gentle voice, with words that cut to the quick" (31); toward Jimmy, "We hesitated between pity and mistrust" (36); the crew's contradictory sentiments are voiced by Belfast's "Knock! Jimmy darlint! . . . Knock! You bloody black beast!" (69); and toward Donkin: "We abominated the creature and could not deny the luminous truth of his contentions" (101). Here the grammatical balance brings into contiguity contradictions and contrasts, rather than echoes and comparisons. In other words, art provides the locus of coherence in which the tale's thematic discordances might be suspended.

In discussing the condition of the narrative in these terms, I am aware of the danger of imprecision—and I want, for a moment, to be even more so by addressing, briefly, the poetic qualities of the prose. The rhythmic balance of Conrad's prose in *The Nigger of the "Narcissus"* that I have identified is consistent with his expressed desire in the "Preface" to make the reader "hear" his written words. This aural quality is present in the description of how the voyage begins:

> The *Narcissus* left alone, heading south, seemed to stand resplendent and
> still upon the restless sea, under the moving sun. Flakes of foam swept past

her sides; the water struck her with flashing blows; the land glided away slowly fading; a few birds screamed on motionless wings over the swaying mastheads. But soon the land disappeared, the birds went away; and to the west the pointed sail of an Arab dhow running for Bombay, rose triangular and upright above the sharp edge of the horizon, lingered and vanished like an illusion. (28)

Poetic qualities, such as rhyme, half-rhyme, assonance, and alliteration underscore the prose and, for all the talk of Conrad's foreignness, the stresses fall, for the most part, where we would expect them to. Look at the trochaic rhythm of: "Flakes of foam swept past her sides," for example. According to Yves Bonnefoy (2005) the respective acts of poetry and prose represent different points of view as to what reality is, the intuitive and the conceptual. The cross-fertilization of these different attitudes to words in *The Nigger of the "Narcissus"* takes various forms. For example, the variable perspective combines with the balance of scene and summary in the narrative to produce a form of *ekphrasis:* reading *The Nigger of the "Narcissus"* one is struck by the sense that the text often appears to be wondering at pictures of the sea, those ornamental sequences that throw the crew's actions into relief and in which the plot seems to confess its subordination to a pictorial form. The resulting portrait of seamanship (and nationalism) is composed of often conflicting elements, where romance and realism coexist, and humdrum routine is transformed into heroic adventure.

Mythology and Nationalism

On the eve of departure, Mr. Creighton looks "dreamily into the night of the East" and sees in it "the caressing blueness of an English sky" (21–22). No less than Donkin, he is going "home." I have argued that the narrative of *The Nigger of the "Narcissus"* synthesizes discordance through aesthetic patterns of balance and proportion. My concern in the rest of this essay will be to show that the different images of seafaring and England are similarly synthesized to yield a national mythology.

The Nigger of the "Narcissus" invites such interpretation: it is, after all, fashioned in the tradition of literary odysseys in which individual lives and actions acquire mythological status. The introduction to the crew in the opening chapter resonates with maritime stereotypes: old sea-salts, "shellbacks," like Singleton; Archie sews while Charley practices tying knots; the crew demand "a bottle" from the liberty men—there is even a ship's cat, "Tom," to complete the portrait. Such stereotypes coexist with a further set of archetypal and mythological references: Allistoun commands the ship from "the Olympian heights of his poop" (31), whence his voice "thundered" (160); while Old Singleton is "Father Time" (24) and, growling at the brake from within "the incult tangle of his white beard" (26), resembles nothing so much as Neptune. His memory is peopled by "a crowd of Shades" (141). Also included in this category are the name of the ship and the description of the Thames as "the dark River of the Nine Bends" (173) that recalls the mythological river Styx of the Underworld.

Added to this, the adjective-noun combinations ensure that the *Narcissus* is described in both micro- and macrocosmic terms simultaneously—"a small planet" (29) and "Our little world" (103)—while the sea offers "an image of life" (155). When James Wait looks out from his sickbed it is upon "a fabulous world made up of leaping fire and sleeping water" (104). Confronting the storm, the crew resemble "men strangely equipped for some fabulous adventure" (52). The worlds of the everyday and the fantastic are everywhere drawn into correspondence. Literal examples of this include Singleton's immersion in Bulwer-Lytton's silver-fork novel *Pelham* (1828), the sailmaker's "impossible stories about Admirals" (32), and the crew's refashioning of their actions during the storm: "We remembered our danger, our toil—and conveniently forgot our horrible scare" (100). Even Podmore envisions himself as "Samson" (115) when trying to "save" Wait. The need to fashion such myths to explain human behavior is an important feature of this narrative and evident in various formulations, including the ideal of seamanship, Podmore's religious belief, and sailor superstitions. These appeals to explanations of human existence suit a tale about extreme experience. The voyage of the *Narcissus* ensures Singleton's completed wisdom (99), for instance, while Wait's death—"what's coming to us all" (127), in Allistoun's phrase—is magnified by persistent sepulchral references: forecastle berths are "like graves tenanted by uneasy corpses" (22); Wait's sickroom is transformed into a potential "coffin" (66) during the storm; and sailors sleeping on deck resemble "neglected graves" (155).

A further aspect of the narrative that suggests a deliberate appeal to a mythical, folkloric register comes in the form of animal imagery. The novella's frame of reference includes a veritable bestiary: thunder squalls resemble "a troop of wild beasts" (104); Belfast leaps "like a springbok" (68); during the storm, Jimmy is "[c]aught like a bloomin' rat in a trap" (64); later he gasps "like a fish" (111); the boatswain compares Podmore's ungainliness on deck to a "milch-cow" (81); Singleton is "[s]trong as a horse" (98); to Donkin the crew "ain't men . . . sheep they are" (110); described as a "cur" (136) by Captain Allistoun, Donkin adopts the slander, referring to himself as "a mangy dorg"

(150). Most apparent are the bird references persistently applied to Donkin: his hand is "like the claw of a snipe" (105); he has a "conical, fowl-like profile" (110); his ears resemble "the thin wings of a bat" (110); to James Wait he is "a poll-parrot" who chatters "like a dirty white cockatoo" (110); after Wait's burial he resembles "a sick vulture" (128); he is described as "pecking" at Jimmy's eyes (111) and as "perched" on the coal locker (144).

For my purposes, it is unnecessary to examine either the archetypal investment in such appellations or the implications of the metamorphosis involved in, say, Donkin's transformation from bird to "mangy dorg." I would, however, note in passing that the *Narcissus* herself is described as a bird: once in the English Channel and "[u]nder white wings" she is compared to "a great tired bird speeding to its nest" (161). This identification, albeit at the level of metaphor, includes Donkin in Wait's claim to "belong to the ship" (18) and, as such, seems designed to trouble any idealized interpretation of the British Merchant Service.

Indeed, idealized interpretations generally are undermined or subverted in this narrative. Podmore's brand of Christianity makes no converts among the crew, but as Wait's funeral demonstrates, nor does religion generally: as Mr. Baker reads the funeral oration, "The words, missing the unsteady hearts of men, rolled out to wander without a home upon the heartless sea" (159).[11] By contrast, Singleton's sailor superstition is proved when Wait dies in sight of land. Poised between first-person and omniscience, the narrating voice offers varying degrees of authority, alternating between speculative belief and final knowledge, allowing different codes to coexist within the narrative.

Composed in 1896 and early 1897 and drawing upon Conrad's two decades as a sailor, including his voyage in the actual *Narcissus* in 1885, *The Nigger of the "Narcissus"* is clearly "of its age," the late-Victorian age of Empire. Like all narratives, it stands unavoidably at a confluence of discourses, those that defined the moment of its composition and those conferred from a distance by its subsequent reception. Although a work of fiction, its idealism is tempered by the realism of its nautical detail and its engagement with issues that bear directly upon prevailing definitions of England and Englishness, through such themes as racism, what constitutes a gentleman, and, perhaps *the* debate of English political identity, the conflict between unquestioning duty—the Nelsonian imperative in the context of the sea—and individual rights.[12]

Old Singleton represents an ideal of unquestioning service and tradition,

11. "Mr. Baker read out: 'To the deep,' and paused" (159). The Anglican *Book of Common Prayer* provides a further repository of language and culture in the novella.

12. According to W. H. Chesson, "'The Nigger' is not an episode of the sea; it is a final expression of the pathology of Fear" (Stape and Knowles 1996, 30).

yet when we meet him in chapter 1 he is already a "relic" of a bygone era. Furthermore, in the face of the contemporary historical reality of labor rights and representation, the determination of such "everlasting children of the mysterious sea" (25) to remain "voiceless" seems stubbornly anachronistic. Described as "old as Father Time" (24), it is, wryly, time itself, in the form of the aging process, that Singleton is made to confront during his thirty hours at the helm during the storm. It is not going to far to claim that, in the novella, Singleton, simultaneously "Father Time" and "a child of time" (24), is forced to acknowledge the passing of time, is brought from timelessness into time. Yet time is measured by change and one aspect of this change is the demand for rights voiced by Donkin. Even Singleton's prediction and explanation of Wait's death appears to assert the claims of the past, voiced as a sailor superstition that, if true, also remains inexplicable. Any Manichean distinction between past and present, therefore, entails setting the appeal of tradition against the veracity of reason.

This is not to decry Singleton's duty but rather to note that the tradition he represents is also presented as antithetical to social and political realities. Significantly, both "the everlasting children of the mysterious sea" and their successors, "the grown-up children of a discontented earth" (25), are presented in qualified terms: Singleton's generation had been "impatient and enduring, turbulent and devoted, unruly and faithful," their contemporary counterparts are "less naughty, but less innocent; less profane, but perhaps also less believing; and if they have learned to speak they have also learned how to whine." The inclusiveness that defines the former—"unruly *and* devoted"—is contrasted with the lack ("less") that defines the latter. That said, according to Captain Allistoun the crew are, "[a] good crowd, too, as they go nowadays" (103).

In the contrast between past and present expressions of seamanship, *The Nigger of the "Narcissus"* historicizes the sea. The conservative maritime ideal embodied in Old Singleton, whose very name (altered from "Sullivan" in the manuscript) contains an appeal to nineteenth-century individualism, encounters forces disruptive to the code of collective responsibility. The "votary of change" (14), Donkin, who deserted from his previous ship, declares: "I stood up for my rights like a good 'un. I am an Englishman, I am" (12).[13] By contrast, Singleton's "inarticulate and indispensable" generation lived "without knowing the sweetness of affections or the refuge of home" (25). According to the third-person narrator, Donkin "knows all about his rights, but knows nothing . . . of the unspoken loyalty that knits together a ship's company"

---

13. Donkin here voices the paradox that impinges on the story: obliged to surrender his individual rights by joining the crew, he has then had to defend these.

(11). When Captain Allistoun reprimands the crew after the near-mutiny it is in terms of "duty" (134); their response is to "stand by and see [Donkin] bullied" (136).

Multiple narrators technically complement the narrative's emphasis upon the crew as a collective. The narrative begins with Mr. Baker wanting to muster "our crowd" (3); it ends with the now-first-person narrator's detached survey: "You were a good crowd" (173). This is a group-fiction, as Conrad acknowledged in his comments on Stephen Crane's *The Red Badge of Courage:* "Stephen Crane dealt in his book with the psychology of the mass—the army; while I—in mine—had been dealing with the same subject on a much smaller scale and in more specialized conditions—the crew of a merchant ship, brought to the test of what I may venture to call the moral problem of conduct" (*Last Essays,* 95). Indeed, the very terms and nature of Donkin's appeal are to a specific socioeconomic group. He will, of course, have become a landlubber by the end of the narrative.

As their designation "children of the sea" suggests, the generation of seamen represented by Singleton are somehow outside human time—at least until mortality and aging are brought home to them by experiences such as the storm off the Cape of Good Hope. With their "home" as the sea—they are described as "without . . . the refuge of home" (25)—they are also detached from home as a physical place: it is Greater Britain rather than Great Britain that houses them. The chapter succeeding the storm scene begins: "On men reprieved by its disdainful mercy, the immortal sea confers in its justice the full privilege of desired unrest" (90). Such "desired unrest" locates the ideal of service outside the conflicted vision of home and belonging that is voiced in the novella. By including Singleton and Donkin, unquestioning maritime duty and subversive social rights, in the same boat, as it were, *The Nigger of the "Narcissus"* offers not only a contrast between the two but also an attempt to historicize and politicize the romantic ideal.

In the contest between past and present codes of conduct it is worth noting that it is Singleton's reading of *Pelham,* the adventures of a gentleman dandy in fashionable society, that introduces, albeit in a minor key, the narrative of what constitutes a gentleman, whose subversive consequences for social hierarchy encourages the reader to view the world of the *Narcissus* as emblematic of broader society. As Magwitch's attempt to buy a gentleman in *Great Expectations* (1860–61) demonstrates, inherited class divisions were becoming increasingly porous. The crew's discussion about their social betters is interrupted by the narrator's observation: "They were forgetting their toil, they were forgetting themselves" (32). But hierarchy itself is implicitly questioned in Allistoun's signing of James Wait: "Sorry for him . . . Kind of impulse" (127).

This allies him with the "latent egoism of tenderness to suffering" (138) that defines the crew's response to "Jimmy."

As Hawthorn has argued, Conrad's choice of James Wait as a central character is historically acute, "for if anything symbolized contradiction and unclarity in the late Victorian popular mind it was the figure of the Negro" (1992, 102). Casual racism inflects the crew's reception of the "St. Kitts nigger" (37). Uncertainty about his illness only exacerbates this, leaving them stranded between "pity and mistrust" (36). Donkin's view is that "damned furriners should be kept under" (13). He "didn't want to 'ave no truck with 'em dirty furriners" (43). Historically, as Conrad himself discovered, the nation's inability to meet the British Merchant Service's demand for sailors meant that international crews were a common feature of the fleet. As second mate in the actual *Narcissus,* "Conrad Korzeniowski," as he signed his name in the "Agreement and Account of Crew," served with sailors whose birthplaces included Norway, Canada, Australia, Sweden, and Germany as well as those in Britain. One of the seamen, Joseph Barron, lists his birthplace as Charlton, which Jerry Allen suggests is Charlton, Georgia, and Ian Watt speculates may be a mistranscription of Charlestown, Nevis, near St. Kitts. It may, of course, simply be Charlton in the East End of London. My point, however, is that, writ large, the racism exhibited toward James Wait simultaneously entails a threat to the prowess of the merchant service that enabled Empire.

Shortly before his death, Wait recalls a "Canton Street Girl" who "[c]ooks oysters just as I like" and who "would chuck—any toff—for a coloured gentleman" (149). Admittedly Wait's "scandalised" addressee, who "could hardly believe his ears" (149), is Donkin, but nonetheless his claim weaves together issues of race and class in a manner that seems designed to threaten inherited ideas of superiority. Put starkly, it poses a challenge to English manhood. Yet, for all of his subversive potential, before being committed to the sea, Wait's coffin rests under a Union Jack (159).

Although my attention has been largely focused upon the crew, the novella's epigraph steers the reader toward the *Narcissus* herself: "My Lord in his discourse discovered a great deal of love to this ship."[14] In Conrad's tale, the romantic portrait of the *Narcissus* is framed between reminders of her commercial functionality. Although, famously, Conrad never identifies the ship's cargo, this is a trading voyage, and the crew's adventure is subordinate, or at least incidental, to the demands of economics. Stripped of her romance, along

14. The ship referred to in Pepys's diary entry (for 30 March 1660) is the *Naseby,* in which Charles II returned to England after the restoration of the monarchy in 1660. As Watts has noted, this connection sustains parallel, underlying motifs concerning the restoration of hierarchy after an "individual rights" revolt (1988, 133).

with her sails and cargo, at the end of the voyage, the *Narcissus* is reclaimed for realism, returned to her true status as a cog within the Merchant Service, to the reason she was born "in the thundering peal of hammers beating upon iron, in black eddies of smoke, under a grey sky, on the banks of the Clyde" (50). Like the belaying pin that Donkin fashions as a weapon, and perhaps like the individual crew members themselves, the *Narcissus*'s true identity is as part of a broader system.

In the actual *Narcissus*, Conrad sailed from Bombay not to London but to Dunkirk. His decision to alter this fact, ensuring that his adopted homeland is the destination of the fictional voyage, dramatizes the relationship between national identity and the British Merchant Service. The portrait of England that results, however, is by turns romantic and grotesque, now the view of an enraptured patriot, now that of an exile within his own community. As Conrad wrote of the tale: "There are so many touches necessary for such a picture" (*CLJC* 1:310).

The Nigger of the "Narcissus" is a Jubilee-year piece. It, too, is celebratory. But the image of England it offers, "A ship mother of fleets and nations! The great flagship of the race" (163), is a night vision, inspired by the comparison between a lighthouse and a ship's riding light. As such it offers itself as an imperfect vision, emphasising this through contrasted attributes: "She towered up immense and strong, guarding priceless traditions and untold suffering, sheltering glorious memories and base forgetfulness, ignoble virtues and splendid transgressions" (162–63). This is not to divest England of her glory, rather to temper such glory with clear-eyed fact. The mythologizing in *The Nigger of the "Narcissus"* is characterized by this combination of idealism and realism, ensuring and ensured by the coexistence of both the poetic and the prosaic. The further up the Thames that the *Narcissus* sails, the less appealing seems England. Dickensian images punctuate the description: "tall factory chimneys appeared in insolent bands and watched her go by" (163). The river journey, like that of the sea voyage, thus serves as a journey of gradual disenchantment in which an elevated image of home is reconstituted by being forced into contiguity with the banal substratum on which it is founded.

In Donkin's words, the crew lead a "dorg's loife for two poun' ten a month" (100).[15] Whatever the truth of their exploitation, the material fact is that they put to sea for the same reason that Conrad wrote novels: economic necessity.

---

15. Donkin is presumably speaking of wages earned by an Ordinary Seaman (O.S.). In the "Agreement and Account of Crew," held at the National Maritime Museum, Greenwich, the monthly earnings of Ordinary Seamen in the actual *Narcissus* was two pounds, two pounds five shillings, or two pounds fifteen shillings. The variance, presumably, relates to their maritime experience.

The literal voyage of the *Narcissus* ends among "the dust of all the continents" and overlooked by warehouses whose windows resemble "the eyes of over fed brutes" (165); that of the crew ends with the payoff—before the narrator takes his "last look" (171) at them, outside the Mint. Economics and romance are further conflicted as the sailors seek the "illusions" dispensed at the Black Horse. But, look at what's on offer: "the illusions [plural] of strength, mirth, happiness" and "the illusion [singular] of splendour and poetry of life" (171).

Before the voyage begins, new hands and liberty-men are rowed out to the ship by "white-clad Asiatics, who clamoured fiercely for payment before coming alongside the gangway-ladder" (4). In the ensuring exchange, the "feverish and shrill babble of Eastern language, struggled against the masterful tones of seamen, who argued against brazen claims and dishonest hopes by profane shouts" (4). This conflict, "over sums ranging from five annas to half a rupee" (4), proves thematically and stylistically directive: commercially it suggests that romance cannot free itself from economic forces, while linguistically it suggests an international presence at the beginning of a narrative that will query and try to give voice to national experience. The last point I want to make about the place of money in the narrative concerns its magical power. Conrad's next composition, "Karain," would extend this theme. In the novella, money is transformative. Donkin's altered fortunes demonstrate this. But this magic appears, playfully, to work both ways in the commercial sleight-of-hand by which the wealth gathered from all the continents is reduced to the twice-mentioned "dust of all the continents" in the London docks. The Midas effect is reversed.

Flaubert identified *Don Giovanni, Hamlet,* and the sea as the "finest things God ever made" (Steegmuller 1980, 83). Conrad, who coincidentally shares the year of his birth with the publication of *Madame Bovary,* was an assiduous pupil. But to him, as this text shows, commerce is one of a matrix of factors that sullies the portrait of the sea. As its treatment of seamen demonstrates, *The Nigger of the "Narcissus"* relocates standard myths within a broader context that incorporates the human and commercial realities they tend to obscure. In Conrad's mythologizing the forces of cohesion are inseparable from the forces of disintegration; thus, the heroism of the common man remains, but so too does his commonness; the romance of seafaring remains, but so too does the economic purpose that sustains it. *The Nigger of the "Narcissus"* negotiates both the nonfictions and the fictions of the sea. To do otherwise would have meant the novella shading into anachronism or pastiche. It has not been my purpose in this essay to charge Conrad with iconoclasm in his treatment of myths, national or maritime; rather I have tried to show how he reconstitutes such myths as unavoidably polyphonic.

SMMONS, "HISTORY, NARRATIVE, AND NATIONALISM"   **159**

Works Cited

Berthoud, Jacques. "The Preface to *The Nigger of the 'Narcissus.'*" In *The Nigger of the "Narcissus"*, edited by Jacques Berthoud. Oxford: Oxford University Press, 1992. 175–82.

Bonnefoy, Yves. "Beyond Words." *Times Literary Supplement*, 12 August 2005. 13.

Cannadine, David. "The Context, Performance and Meaning of Ritual: The British Monarchy and the 'Invention of Tradition,' c. 1820–1977." In *The Invention of Tradition*, edited by Eric Hobsbawm and Terence Ranger. London: Canto 1992. 101–64.

Garnett, Edward, ed. *Letters from John Galsworthy: 1900–1932*. London: Jonathan Cape, 1934.

Hawthorn, Jeremy. *Joseph Conrad: Narrative Technique and Ideological Commitment*. London: Edward Arnold, 1992.

Hyde, H. Montgomery, ed. *The Annotated Oscar Wilde*. London: Orbis, 1982.

Lycett, Andrew. *Rudyard Kipling*. London: Weidenfield & Nicolson, 1999.

McDonald, Peter. "Men of Letters and Children of the Sea: Conrad and the Henley-Circle Revisited." *Conradian* 21.1 (1996): 15–56.

Millar, J. H. "William Blackwood and His Men." *New Review* 103 (December 1897): 646–56.

Simmons, Allan H. "Introduction." In *The Nigger of the "Narcissus"*, edited by Allan H. Simmons. London: Everyman, 1997. xvii–xxxvii.

Stape, J. H., and Owen Knowles, eds. *A Portrait in Letters: Correspondence to and about Conrad*. Amsterdam: Rodopi, 1996.

Steegmuller, Francis, ed. and trans. *The Letters of Gustave Flaubert, 1830–1857*. London: Faber, 1980.

Thierry, C. de. "Imperialism." *New Review* 100 (September 1897): 316–33.

Watts, Cedric. "Commentary." In *The Nigger of the "Narcissus"*, edited by Cedric Watts. Harmondsworth: Penguin, 1988. 129–42.

———. *Joseph Conrad: A Literary Life*. London: Macmillan, 1989.

Willy, Todd G. "The Conquest of the Commodore: Conrad's Rigging of 'The Nigger' for the Henley Regatta." *Conradiana* 17 (1985): 163–82.

Wilson, A. N. *The Victorians*. London: Hutchinson, 2002.

8

"Material Interests"

Conrad's *Nostromo* as a Critique of Global Capitalism

J. HILLIS MILLER

Joseph Conrad's *Nostromo* is extremely complicated in its narrative organization. It offers narratologists great opportunities to demonstrate in detail the various kinds of narrative complexity employed by modernist authors such as Faulkner, Woolf, James, or Conrad himself. Just about every narrative device specialists in narrative form have identified is employed in one way or another: time shifts; analepsis; prolepsis; breaks in the narration; shifts in "focalization" from one character's mind to another by way of the "omniscient" (or, as I should prefer to say, following Nicholas Royle, "telepathic")[1] narrator's use of free indirect discourse, or by way of interpolated first person narration or spoken discourse; shifts by the narrator from distant, panoramic vision to extreme close-ups; retellings of the same event from different subjective perspectives; citations of documents, and so on.[2] The chronological trajectory of Sulaco history can be pieced together from these indirections. The story begins in the middle and then shifts backward and forward in a way that the reader may find bewildering, as he or she wonders just where on a time scale a given episode is in relation to some other episode. It is as though all these

1. See Royle 2003, 256–76.
2. The best interpretation of Conrad's work from a narratological perspective is Lothe 1989.

episodes were going on happening over and over, continually, in the capacious and atemporal mind of the narrator, like the endless succession of similar days and nights over the Golfo Placido in the setting of *Nostromo.* The story is presented in an almost cubist rendering, rather than by way of the impressionist technique Conrad is often said to have employed. I suggest that if the goal of *Nostromo* is to reconstruct the history of an imaginary Central American country, the formal complexity of the novel does more than implicitly claim that form is meaning, that is, that the complexity was necessary if Conrad was to tell at all the story he wanted to tell. *Nostromo*'s narrative complications also oppose what it suggests is false linear historical narration to another much more complex way to recover through narration "things as they really were." I shall return at the end of this essay to the question of the social, political, and ethical "usefulness" of modernist narration of this sort.

Fredric Jameson's slogan, "Always Historicize," means that we should read modernist English literature, or any other literary work of any time, in its immediate historical context. He is no doubt right about that. Nevertheless, certain works of English literature from the beginning of the twentieth century have an uncanny resonance with the global situation today. Examples would be the exploitation of Africa by the Wilcox family in E. M. Forster's *Howards End,* or the presentation of the effects of combat on Septimus Smith in Virginia Woolf's *Mrs. Dalloway.* Charles Gould and the American financier Holroyd, in Joseph Conrad's *Nostromo,* are even better examples. Their collaboration is remarkably prophetic of the current course of American global economic aspirations as well as of the effects of these on local cultures and peoples around the world. I shall indicate some of those disquieting consonances later.

If *Nostromo* is a novel not so much about history as about alternative ways to narrate history, this means its goal is not to recover a single life story (as, say, *Lord Jim* does), but to recover the story of the ways a whole group of individuals were related, each in a different way, to their surrounding community as it evolved through time. *Nostromo* is a novel about an imagined community, a fictitious one based on Conrad's reading about South American history.

A spectrum or continuum of different ways the individual may be related to others can be identified, going from smaller groups to larger. At the small end is my face-to-face encounter with my neighbor, with my beloved, or with a stranger, in love, friendship, hospitality, or hostility. A family, especially an extended family or a clan, is a larger group, in this case bound by ties of blood or marriage. A community is somewhat larger. A community is a group of people living in the same place who all know one another and who share the same cultural assumptions. They are not, however, necessarily related by blood or marriage. A nation is larger still. Most commonly a nation is made of a large number of overlapping but to some degree dissonant communities. Largest of all is the worldwide conglomeration of all human beings living on the same planet and all more and more subject to the same global economic and cultural hegemony. At each of these levels the individual has a relation to others, different in each case and subject to different constraints and conventions. It is of course often, in a given case, difficult, if not impossible, to maintain a sharp boundary between the different-sized groups.

Each form of living together, or of what Heidegger called "Mitsein," has been the object of vigorous theoretical investigation in recent years, for example, Lévinas's focus on the face-to-face encounter of two persons, or Jacques Derrida's similar focus in *The Politics of Friendship,* or work by Bataille, Blanchot, Nancy, Lingis, and others on the concept of community. In what I shall say about Conrad's *Nostromo* I shall interrogate primarily the relation of the individual to the community, or lack of it, in this novel, in the context of an intervention by one stage of global capitalism.

It can certainly be said that the citizens of Sulaco, the province of Conrad's imaginary Central American country of Costaguana, the setting for *Nostromo* (1904), form a community, at least in one sense of the word "community." The inhabitants all live together in the same place. All share, more or less, the same moral and religious assumptions. Whether rich or poor, white, black, or native American, they have been subjected to the same ideological interpellations, the same propaganda, the same political speeches, proclamations, and arbitrary laws. Most of all, they share the same history, what Don José Avellanos calls, in the title of his never-to-be-published manuscript, "Fifty Years of Misrule" (though the narrator, magically and quite improbably, has read it and can cite from it [Conrad 1951, 157; henceforth identified by page number alone]). Though Sulaco is a community of suffering, as one revolution after another brings only more injustice and senseless bloodshed, nevertheless, it can be argued, it is a true community. It is small enough so that most people know one another. Don Pépé, who runs the mine, knows all of the workers by name. Almost all belong to a single religious faith, Catholic Christianity.

If the reader reconstructs the story from a distance, putting the broken pieces of narration back in chronological order, *Nostromo* appears as a tale of nation-building, the creation of one of those "imagined communities" Benedict Anderson describes in his book of that name. After fifty years of misrule by the central government of Costaguana in Santa Marta, Sulaco, through a series of seriocomic events and accidents, becomes a prosperous, modern, peaceful, independent state, the Occidental Republic of Sulaco. An example of the fortuitous "causes" of this historical change is the cynical plan for secession devised by the skeptic Decoud shortly before his death. His plan is motivated not by political zeal or belief, but by his love for Antonia Avellanos. Nevertheless, Captain Mitchell, in his fatuous incomprehension, recounts the creation of the Republic of Sulaco as a connected story whose destined endpoint is the present-day prosperous nation. He recounts the sequence, in tedious detail, "in the more or less stereotyped relation of the 'historical events' which for the next few years was at the service of distinguished strangers visiting Sulaco" (529).

The pages following the citation just made give an example of Captain Mitchell's version of Sulaco history. Captain Mitchell is the spokesperson for an exemplary "official history," with its naïve conception of "historical events" as following one another in a comprehensible linear and causal succession. Conrad quite evidently disdains such history-writing. That false kind of history is represented, in one degree or another, by those source books on South American history, by Masterman, Eastlake, Cunninghame Graham, and others that Conrad had read.[3] Though *Nostromo* is about the nation-building of an imaginary South American republic, not a real one, nevertheless it is, among other things, a paradigmatic example of an alternative mode of history-writing, much more difficult to bring off. Conrad implicitly claims that this counterhistory is much nearer to the truth of human history and much more able to convey to readers the way history "really happens."

If the reader looks a little more closely at what the narrator says about Sulaco society, however, it begins to look less and less like a community of the traditional kind, that is, less and less like a community of those who have a lot in common, like those egalitarian rural English villages on the Welsh border Raymond Williams, in *The Country and the City*, so much admires, even though he resists idealizing them. For one thing, Sulaco "society" is made up of an extraordinary racial and ethnic mixture, product of its sanguinary history, as the narrator emphasizes from the beginning. The Spanish conquistadores enslaved the indigenes, the Native Americans. Wars of liberation from Spain led to wave after wave of military revolutions, one tyranny after another, with incredible bloodshed, cruelty, and injustice. Nevertheless, a large class of aristocratic hacienda-owning, cattle-ranching, pure-blooded Spanish people, "creoles," remain. They are the core of the "Blanco" party. Black slaves were imported. Then a series of migrations from Europe, people coming either as workmen, political exiles, or as imperialist exploiters, brought English, French, Italians, even a few Germans and Jews. Sailors, like Nostromo, deserted from

---

3. See Cedric T. Watts's succinct account of Conrad's sources in "A Note on the Background to 'Nostromo,'" in Conrad 1969, 37–42. A fuller account is given in Watts 1990.

merchant ships to add to the mix. Much intermarriage of course has occurred. Bits of three languages other than English exist in the novel: Spanish, French, and Italian. The narrator often uses Spanish names for occupations and ethnic identifications, as well as for place names like Cordillera, the name of the overshadowing mountain range. A good bit of the conversation in the novel must be imagined to be carried on not in the English the narrator gives, but in Spanish. Decoud and Antonia are native-born Costaguanans, but they have been educated in France. They talk to one another in French. Giorgio Viola, the old Garibaldino, and his family are Italian, as is Nostromo. They speak Italian to one another. This is signaled even in this English-language book by the way Nostromo addresses Viola as "Vecchio," Italian for "old man." Conrad does not specify what language the descendants of black slaves and the indigenes speak, but presumably some original languages persist beneath their Spanish. Charles Gould and all his family are English, though Gould was born in Costaguana and educated in England, as is the custom in that family. His wife is English, though her aunt has married an Italian aristocrat, and Charles Gould meets his future wife in Italy. The railroad workers are partly locals, "Indios," but engineers from England run the operation, and some workmen are European.

Sulaco, I conclude, is a complex mixture of races, languages, and ethnic allegiances. Sulaco is not all that different in this from the United States, by the way, though we have had, so far, only one, successful, "democratic revolution," ushering in government of the people, by the people, and for the people, with liberty and justice for all. I say those words with only a mild trace of irony, though the liberty, justice, and equality did not of course in 1776 extend to black slaves, or to Native Americans, or to women. My houses in Maine are on land taken from the Native Americans who had lived in the Penobscot Bay region for at least seven thousand years before the white man came and destroyed their culture in a few generations. "Liberty and justice for all" still has a hollow ring for many Americans, for example, the African American men and women who populate our prisons in such disproportionate numbers, or who swell the ranks of the unemployed.

The Sulaco noncommunity exists, moreover, like the United States one, as a complex layering of differing degrees of power, privilege, wealth, with the African Americans and Indios at the bottom, extending up through European working-class people, to the Creoles and the dominating quasi-foreigners like Charles Gould. Though the Gould family has been in Sulaco for generations, they are still considered Anglos, Inglesi. They are English in appearance, sensibility, mores, and language. The chief form of social mobility in Sulaco is through bribery, chicanery, or outright thievery, such as Nostromo's theft of the silver, or by way of becoming the leader of a military coup and ruling the country through force, as the indigene Montero momentarily does in *Nostromo*. It isn't much of a community.

Martin Decoud at one point sums up succinctly the nature of the Sulaco noncommunity in a bitter speech to his idealistic patriotic beloved, Antonia Avellanos. He quotes the great "liberator" of South America, Simón Bolívar, something for which the "Author's Note," oddly enough, apologizes. I suppose that is because the citation is a parabasis suspending momentarily the dramatization of a purely imaginary Central American state with an intrusion from actual history. In the "Note" Conrad has been defending, ironically, the "accuracy" of his report of Sulaco history, based as it is on his reading of Avellanos's "History of Fifty Years of Misrule." The joke (almost a "postmodern" rather than "modernist" joke) is that Avellanos's "History" is fictitious, along with the whole country of which it tells the story. No way exists to check the accuracy of Conrad's account against any external referent, nor any way to check what the narrator says against what Avellanos says. This reminds Conrad that some actual historical references do exist in the novel, and that these are a discordance:

> I have mastered them [the pages of Avellanos's "History"] in not a few hours of earnest meditation, and I hope that my accuracy will be trusted. In justice to myself, and to allay the fears of prospective readers, I beg to point out that the few historical allusions are never dragged in for the sake of parading my unique erudition, but that each of them is closely related to actuality—either throwing a light on the nature of current events or affecting directly the fortunes of the people of whom I speak. (5)

"Actuality"? "Current events"? The words must refer here to the pseudo-actuality of Costaguana history. One such parabasis-like intrusion is Decoud's citation of Bolívar: "After one Montero there would be another," the narrator reports, in free indirect discourse, Decoud as having said,

> the lawlessness of a populace of all colors and races, barbarism, irremediable tyranny. As the great liberator Bolívar had said in the bitterness of his spirit, "America is ungovernable. Those who worked for her independence have ploughed the sea." He did not care, he declared boldly; he seized every opportunity to tell her [Antonia] that though she had managed to make a Blanco journalist of him, he was no patriot. First of all, the word had no sense for cultured minds, to whom the narrowness of every belief is odious; and secondly, in connection with the everlasting troubles of

this unhappy country it was hopelessly besmirched; it had been the cry of dark barbarism, the cloak of lawlessness, of crimes, of rapacity, of simple thieving. (206)

It should be remembered that though what the narrative voice reports Decoud as having said agrees more or less with what the narrative voice itself says, speaking on its own, nevertheless Decoud is explicitly presented as an "idle boulevardier," who only thinks he is truly Frenchified. His corrosive skepticism leads ultimately to suicide. One might say that Decoud is a side of Conrad that he wants to condemn and separate off from himself, leaving someone who is at least earnestly committed to the endless hard work of the professional writer who earns his daily bread by putting words on paper. Conrad's letters to Cunninghame Graham often express, it must be said, a skeptical pessimism that is close to Decoud's, as in one famous passage about the universe as a self-generated, self-generating machine: "It knits us in and it knits us out. It has knitted time, space, pain, death, corruption, despair, and all the illusions—and nothing matters" (Conrad 1969, 57). In any case, what Decoud says matches closely what the narrator says about Sulaco's deplorable history.

How did Sulaco come to be such a noncommunity, or, to give Jean-Luc Nancy's term a somewhat different meaning from his own, how did Sulaco come to be an inoperative or "unworked" community, a *communauté désoeu-vrée*? Nancy's book begins with the unqualified statement that "The gravest and most painful testimony of the modern world, the one that possibly involves all other testimonies to which this epoch must answer (by virtue of some unknown decree or necessity, for we bear witness also to the exhaustion of thinking through History), is the testimony of the dissolution, the dislocation, or the conflagration of community" (Nancy 1991, 1). *Nostromo,* it might be said, is a parabolic fable or allegory, a paradigmatic fiction, of the dissolution, dislocation, or conflagration of community. Just how does this disaster come about, according to Conrad? Who are the villains in this sad event? It is an event that can no longer even be understood historically. Nancy's view of "thinking through History," the reader will note, is quite different from Jameson's. The dislocation of community must be borne witness to as something that we, or rather I, have experienced even if we (I) cannot explain it: "I have witnessed the conflagration of community. I testify that this is what has happened. I give you my personal word for it." The magically telepathic narrative voice in *Nostromo* is such a witness.

No doubt, Conrad, quite plausibly, ascribes a lot of stupidity, knavery, limitless greed, thievery, and wanton cruelty to his Costaguanans. Someone had to obey orders and torture Dr. Monygham or Don José Avellanos. Someone had to do as they were told and string Señor Hirsch up to a rafter by his hands tied behind his back, just as someone has had to commit all the recent violence in Iraq, Rwanda, Kosovo, and elsewhere. We have seen a lot of examples of this human propensity for murder, rape, and sadistic cruelty all over the world in recent years. *Nostromo* provides a parabolic representation of this aspect of human history. These traits of human nature, organized in civil wars and revolutions, have certainly stood in the way of Sulaco, in Conrad's fictitious history, becoming a community, to put it mildly.

Nevertheless, one needs to ask just what has made these deplorable aspects of "human nature," aspects that always stand in the way of law, order, democracy, and civil society, especially active in Sulaco. The answer is twofold. First there was the murderous invasion of South America by the Spanish that killed many of the indigenous population and enslaved the rest, driving them to forced labor and destroying their culture. Mrs. Gould has a sharp eye for the present condition of the indigenous population. She sees them during her travels all over the country with her husband to get support for the new opening of the mine and to persuade the Indios to come as workmen for the mine:

> Having acquired in southern Europe a knowledge of true peasantry, she was able to appreciate the great worth of the people. She saw the man under the silent, sad-eyed beast of burden. She saw them on the road carrying loads, lonely figures upon the plain, toiling under great straw hats, with their white clothing flapping about their limbs in the wind; she remembered the villages by some group of Indian women at the fountain impressed upon her memory, by the face of some young Indian girl with a melancholy and sensual profile, raising an earthenware vessel of cool water at the door of a dark hut with a wooden porch cumbered with great brown jars. (98)

This passage is a good example of that shift from a panoramic view to the specificities of an extreme close-up, in this case in a report of Mrs. Gould's memory, as it diminishes from her general knowledge of "the great worth of the people" to that "earthenware vessel of cool water at the door of a dark hut with a wooden porch cumbered with great brown jars." Conrad's narrator observes that many bridges and road still remain in Sulaco as evidence of what slave labor by the Indios accomplished (99). Whole tribes, the narrator says, died in the effort to establish and work the silver mine. At several places the narrator describes the Native American remnant in their sullen reserve.

"For whatsoever a man soweth, that shall he also reap" (Gal. 6:7). The consequences of the Spanish conquest still remain as the inaugural events in that whole region. The effect of these events cannot be healed or atoned for even after hundreds of years. They still stand in the way of the formation of any genuine community, Christian or secular, in the usual sense of the word community. This "origin" was not a unified and unifying originating event, like the big bang that initiated our cosmos, from which Costaguanan history followed in a linear and teleological fashion toward some "far off divine event" of peace and justice for all. It was rather a moment of what Jean-Luc Nancy calls, in a play on the word, "dis-position." The indigenous community, whatever it was like (and it will not do to idealize it too much; pre-Columbian history in South America was extremely bloody too), was disposed of by being displaced, posed or placed beside itself, unseated, dis-posed. This happened through the violent occupying presence of an alien culture bent on converting the savage heathens to Christianity and on enslaving them as workers in the Europeanizing of Sulaco.

This divisive violence at the origin, or origin as *polemos,* division, dis-position, also helps account for the way South American history, in what Conrad in *A Personal Record* calls this "imaginary (but true)" version of it (Conrad 1923, 98), is a long story of civil wars, tyrannies, and revolutions. Nor has this history come to an end. Twentieth-century events in Brazil, Argentina, Panama, Uruguay, Chile, or in Haiti bear witness to this. (A bloody rebellion against the Haitian government of Jean-Bertrande Aristide, led by armed paramilitary forces and parts of the army, was taking place at the moment I first drafted this essay, on 10 February 2004. The Bush government, in typical United States interventionist fashion, put its support behind Aristide's ouster. Never mind that he was the democratically elected president. The issue is the privatization of Haitian state-owned companies. The parallel with the central political event in *Nostromo* is striking.) These sad "true" histories are the background, or the assumed subsoil, of the "imaginary" story Conrad tells.

The next phase of Sulacan society the narrator records is the subsequent invasion of Europeans, in a second wave, after South American republics achieved independence. This was the invasion of global capitalism. It was already in full swing in Conrad's day. Of course that invasion is still going on today. It is more often now transnational corporations, often, but not always, centered in the United States, rather than in Europe, that are doing the exploiting. *Nostromo*'s main action is a fable-like exemplum of the effects of Western imperialist economic exploitation. The novel can be read with benefit even today as an analysis of capitalist globalization. The novel circles around one signal event in such a history, the moment when foreign capital, what Conrad calls "material interests," makes it possible to resist a threatened new local tyranny. This happens by way of a successful counterrevolution, and the establishment of a new regime. The Occidental Republic of Sulaco will allow foreign exploitation, in this case the working of the San Tomé silver mine, to continue operating peacefully in a stable situation, a nation with law and order. The silver will flow steadily north to San Francisco to make rich investors constantly richer. This prosperity leaves the men who work the mine still earning peasants' wages, though they now have a hospital, schools, better housing, relative security, and all the benefits that the Catholic Church can confer. Nevertheless, references to labor unrest, strikes, and the like are made toward the end of the novel. Conrad's narrator gives a haunting picture of the mine workers at a moment of the changing of shifts:

> The heads of gangs, distinguished by brass medals hanging on their bare breasts, marshaled their squads; and at last the mountain would swallow one-half of the silent crowd, while the other half would move off in long files down the zigzag paths leading to the bottom of the gorge. It was deep; and, far below a thread of vegetation winding between the blazing rock faces, resembled a slender green cord, in which three lumpy knots of banana patches, palm-leaf roofs,[4] and shady trees marked the Village One, Village Two, Village Three, housing the miners of the Gould Concession. (111)

What is most terrifying about this process of exploitation is Conrad's suggestion of its inevitability, at least in the eyes of the capitalist exploiters. It does not matter what are the motives of the agents of global capitalism, how idealistic, honest, or high-minded they are. They are co-opted in spite of themselves by a force larger than themselves. Charles Gould has inherited the Gould Concession from his father, who was destroyed by it, since, though he was not working the mine, constant levies were made on him by the central government in Santa Marta, until he was ruined financially and spiritually. "It has killed him," says Charles Gould, when the news of his father's death reaches him in England. He resolves to atone for that death by returning to Sulaco, raising capital on the way, and working the mine, just as, it might be argued, one of George W. Bush's motives for the invasion of Iraq was a desire to make up for his father's failure to "take out Saddam Hussein" and secure Iraqi oil for Western use.

Charles Gould was, as I have said, born in Sulaco. His sentimental and idealistic belief is that what he calls "material interests" will eventually bring

---

4. The text has "roots," as does the Dent edition, but surely that is a misprint for "roofs." "Palm-leaf roots" doesn't make sense.

law and order to his unhappy homeland, since these will be necessary to the working of the mine. "What is wanted here," he tells his wife,

> is law, good faith, order, security. Anyone may declaim about these things, but I pin my faith on material interests. Only let the material interests once get a firm footing, and they are bound to impose the conditions on which alone they can continue to exist. That's how your money-making is justified here in the face of lawlessness and disorder. It is justified because the security which it demands must be shared with an oppressed people. A better justice will come afterwards. That's your ray of hope. (92–93)

That noble but naïve confidence finds its echoes in today's neoconservative arguments for bringing democracy to Iraq by way of securing the smooth working of the oil industry there, our present-day form of "material interests." The latter (oil exploitation) is bound to bring the former (Western-style capitalist democracy)—in good time—since oil exploitation requires law and order.

Actually Gould is, in spite of his English sentimental idealism and practical efficiency, no more than a tool of global capitalism. The latter is represented, as every reader of the novel will remember, by the sinister American businessman and entrepreneur from San Francisco, Holroyd. Holroyd funds the reopening of the San Tomé mine as a kind of personal hobby. It is one small feature of his global enterprise. That enterprise includes, as a significant detail, a commitment to building Protestant churches everywhere the influence of his company reaches. Or, rather, Holroyd funds not the mine, but Charles Gould. It is Gould he has bought, not the mine, out of his confidence in Gould's integrity, courage, practicality, mine engineering know-how, and fanatical devotion to making the mine successful at all costs. Holroyd's recompense is the steady flow of large amounts of silver north by steamer to San Francisco from the port of Sulaco.

Holroyd has a canny sense of the precariousness of the San Tomé enterprise. He is ready at a moment's notice to withdraw funding if things go badly, for example, through a new revolution installing another tyrannical dictator who will take over the mine for his own enrichment. Nevertheless, Holroyd sees global capitalism as destined to conquer the world. He states this certainty in a chilling speech to Charles Gould. Gould does not care what Holroyd believes as long as he gets the money necessary to get the mine working. Holroyd's speech is chilling because it is so prescient. A CEO of ADM, "Supermarket to the World," or Bechtel, or Fluor, or Monsanto, or Texaco, or Halliburton, or Dick Cheney, for example, might make such a speech today, at least in private, to confidantes or confederates. It is not insignificant that Holroyd's big office building of steel and glass is located in San Francisco, since so many transnational corporations even today are located in California, if not in Texas. Conrad foresaw the movement of global capitalism's center westward from Paris and London first to New York and then to Texas and California. What Conrad did not foresee is that it would be oil and gas rather than silver or other metals that would be the center of global capitalism. Nor did he foresee that the development and use of oil and gas would cause environmental destruction and global warming that would sooner or later bring the whole process of economic imperialism to a halt, if nuclear war does not finish us all off before that.

Western-style industrialized and now digitized civilization, as it spreads all over the world, requires oil and gas not just for automobiles and heating, but for military might and explosives; for the airplanes that span the globe; for plastics, metal, and paper manufacture; for producing fertilizers and pesticides that grow the corn and soybeans that feed the cattle that make the beef that feeds people, and now for the production of personal computers, television sets, satellites, fiber optic cables, and all the rest of the paraphernalia of global telecommunications and the mass media. Surprisingly, it takes two-thirds as much energy to produce a PC as to produce an automobile, a large amount in both cases. When the oil and gas are gone, in fifty years or less, we are going to be in big trouble.

Holroyd, by the way, is a perfect United Statesian, that is, a mixture of many races. He is also a splendid exemplar of religion's connection to the rise of capitalism, this "millionaire endower of churches on a scale befitting the greatness of his native land" (84). "His hair was iron gray," says the narrator, "his eyebrows were still black, and his massive profile was the profile of a Caesar's head on an old Roman coin. But his parentage was German and Scotch and English, with remote strains of Danish and French blood, giving him the temperament of a Puritan and an insatiable imagination of conquest" (84). Here is this insatiable capitalist's prophetic account of the way United States–based global capitalism is bound to take over the world:

Now what is Costaguana? It is the bottomless pit of ten per cent loans and other fool investments. [The reader will remember the huge losses the Bank of America and other banks incurred not long ago from bad South American loans.] European capital has been flung into it with both hands for years. Not ours, though. We in this country know just about enough to keep in-doors when it rains. We can sit and watch. Of course, some day we shall step in. We are bound to. But there's no hurry. Time itself has got to wait on the greatest country in the whole of God's universe. We shall be giving the word for everything—industry, trade, law, journalism, art, politics, and religion, from Cape Horn clear over to Smith's Sound, and beyond too, if anything worth taking hold of turns up at the North Pole. And then we shall have the leisure to take in hand the outlying islands and continents of the earth. We shall run the world's business whether the world likes it or not. The world can't help it—and neither can we, I guess. (85)

Holroyd makes this remarkable statement to Charles Gould, during the latter's visit to Holroyd's office in San Francisco to raise venture capital for the mine. The "great Holroyd building" is described as "an enormous pile of iron, glass, and blocks of stone at the corner of two streets, cobwebbed aloft by the radiation of telegraph wires" (89). That sounds pretty familiar, except that today such a building would have more glass and less visible iron and stone. The cobweb of telegraph wires would be replaced by invisible underground optic cables or by discrete satellite dishes. Nevertheless, Conrad's circumstantial account of the determining role of the telegraph and of transoceanic cables in Sulaco's affairs anticipates the role of global telecommunications today.

Gould's reaction to Holroyd's speech about the way the United States will take over the world is a slight disagreeable uneasiness caused by a sudden insight into the smallness, in a global perspective, of the silver mine that fills his whole life. Holroyd's "intelligence was nourished on fact," says the narrator, and, oddly, says his words were "meant to express his faith in destiny in words suitable to his intelligence, which was unskilled in the presentation of general ideas" (85). This commentary is odd, because Holroyd's speech, it seems to me, expresses with great eloquence the "general idea" or ideological presuppositions of United States' "exceptionalism," its presumption that it is our destiny to achieve imperialist economic conquest of the world, with military help when necessary. Holroyd's grandiose conceptions are not all that solidly nourished on fact. Charles Gould, on the other hand, "whose imagination had been permanently affected by the one great fact of the silver-mine, had no objection to this theory [Holroyd's] of the world's future. If it had seemed distasteful for a moment it was because the sudden statement of such vast eventualities dwarfed almost to nothingness the actual matter in hand. He and his plans and all the mineral wealth of the Occidental province appeared suddenly robbed of every vestige of magnitude" (85).

My own reaction to Holroyd's speech is that chill or frisson I mentioned as a reaction to Conrad's prescience. It is also the reflection that United States global economic imperialism may already be coming to an end, like all imperialisms, as China is about to become the world's largest economy, as Indian software displaces Silicon Valley, as United States jobs flee by the hundreds of thousands to worldwide "outsourcing" and manufacturing (a million jobs lost to China alone in the last few years), and as non-Americans like the Australian Rupert Murdoch are coming to dominate the worldwide cable and satellite media. The triumph of global capitalism means the eventual end of nation state imperialist hegemony. That includes the United States. We should make no mistake about that.

Somewhat paradoxically, one of the best ways to understand what is happening now in our time of globalization is to read this old novel by Conrad, written just a hundred years ago. That is one answer to the question of literature's "usefulness" I posed at the beginning of this essay. The way military intervention by the United States is necessary to secure and support its worldwide economic imperialism is indicated in one small detail in *Nostromo.* The narrator notes that at the climax of the successful secession and establishment of the new Occidental Republic of Sulaco, a United States warship, the *Powhatan* (ironically named by Conrad for a Native American nation located in the eastern United States), stands by in the offing to make sure that the founding of the new Republic does not go amiss (544). This parallels the historical fact that when Panama, through United States conniving, split off from Colombia after Colombia refused to approve the Panama Canal, an American naval vessel, the *Nashville,* stood by to make sure the split really happened and the Columbians did not try to take Panama back.

It would be too long a tale here to tell the whole story of United States military and economic intervention, not to speak of covert action, in South America. Conrad's *Nostromo* gives an admirable emblematic fictional example of it. Whether or not Conrad himself agreed unequivocally with Holroyd's economic determinism is another question, just as it is questionable whether Conrad expresses without qualification his own radical skepticism in the Parisian dandy Decoud, "the man with no faith in anything except the truth of his own sensations," as though he were a perfect "impressionist." I think the answer is no in both cases.

The biographical evidence, for example, that provided succinctly by Cedric Watts, indicates that though Conrad learned a lot about South American history and topography from Eastlake, Masterman, and others, it was especially through his friendship and conversations with the Scottish socialist aristocrat R. B. Cunninghame Graham, descendent of Robert the Bruce, and through reading Graham's writings, that Conrad achieved his understanding of, and attitude toward, the bad things Western imperialism over the centuries had done in South America.

I conclude that, as many distinguished previous critics, for example, Edward Said and Fredric Jameson, have noted, *Nostromo* is, among other things, an eloquent and persuasive indictment of the evils of military and economic imperialism exercised by first-world countries, especially the United States, against so-called third-world countries everywhere. The reader needs, however, to be on guard against confusing analogy with identity. I have used words like "allegory" or "parable" or "fable" or "consonance" or "uncanny resonance" to indicate that *Nostromo* is a commodious emblem of historical events, economic imperialism in this case. Such historical events have recurred from time to time in post-Renaissance world history. They always happen, however, in significantly different ways at different moments in history, as, for example, oil and gas have replaced silver as the preferred loot from third-world countries, or as new telecommunications, e-mail, cellphones, and the Internet have replaced the telegraph lines and undersea cables of Conrad's day. The differences, we must always remember, are as important as the similarities. A parable is not a work of history. It is a realistic story that stands for something else in an indirect mode of reference. One might call each such literary work a reading of history. Literature, to express this in Conrad's own terms, is a way of using language in a mode that is "imaginary (but true)."

The claim I am making is complex and problematic. I am sticking my neck out in making this claim. It is impossible to do justice to the complexity in question in a short paper. A parable is not the same mode of discourse as an allegory, nor is either the same as an emblem, or as a paradigm, or as a reading. Careful discriminations would need to be made to decide which is the best term for Conrad's procedure of making an imaginary story "stand for" history in *Nostromo*. That little word "for" in "stand for" is crucial here, as is the word "of" in the phrases "parable of," or "emblem of," or "allegory of," or "paradigmatic expression of," or "reading of." What displacement is involved in that "for"? What is the force of "of" in these different locutions? What different ligature or separation is affirmed in each case? The differences among these "ofs" might generate a virtually endless analysis of *Nostromo* in their light.

I have used a series of traditional words for Conrad's displacement of "realist" narration to say something else. The multiplicity is meant to indicate the inadequacy of all of them. *Nostromo* is neither a parable, nor an emblem, nor an allegory, nor a paradigm, nor a reading. Each of these words is in one way or another inadequate or inappropriate. A parable, for example, is a short realistic story of everyday life that stands for some otherwise inexpressible spiritual truths. An example is Jesus' parable of the sower, in Matthew 13:3–9. *Nostromo* is hardly like that. All the other words I have used can be disqualified in similar ways. Nevertheless, it is of the utmost importance not to read *Nostromo* as a straightforward piece of "historical fiction." Historical realities as Conrad knew them, primarily from reading, but also through conversations with Cunninghame Graham, not from direct experience, are used as the "raw material" for the creation of a fictive "world" that is "imaginary (but true)." Conrad's own phrase is perhaps, after all, the best way to express the use of realist narrative techniques to create a place swarming with people and events that never existed anywhere on land or sea except within the covers of copies of *Nostromo,* and in Conrad's imagination, of course. The magnificent opening description of the sequestered province of Sulaco, cut off from the outside world by the Golfo Placido and by the surrounding mountains, is one way this isolation of Sulaco's imagined (non)community is expressed in *Nostromo.* The second part of Conrad's phrase, "but true," argues that the fictive events that take place in *Nostromo* correspond to the way things really happened in Central America at that stage of its history, that is, the moment of United States imperialist and global capitalist interventions. The words "but true" suggest a claim by Conrad that this transformation of historical fact into a complex modernist narrative form is better than any history book at indicating the way history actually happens. History happens, that is, in ways that are distressingly contingent. History is "caused" by peripheral factors such as Decoud's love for Antonia Avellanos or Nostromo's vanity. Conrad's phrase, "imaginary (but true)," is, after all, echoing, with his own modernist twist, what Aristotle said in the *Poetics* about the way poetry is more philosophical than history because "[history] relates what has happened, [poetry] what may happen" (*Poetics,* 1451b; Aristotle 1951, 35). The "modernist twist" is the implicit claim that the narrative complexities and indirections I have been identifying get closer to "what has happened" than "official" histories. Aristotle would probably not have approved of those complexities, any more than Plato, in *The Republic,* approved of Homer's "double diegesis" in pretending to narrate as Odysseus.

In spite of these complexities, the bottom line of what I am saying is that *Nostromo*'s indirect way of "standing for" the real South American history he knew from books and hearsay also means that, *mutatis mutandis,* it is also an indirect way of helping to understand what is going on in the United States and in the world today, in 2007.[5] That understanding would then make possible, it

5. F. R. Leavis, in *The Great Tradition,* first published in 1946, makes a strikingly similar claim for the relevance of *Nostromo* to understanding the history of Leavis's own time. Speaking of "Charles Gould's quiet unyieldingness in the face of Pedrito's threats and blandishments," Leavis says this episode "reinforce[s] dramatically that pattern of political significance which has a major part in *Nostromo*—a book that was written, we remind ourselves in some wonder, noting the topicality of its themes, analysis, and illustrations, in the reign of Edward VII [1901–1910]" (Leavis 1962, 218). I owe this reference to Jeremy Hawthorn. I am no Leavisite, but am, nevertheless, always happy to find myself in agreement with Leavis. Leavis would no doubt have had little sympathy with my insistence on the way *Nostromo* is "parabolic," that is, "imaginary (but true)."

might be, responsible action (for example by voting) as a way of responding to what is going on. This, I am aware, is an extravagant claim for the social, ethical, and political usefulness of literature.

I conclude also, finally, that *Nostromo* demonstrates, to my satisfaction at least, that all its notorious narrative complexities of fractured sequence, reversed temporality, and multiple viewpoints are not goods in themselves. Not telling a story by way of a single point of view and in straightforward chronological order can be justified only if, as is the case with *Nostromo,* such extravagant displacements or "dis-positions" are necessary to get the meaning across more successfully to the reader's comprehensive understanding.

Works Cited

Acts of Narrative. Edited by Carol Jacobs and Henry Sussman. Stanford, CA: Stanford University Press, 2003. 93–109.

Aristotle. *Poetics.* In Aristotle's *Theory of Poetry and Fine Arts,* critical text, translation, and commentary by S. H. Butcher. N.p.: Dover, 1951.

Conrad, Joseph. *A Personal Record.* London: Dent, 1923.

———. *Nostromo.* New York: Modern Library, 1951. All references to *Nostromo* are to this edition. I have used it because it reprints the first book version and has some passages Conrad later cut.

———. *Letters to Cunninghame Graham.* Edited by Cedric T. Watts. Cambridge: Cambridge University Press, 1969.

Leavis, F. R. *The Great Tradition.* Peregrine Books edition. Harmondsworth: Penguin, 1962.

Lothe, Jakob. *Conrad's Narrative Method.* Oxford: Clarendon Press, 1989.

Nancy, Jean-Luc. *The Inoperative Community.* Edited by Peter Connor, translated by Peter Connor, Lisa Garbus, Michael Holland, and Simona Sawhney. Minneapolis: University of Minnesota Press, 1991.

Royle, Nicholas. "The 'Telepathy Effect': Notes toward a Reconsideration of Narrative Fiction." In *The Uncanny.* Manchester: Manchester University Press, 2003. 256–76; also available in *Acts of Narrative,* edited by Carol Jacobs and Henry Sussman. Stanford, CA: Stanford University Press, 2003, 93–109.

Watts, Cedric T. "A Note on the Background to 'Nostromo,'" in Conrad 1969, 37–42.

———. *Conrad's "Nostromo."* London: Penguin, 1990.

9

Nostromo and the Writing of History

DAPHNA ERDINAST-VULCAN

In their foreword to a recent issue of *The Conradian* marking the centenary of *Nostromo*'s publication, Allan Simmons and J. H. Stape quote Conrad's observation that the novel is mentioned "sometimes in connection with the word 'failure' and sometimes in conjunction with the word 'astonishing'" (*A Personal Record*, 98), and note that "*Nostromo* is still oddly absent from the academy that ritually proclaims it 'great'" (vi). Rather than rescue the novel from this ambivalence, I wish to consider the economy of writing which, I believe, is at the core of both its greatness and its failure.

Nostromo is a novel without a protagonist, a text which does not enable or invite sustained emotional engagement with any one of the characters. There is obviously much more to be said about this very fundamental frustration of a desire from which—I would suggest and hope—even sophisticated readers cannot exempt themselves, and which is only partly due to the jerky narrative movement among the various characters and the constant shifts of action in time and space. But in the meantime, in the absence of a protagonist, let me begin with a parrot.

This parrot, one of several representatives of the species who will make their appearance in the narrative, is green, "brilliant like an emerald," and housed in a golden cage at the casa Gould. Obviously not content to serve for mere decorative effect, it watches over the conversation between Emilia and Charles Gould with "an irritated eye," and even makes an occasional comment of his own, screeching out ferociously "viva Costaguana!" before taking "refuge in immobility and silence" (69). At the end of the exchange—or rather a monologue—which follows the departure of the almighty Holroyd and marks Charles's alliance with material interests, the couple stop near the cage:

> The parrot, catching the sound of a word belonging to his vocabulary, was moved to interfere.
>
> Parrots are very human.
>
> "Viva Costaguana!" he shrieked, with intense self-assertion, and, instantly ruffling up his feathers, assumed an air of puffed-up somnolence behind the glittering wires. (82)

Parrots are very human. But humans, it seems, are somewhat parrot-like too, as we can hear if we join the guided tour of Sulaco offered by Captain Mitchell a few years later. Captain Mitchell, now the "Oceanic Steam Navigation (the O.S.N. of familiar speech) superintendent in Sulaco for the whole Costaguana section of the service," also known as "Our excellent Señor Mitchell," or simply as "Fussy Joe," prides himself on his "profound knowledge of men and things in the country—cosas de Costaguana" (10–11). He is thus best qualified, at least in his own view, to relate the history of the new republic, in which he played his own role, to a succession of unnamed "privileged visitors" (an obvious echo of the privileged reader of *Lord Jim*), and offer an official version which frames the narrative of what-really-happened.

Mitchell's guided tour is wonderfully generic, moving predictably along famous buildings, landmark spots, historical celebrities, and memorable dates, and peppered with the tag-phrases of an official historiography. Coming very near the end of the novel, it has the obvious effect of ironic juxtaposition, as the reader already knows at this point that the history of the separation was not exactly the work of a unified community, struggling for a common cause and led by wise statesmen and self-sacrificing heroes. What the reader does not yet know is the secret of Nostromo's treasure and the story of Decoud's suicide, which will follow Mitchell's account and further undermine its credibility.

It is not just a question of Mitchell's naivete or obtuseness. That "closing of the cycle" which ends Captain Mitchell's account (489) is as misleading as the framing structure itself: the end of his story is not the happy ending of bloodshed, revolution, and counterrevolution in Costaguana. Captain Mitchell will go home to England, comfortably obtuse and complacent, but the story of material interests will go on, and yet another revolution—perhaps the revolution of the "annexation"—is already in the offing (509). The consolation of narrative framing, seductive as it is, is not available in *Nostromo*.

But Captain Mitchell, though openly ridiculed by the narrative for the "more or less stereotyped account," the pomposity of his delivery, and his delusion of "being in the thick of things" (473), should not be so easily dismissed. Being only one of a series of historian figures, his version of "viva Costaguana!" is only marginally more parrotlike than that which is heard in the voice of the other writers, or, for that matter, the makers of history in the novel.

Don Jose Avellanos, the "Nestor of the Ricos" (148), venerable author of "Fifty Years of Misrule" (which, though never published, is claimed in Conrad's "Author's Note" to be the documentary origin of the narrative, and hence the source of its authority), is treated more charitably and respectfully than the misguided Captain Mitchell, but his blind patriotism and his love of rhetoric make him ineffectual and pathetically incompetent for dealing with anything which does not fit in with his historical vision: we find him at the casa Gould, seated comfortably in "a rocking-chair of the sort exported from the United States," pontificating "upon the patriotic nature of the San Tome mine for the simple pleasure of talking fluently" (51); we witness his oratorical efforts at the departure of General Barrios, where Emilia—clearly skeptical and apprehensive of his venture—surreptitiously attempts to give him the physical support he needs (140); we hear him relating to Decoud as the "'defender of the country's regeneration . . . expounder of the party's political faith'"(156), turning a deaf ear to the young man's indictment of his compatriots. The vulnerability of the old body is far more real and persuasive than the eloquence of the voice.

The evident inadequacy of these historian-figures foregrounds the historical account of the Separationist Revolution, told by an apparently omniscient, unnamed, and disembodied narrator, an intriguing presence to which I will come back at the close of this essay. But for now, we should note that far from a straightforward juxtaposition of "truth" and "untruth," the relation of historiography and history is triangulated through the introduction of another set of terms—fiction, myth, legend, and story. This invasion of what is ostensibly alien to the scientific project of history, is hardly news at the turn of the twenty-first century following the "constructivist turn" of the mid-1970s. Hayden White (1976, 1978) and Louis Mink (1978), to name the most notable proponents of this paradigm shift, have problematized the dual reference of "history" as both the event and its textual record—that identification which had served as the foundation of the Hegelian project and of Rank's imperative to "tell it as it was." Against the traditional self-positing of historiography as an objective, scientific endeavor, White and Mink highlight its status as a textual, discursive artifice, a product of selection, emplotment, and rhetorical formulation. A third position, pitted against the extreme version of the contructivist view, which was taken by many as a wholesale subversion of the truth-claims of historiography, and the equally sweeping countermoves of historians who sought to reinstate the epistemic legitimacy of their practices, was offered in the philosophical projects of Alasdair MacIntyre (1984) and David Carr (1986), who conceive of narrative not only as the historiographer's medium, but as part of the subject matter itself. Narrative, for both these philosophers, is fundamental to the way human agents construe their actions and lives—before, during, and after the events. The distinction between the experiential perception of the same events by the historical protagonists in real time and the subsequent narrative representation of events in a historical account is, thus, no more than a question of the specific historical context of the lived, or the narrated story. As we shall soon see, narrative self-perception is precisely what is at stake for many characters in Conrad's novel.

But *Nostromo* is not a postmodernist novel.[1] It does, as we have seen, highlight the gaps between discourse and event, and one can certainly point to some deconstructive effects (mostly confined to the Author's Note),[2] but it is, after all, an hour-by-hour account of what-really-happened during those few days of the Separationist Revolution, dappled throughout with the "effects of the real" as Barthes has called them—touches of local color and geography, familiar place names and historical allusions, Spanish phrases—convincing enough for readers who have tried to reconstruct the spatial layout of Costaguana and the temporal chronology of the events.[3] The differences between the various reconstructions are not as significant as that sense of authenticity which has prompted them in the first place. It seems, then, that the narrative conforms to the requirements of historicity—noted by J. Hillis Miller in "Narrative and History" (1974)—in a most traditionally scrupulous manner.

I would suggest that it is precisely this conformity to the discursive—and, more importantly, to the conceptual—parameters of historiography which makes the novel so problematic. To understand the dynamics of this fictional

1. Given the constructivist turn of the 1970s, the postmodernist context is, of course, highly seductive for a reading of *Nostromo,* as evidenced in the readings offered by Edward Said (1975); Pamela Demory (1993); and Christophe Robin (2002). Notwithstanding the fundamental divergence of my own approach, it seems to me that Robin's essay offers a particularly illuminating and rich reading of the novel.

2. I have discussed these deconstructive effects at some length in *Joseph Conrad and the Modern Temper* (1991), 67–85.

3. Such reconstructions have been offered by Jacques Berthoud (1978), 98–99; Cedric Watts (1982), 152–63; and Keith Carabine (1984), xxvi–xxx.

historiography, let us turn for a moment to the work of Michel de Certeau which revolves on the inextricability of historiography and history, of the writing and the making of history.

Historiography, for de Certeau, is a formative historical practice, which helps in the establishment of social cohesion; legitimizes the power of a contemporary regime; and answers the need of a community for a sense of origin, structure, and order. Historiography, he says, is "a discourse based on conjunction, which fights against all the disjunctions produced by competition, labor, time, and death" (1983, 205).

But this work of conjunction, essential for the cohesion of the social body (the sense of an "us" in Conradese), is effected by historiography through the assumption of a rupture with the past, a separation from what is other to a present state. In the case of European historiography it is a "*writing that conquers*. It will use the New World as if it were a blank, 'savage' page on which Western desire will be written. It will transform the space of the other / into a field of expansion for a system of production" (xxv–xxvi). But what is obviously the case with the colonized "other" also holds true for the past self of the social body—the writing of history is inaugurated by an act of differentiation between past and present, civilization and nature, the narrating subject and the narrated object. Historiography is, in fact, a "discourse of separation" (1975, 3). The underside of this historical practice is the suppression of alterity, which needs to be domesticated, buried, or forgotten in the effort of self-creation.

In the West, writes de Certeau, "the group (or the individual) is legitimized by what it excludes," and historiography accomplishes this act of exclusion in that "what is *perishable* is its data; [and] *progress* is its motto. The one is the experience which the other must both compensate for and struggle against . . . it is a breakage everywhere reiterated in discourse, and that yet denies loss by appropriating to the present the privilege of recapitulating the past as a form of knowledge" (1975, 5; emphasis in original). As we can see, the gesture of separation, differentiation, and exclusion, which is the inaugural act of historiography, is conceptualized by de Certeau in psychoanalytic terms as an act of repression.[4] What follows is, almost needless to say, the return of the repressed.

Historiography promotes a selection between what can be *understood* and

---

4. Unlike Jameson's "political unconscious" which focuses on "all the things which Conrad preferred not to see" (and, in the case of *Nostromo*, the moral and ideological division of English-speaking or foreign characters from the Latino-American ones), and generates a quasi-structuralist interpretation of the novel (1981, 269–80), my own approach is inspired by de Certeau's perspective which relates to the unconscious dynamics of both the *making* and the *writing* of history.

what must be *forgotten* in order to obtain the representation of a present intelligibility. But whatever this new understanding of the past holds to be irrelevant—shards created by the selection of materials, remainders left aside by an explication—come back, despite everything, on the edges of discourse or in its rifts and crannies: "resistances," "survivals" or delays discreetly perturb the pretty order of a line of "progress" or a system of interpretation. These are lapses in the syntax constructed by the law of a place. Therein they symbolize a return of the repressed, that is, a return of what, at a given moment, has *become* unthinkable in order for a new identity to become *thinkable.* (1975, 4; original italics)

The narrative of *Nostromo,* which so clearly revolves on the "Separation" and the "Separationist revolution" as an inaugural event, is an exemplary historiography, the story of "the birth of a state," its liberation from tyranny and lawlessness, and—most importantly—its accession to modernity.

The excluded other in this case is not only the past of Costaguana, ostensibly over and done with after the Separationist Revolution, but also, primarily, I believe, a different narrative conception which is relegated to the past and allowed to appear only in the margins of the historical narrative, as a piece of folklore, a mere exotic relic of otherness. The most visible form of this narrative conception is the mythical legend of the accursed treasure:

The peninsula of Azuera, a wild chaos of sharp rocks and stony levels cut about by vertical ravines . . . [is] utterly waterless . . . it has not soil enough—it is said—to grow a single blade of grass, as if it were blighted by a curse. The poor, associating by an obscure instinct of consolation the ideas of evil and wealth, will tell you that it is deadly because of its forbidden treasures. The common folk of the neighborhood, peons of the estancias, vaqueros of the seaboard plains, tame Indians coming miles to market with a bundle of sugar-cane or a basket of maize worth about threepence, are well aware that heaps of shining gold lie in the gloom of the deep precipices cleaving the stony levels of Azuera. Tradition has it that many adventurers of olden time had perished in the search. The story goes also that within men's memory two wandering sailors—Americanos, perhaps, but gringos of some sort for certain—talked over a gambling, good-for-nothing mozo, and the three stole a donkey to carry for them a bundle of dry sticks, a water-skin, and provisions enough to last a few days. Thus accompanied, and with revolvers at their belts, they had started to chop their way with machetes through the thorny scrub on the neck of the peninsula. . . .

The sailors, the Indian, and the stolen burro were never seen again. As to the mozo, a Sulaco man—his wife paid for some masses, and the poor four-footed beast, being without sin, had been probably permitted to die; but the two gringos, spectral and alive, are believed to be dwelling to this day amongst the rocks, under the fatal spell of their success. Their souls cannot tear themselves away from their bodies mounting guard over the discovered treasure. They are now rich and hungry and thirsty—a strange theory of tenacious gringo ghosts suffering in their starved and parched flesh of defiant heretics, where a Christian would have renounced and been released.

These, then, are the legendary inhabitants of Azuera guarding its forbidden wealth. (4–5)

This folktale bears all the markers of narrative distancing, repeated expressions, and phrases of disassociation—"the poor . . . will tell you; the common folk . . . are well aware"; "tradition has it"; "the story goes also"—relegating the legend to the status of mere folklore. The story is also literally marginalized, offered as part of the panoramic geography of the Occidental Republic which prefaces the narrative itself, and set outside the account of Costaguana history, which does not begin until the following chapter.

Against this folktale, told by ignorant people steeped in superstition, we are offered a "proper" historical narrative—"proper" in that it is founded on the discursive proprieties of Western rationality and establishes its property rights. It is the discourse of "facts," of "material interests," of "progress" and "modernity": the construction of the National Railway is a "progressive and patriotic undertaking" (34); "The sparse row of telegraph poles . . . [is like] a slender, vibrating feeler of progress" (166). The San Tomé mine becomes, in the hands of the new regime, "an institution, a rallying point for everything in the province that needed order and stability to live" (110); the "fact—very modern in its spirit—of the San Tomé mine had already thrown its subtle influence" (96–97). It is, as Sir John, the Chairman of the Railway Company, perceives, the most important of those "reassuring facts" behind the ceremonies, the speeches, and the proclamations which inaugurate the new era (37–38).

The principal actor in this shift from legend to history is Charles Gould, whose claim to the title "el rey de Sulaco" is given legitimacy through the "familial, political, [and] moral genealogy" (de Certeau 1975, 6–8) provided by the historical narrative. Charles Gould has consciously chosen to defy his father's wishes and take up the concession. For the father, "well-read in light literature" (like other Conradian characters), the mine took "the form of the Old Man of the Sea fastened upon his shoulders" (56). But the son—the maker of history—shuts off the myth, dismisses his father's superstitions, and expurgates the facts from the mist of legend: "[W]ith advancing wisdom, he managed to clear the plain truth of the business from the fantastic intrusions of the Old Man of the Sea, vampires, and ghouls, which had lent to his father's correspondence the flavor of a gruesome Arabian Nights tale" (58).

The legend, however, creeps back into the making and the writing of history. In his role as a maker of history, Charles Gould, obsessed with "the tearing of the raw material of treasure from the earth" (60), will also turn the possession of the mine into a curse which will blight his own life. This is, to use de Certeau's uncannily resonant phrase, the "tautology of legend" (1983, 84), as the folk story of the cursed gringos, the mozo, and the treasure of the Azuera resurfaces through the cracks in the historical narrative.

The most obvious instance of this return of the repressed is the case of Nostromo himself. Initially described as a legendary popular hero, picturesque on his silver-grey mare, Nostromo straddles both myth and history. Paradoxically, it is his legendary charisma—self-consciously enhanced by spectacular displays of bravura and generosity—this larger-than-life, epic quality, which turns him into one of the makers of the new age of Costaguana. He is thus a halfway figure, uneasily poised between legend and history. But the narrative ends with his unconditional surrender to the legend. From the moment of contact with the silver of the mine, Nostromo becomes its slave, taking on the role of the cursed Gringos on Azuera (526–27, 531).[5]

But the tautology of legend seems to assert itself in yet more insidious ways. The modern representations of change and progress turn out to be uncomfortably similar to those of the past. Against the supposed linearity of historical progression and its underlying teleology, the regime of legend and myth seems to engender a cyclical conception of human life. Neither Mitchell's complacent historical summation, which ends with the establishment of the prosperous Occidental Republic, nor the narrator's description of present-day Sulaco "with cable cars" "carriage roads," and "a vast railway goods yard by the harbor, which has a quay-side, a long range of warehouses, and quite serious, organized labor troubles of its own" (95)—neither one of these claims of accomplishment can dispel the sense that the cycle of revolution and counter-revolution is not over.

By the end of the novel we are left with a set of superimpositions rather

---

5. See also pp. 460, 491, 529. We should note that the legendary curse which attaches to the silver is not confined to the mind of Nostromo himself who is, after all, a man of the people, and thus presumably susceptible to superstition. The narrative itself seems to take over the terms of the legend: following the description of Decoud's suicide, Nostromo appears on the island, and "the spirit . . . the silver of San Tomé was provided now with a faithful and lifelong slave" (501). No wonder then that even to Captain Mitchell he appears like "a haunting ghost" (487).

than oppositions: the figure of Gould, "el rey de Sulaco," riding his horse along the Camino real, the old Spanish road, is superimposed on the ancient weather-stained equestrian statue of Charles IV (58–59); and Captain Mitchell's comment on the removal of the statue which was "an anachronism" (482) sounds like an ominous prediction of what is to come. Gould's optimistic sense of having "mastered the fates" through action (66), is echoed in the description of Nostromo, now known as Captain Fidanza bound for the Great Isabel "before all men's eyes, with a sense of having mastered the fates" (530); the dead weight of the silver around the neck of Gould's father is transformed into a "monstrous and crushing weight" around his wife's neck (221); the clanking of wheels heard at the approach of the train, that vehicle of modernity, is replicated in the clanking of the invisible silver fetters which bind Nostromo to the treasure (546).

Myth, then, is not the opposite, but the suppressed underbelly of historiography and of history itself. These two discursive regimes converge in the paternal figure of the almighty Holroyd, the head of silver and steel interests, who "serves the progress of the world" (378). Looming large behind the scenes like the puppet master of the show, Holroyd is a later avatar of Kurtz, both in his status as the agglomerate creature of European civilization and in his insatiable omnivorous imperialism,[6] but his political rhetoric is explicitly—indeed uncomfortably—American (and even more uncomfortably contemporary):

> "Time itself has got to wait on the greatest country in the whole of God's Universe. We shall be giving the word for everything: industry, trade, law, journalism, art, politics, and religion, from Cape Horn clear over to Smith's Sound, and beyond, too, if anything worth taking hold of turns up at the North Pole. And then we shall have the leisure to take in hand the outlying islands and continents of the earth. We shall run the world's business whether the world likes it or not. The world can't help it—and neither can we, I guess."
>
> His intelligence was nourished on facts; and Charles Gould, whose imagination had been permanently affected by the one great fact of a silver mine, had no objection to this theory of the world's future. (77)

It is in this suspension of time that history and myth most clearly intersect, as the silver, too, is perceived as immune to the ravages and corruption of time. An incongruous echo of Holroyd's "time itself has got to wait" is heard

---

6. Holroyd's "massive profile [is] the profile of a Caesar's head on an old Roman coin"; "and his parentage is German and Scotch and English, with remote strains of Danish and French giving him the temperament of a Puritan and an insatiable imagination of conquest" (76).

in Nostromo's assertion that "time is on our side, señor. And silver is an incorruptible metal that can be trusted to keep its value for ever . . . an incorruptible metal" (299–300). The mythicity—the desire of sameness, self-identity, and totality—is the real curse, or the nightmare of history. It is same desire, I believe, which accounts for the lack of emotional focus, and the absence of a protagonist in *Nostromo*.

The eponymous character himself, who makes a belated, if spectacular, entrance into the novel, initially seems to have no interiority at all, and his existence is predicated on being seen, paraded, trusted, and adored. With neither the space nor the need to exhaust the textual evidence for this mode of existence, which is laid on quite thick throughout the narrative, let me just point to a few illustrative passages, beginning with his introduction by Mitchell who modestly claims to be "a pretty good judge of character," and then proceeds to tell the disembodied listener of this local legendary hero, a man, "absolutely above reproach, [who] became the terror of all the thieves in the town. . . . That's what the force of character will do for you" (13).

True to his role as the "lordly Capataz de Cargadores, the indispensable man, the tried and trusty Nostromo, the Mediterranean sailor come ashore" (130), he takes on the heroic mission of saving the silver, in order—as he explains to the dying Teresa whose request for a priest he has just refused—to "keep on being what I am: every day alike" (253). This odd reply points to a sense of selfhood which is entirely embedded in and authored by a public narrative: "They shall learn I am just the man they take me for" (267). This sense of character as public property will later reverberate in Dr. Monygham's exhortation: "you must be true to yourself" (457), which will come at the very moment when this local hero is about to betray his mission. But this shift of loyalties, presumably brought about by a breach in Nostromo's public identity, is only the mythical flipside of the same historical currency: no longer in the service of the mine and its historical-political function–Nostromo is now the slave of the forbidden silver, totally identified with and subjected to its legendary curse. In both these phases he does remain true to himself, insofar as his sense of selfhood is entirely authored by public narratives.[7]

---

7. Two comments which might be relevant here: first of all, Nostromo identifies himself with the cursed treasure hunters on the Azuera long before he shifts his loyalties, referring to the silver cargo as "a greater treasure than the one which they say is guarded by ghosts and devils in Azuera" (255), and to the mission as "taking up a curse upon me" (259; see also 265). For him, too, the service of material interests, ostensibly on the side of history-making, is bound up with the mythical, repressed legend of the treasure. Second, Nostromo's acts of charity, even when performed in private, are tinged with contempt for "those beggarly people accustomed to my generosity" (297; see also 247), rather than compassion, and are aimed primarily to promote his fame.

Writing to his sister about this local hero who has a "particular talent for being on the spot whenever there is something picturesque to be done" (224), Decoud explains: "'Exceptional individualities always interest me, because they are true to the general formula expressing the moral state of humanity'"(246). This is actually less paradoxical than it sounds. In the same way that Mitchell is like other historiographers only more so, Nostromo is an exaggerated but exemplary version of the species which I would call *homo historicus,* and his difference from other characters is a matter of degree.

Nostromo's mode of being is shared by other characters in the novel, heroes and villains alike, who seem to author themselves through some sort of public, historical perception, each living up to or making use of his or her reputation: Dr. Monygham, who cannot exorcise his past, with "the dark passages of his history" (311) indelibly inscribed on his body, his hobbling gait and his dam-aged feet (347), is also "the slave of a ghost" (374). He, too, is trading on his (false) reputation as a man who had once betrayed his friends. In the depth of his personal abasement, his "conception of his disgrace," this eminently loyal man has come to believe that his own usefulness consists in his "character" (409), and offers to serve the woman he loves "to the whole extent of [his] evil reputation" by playing the "game of betrayal" (410).

Antonia, too, is described by Captain Mitchell as "a historical woman," a "character" (476). Indeed, in her few appearances in the novel, attending to her father, engaged in the drafting of state papers and proclamations, convert-ing her poor lover into a patriot, or sending him off on his deathly mission without as much as a tear, she is seen—even through Decoud's eyes—as a "Charlotte Corday" (which she takes as a compliment), "stately," "lovely and statuesque," but never a real creature of flesh and blood.[8]

Charles Gould, too, is a "public character, subjectified by and subjected to his role as "el rey de Sulaco" (316), with an "almost mystic view of his right" (402). With her acute political senses, Antonia Avellanos quite rightly per-ceives this when she tells Gould: "It is your character that is the inexhaustible treasure which may save us all yet; your character, Carlos, not your wealth" (361). Indeed, it is his heritage as "the descendant of adventurers enlisted in

8. It is not only the exclusive focus on "the great cause" which makes the relationship inconceivable in terms of romance, but Antonia's body language. Following Decoud's passionate declaration of love (during which we are told that "she never looked at him"; "she turned her head a little"; "her hand closed firmly on her fan"), Antonia finally "opens her red lips for the first time, not unkindly" only to say that "men must be used as they are" (177). Even Conrad's notorious limitations in handling love scenes cannot fully account for the coldness, the austerity, and the reticence of this character. Finally, she is seen at the very end of the novel accompanying her uncle, the fierce Bishop Corbelan on a visit to the casa Gould, trying to promote the idea of the annexation with her usual "earnest calm of invincible resolution" in the name of her dead lover (509).

a foreign legion, of men who had sought fortune in a revolutionary war, who had planned revolutions, who had believed in revolutions" (366), which will make it possible for him to harness the mine, by threatening to blow it up, into the service of those material interests in the name of the father, the almighty Holroyd, he has elected to serve.

The novel is an exemplary historiography, then, not only because it is so carefully crafted in terms of action, time, and place, but primarily because most of the characters themselves are blighted by the same desire diagnosed by de Certeau in the workings of historiography. It is a desire for sameness and absolute self-coherence through the exclusion of alterity. Most of the characters are incapable of breaking through their mythicized histories or historical myths, imprisoned within their own conceptions of themselves as "public characters," static, insular, indeed nearly autistic in their encounters with others.[9]

In spite of the various focalizations offered in the narrative, the novel is not polyphonic in any Bakhtinian sense. "Poly-monologic" seems to be a little more apt. The human encounters in the novels are not only few and far between; they also, for the most part, involve characters who are cocooned in their own narratives and talking at cross purposes. This is particularly noticeable in the conversation between Nostromo and Dr. Monygham, where the former is desperate for a word which would "restore his personality to him" (434), and the latter is only interested in the "instrumentality" of the Capataz; or in the dialogues of Decoud and Nostromo, bound on their dangerous mission, risking their lives presumably for the same cause, but entirely at odds as far as their motives go. But, more poignantly, even encounters of characters who supposedly love each other—Charles and Emilia Gould, Antonia and Decoud, Nostromo and Giselle—where one party desperately reaches out to the other only to met with silence—do not involve that genuine intimacy.

Paradoxically, perhaps, this insularity of the "public characters" hollows out the historiographical desire of conjunction. The political history of the land, made as it is by conflicting interests and random coincidences, does not yield a sense of community either before of after the Separation.[10] The name—or rather the title—"Nostromo" (our man) is thus problematic not

9. What is true for the heroic figures applies to the villains as well. They, too, live up to their public images within their own narrative contexts: Pedrito Montero "had been devouring the lighter sort of historical works in the French language." Struck by the splendor of the brilliant court of the second Empire, he had "conceived the idea of an existence for himself." This, we are told "was one of the immediate causes of the Monterist Revolution" (387); Sotillo brazens out the danger of being deserted by his troops "on the strength of his reputation with very fair success" (450). And even Captain Mitchell, refusing to let go of his gold chronometer with admirable tenacity (which borders on stupidity), insists "I am a public character, sir" (347).

10. For an illuminating discussion of nation-building discourse in *Nostromo,* see Mallios 2001.

only because the illustrious Capataz de Cargadores eventually betrays his mission, but because there is no first-person plural in the novel. There is no "us" in Sulaco.

Against the history made and written in the shadow of Holroyd, the Father, we have the two maternal figures, Teresa Viola and Doña Emilia Gould. Teresa Viola, Nostromo's adoptive mother, is the only character who sees through him with extraordinary clarity. "He has not stopped very long with us. There is no praise from strangers to be got here," Signora Teresa said tragically. "Avanti! Yes! That is all he cares for. To be first somewhere—somehow—to be first with these English. They will be showing him to everybody. 'This is our Nostromo!'" She laughed ominously. "What a name! What is that? Nostromo? He would take a name that is properly no word from them." (23). But she is a woman of no consequence, as "unreasonable," her husband believes, as the rest of them, and so she remains all alone with her pain and her homesickness (25).

Emilia Gould is a much more powerful maternal counterforce, "highly gifted in the art of human intercourse" and "always sorry for homesick people" (46). Fully aware of the history of the mine—"worked in the early days mostly by means of lashes on the backs of slaves, its yield had been paid for in its own weight of human bones" and the corpses "thrown into its maw" (52), she is not concerned "with the erection or demolition of theories any more than with the defense of prejudices" and has "no random words" at her command (67). She is childless, but closely associated with the wooden figure of "a Madonna in blue robes with the crowned child sitting on her arm" (67, 206), which the almighty Holroyd, the endower of churches, clearly finds tawdry and cheap.

Unlike her husband, the champion of facts and material interests, Emilia sees "the man under the silent, sad-eyed beast of burden . . . ; she remembered the villages by some group of Indian women at the fountain impressed upon her memory, by the face of some young Indian girl with a melancholy and sensual profile, raising an earthenware vessel of cool water at the door of a dark hut with a wooden porch cumbered with great brown jars" (88; see also 67).

But Emilia is disempowered. She does not speak out again after her initial and tentative expression of misgivings at the beginning of Gould's partnership with Holroyd (67–71). The potential conflict with her husband is channeled by the narrative into the metaphor of the waterfall with its dark-green, lush fernery, dried up and supplanted by the San Tome mine.

> There was no mistaking the growling mutter of the mountain pouring its stream of treasure under the stamps; and it came to his heart with the peculiar force of a proclamation thundered forth over the land and the marvellousness of an accomplished fact fulfilling an audacious desire. . . .
> The waterfall existed no longer. The tree-ferns that had luxuriated in its

spray had died around the dried-up pool, and the high ravine was only a big trench half filled up with the refuse of excavations and tailings. The torrent, dammed up above, sent its water rushing along the open flumes of scooped tree trunks striding on trestle-legs to the turbines working the stamps on the lower plateau—the mesa grande of the San Tome mountain. Only the memory of the waterfall, with its amazing fernery, like a hanging garden above the rocks of the gorge, was preserved in Mrs. Gould's water-color sketch. (106; see also 209)

The recurrent association of Emilia with water acts like an antidote to and a reminder of the curse of the treasure on the "utterly waterless" Peninsula of the Azuera, haunted by the two gringos, "spectral and alive," who "are believed to be dwelling to this day amongst the rocks, under the fatal spell of their success . . . rich and hungry and thirsty" (5). By the end of the novel, however, the two maternal characters are entirely defeated. Teresa is dead, and Emilia's life is blighted by the mythicity of history, not only in the obvious sense of her helplessness before those economic and political powers represented by her husband, but also—primarily, I think—in that her voice is no longer heard in the narrative itself. Perhaps, after all, she cannot break away from the narrative of history because she remains at home, exactly where she is supposed to be, attending to the needy with her "lieutenants," the doctor and the priest (146), silently looking on from the margins of history, as mothers have always done.

Between these two sets of characters—the "public figures," authored by the narrative of the father and the "maternal" figures, who are silenced and defeated, there is one character who presents the greatest difficulty. Martin Decoud, less deluded and more self-consciously complex than the "paternal" characters, and having more agency than the "maternal" ones, seems to be the only potential Conradian protagonist in this novel. Why, then, does Conrad have him commit suicide shortly after his introduction into the narrative?

The problem becomes even more pressing when we consider the narrative voice. The concept of the 'omniscient narrator' has recently been probed and problematized in theoretical discussion, and the case of *Nostromo* would certainly reinforce the call for a reconceptualization of the term.[11] The narrative voice in the novel—that is, the teller of the "real" historical course of events—is apparently omniscient as it seems to have unlimited access to the various plotlines and events which make up the history of Costaguana and to the minds of the various characters as it moves between different focalizers. But throughout these movements, the voice remains relatively constant:

---

11. For a seminal discussion of this concept, see Jonathan Culler 2004, 22–34. There is, obviously, much more to be said about the narrator function in *Nostromo*, which is beyond the scope of the present discussion.

urbane, skeptical, modulated by irony, and often quite scathingly sarcastic. In fact, it is very much like the voice of Martin Decoud, whose observations of the other characters—when expressed in his own voice—are strikingly similar to those of the disembodied narrator.[12]

This merging of Decoud's voice and outlook with that of the narrator is particularly disturbing in the account of Decoud's suicide. It sounds, in fact, as though it is Decoud himself who is telling of his own death, as though he commits a "double suicide," both at the level of story and at the level of discourse.

The issue becomes even more problematic when we bear in mind the indications—far too many to ignore—of autobiographical elements which clearly relate Decoud to his author. Like Conrad, he is a writer who has chosen to live away from his native country and is slightly "frenchified" (152). He is, to use Bishop Corbelán's scornful epithet "neither the son of his own country nor of any other" (198). Most significantly, perhaps, in his playful author's note to this "most anxiously meditated of the longer novels," Conrad makes repeated autobiographical allusions to "the beautiful Antonia," moving between a fairly conventional metaphoric description of the writing as an extended visit to Sulaco, where Antonia is a fictional figure "modeled on" the author's first love, and a literalization of the metaphor, which relates to Antonia as real person: "Of all the people who had seen with me the birth of the Occidental Republic, she is the only one who has kept in my memory the aspect of continued life"; "If anything could induce me to revisit Sulaco (I should hate to see all these changes) it would be Antonia" (xlvi). This playful equivocation should not blind us to the deep underlying anxiety. Fortunately for us, Conrad did not come to the same end as poor Martin Decoud. But having set up this character as a fictional counterpart only to have him commit suicide does raise some disturbing questions.

I would suggest that the answer to some of these questions may have to do with Conrad's conception of language, which, unlike the legendary silver, is highly corruptible, particularly when stamped and molded by the discourse of politics, ideology, and historiography. Political violence, that "puerile and bloodthirsty game of murder . . . played with terrible earnestness by depraved children," passes in Costaguana as "the saving of the country" (49). The mur-

---

12. Decoud's perception of Charles Gould's obsession with the mine as a form of marital infidelity—"a subtle wrong . . . that sentimental unfaithfulness which surrenders her happiness, her life, to the seduction of an idea. The little woman has discovered that he lives for the mine rather than for her" (244–45)—is echoed by the narrative voice which refers to that "subtle conjugal infidelity through which his wife was no longer the sole mistress of his thoughts" (366). Decoud's jaded views of the mine, of Sulaco politics and history are similarly echoed by the narrative (see 16, 182, 199).

derous tyrant is known as "The Citizen Saviour of the Country" (138) or "The supreme chief of democratic institutions" (140). His band of hooligans is "The Army of Pacification" (137). Montero overthrows the government "in the name of national honor" (145) and of "'a justly incensed democracy'" (190); and the Junta of Notables, the "Great Parliamentarians," headed by Don Juste Lopez who, Mitchell tells us, is "a first-rate intellect" (478), is ready to welcome the change of regime for the sake of "Democratic aspirations" and "the inscrutable ways of human progress" (238). There is more, much more, of the same corrupt rhetoric, which is by no means the monopoly of the villains in the historical drama.

Martin Decoud, a writer in exile, is painfully aware of the corruptibility of language, and refuses to take part in the parrot-talk. His apparent alienation from his community and from the patriotic cause is not the indifference of a Parisian dandy, but an attempt to preserve his own voice, which is, quite literally in his case, a matter of life and death. He knows that "the noise outside the city wall is new, but the principle is old" (173); that this is "history, as that absurd sailor Mitchell is always saying" (172). He has no illusions about "our friends, the speculators" (175), nor any faith in the parrotlike slogans he churns out in the service of the great cause, that "deadly nonsense" which, he says, has already killed his self-respect and is, for him, "a sort of intellectual death" (180):

> He was no patriot. First of all, the word had no sense for cultured minds, to whom the narrowness of every belief is odious; and secondly, in connection with the everlasting troubles of this unhappy country it was hopelessly besmirched; it had been the cry of dark barbarism, the cloak of lawlessness, of crimes, of rapacity, of simple thieving. (186–87; see also 189, 191)

Decoud's letter to his sister, written under the portrait of "The Faithful Hero" at the Albergo of United Italy, by a "man with no faith in anything except the truth of his own sensations," is not a public or historical document. Decoud—laboring against that typically Conradian "impenetrable darkness" outside—feels "a desire to leave a correct impression of the feelings, like the light by which the action may be seen when personality is gone . . . the truth which every death takes out of the world" (229–30). It is the need, as Conrad has famously put it, to make us see.

Conrad was undoubtedly just as aware as our own contemporaries (or perhaps more so, given his own historical and biographical background) of human lives as thoroughly historicized, of human subjectivity as interpellated by culture and ideology, of the idea that we are, in fact, "spoken by" language. These are by no means the discoveries of postmodernism. But this, I would argue, is precisely why literature matters. It matters because, as Lukacs put it, it can say "and yet!" to life. Or to historiography, for that matter. And it is not through a willed, blind optimism that this fundamental challenge can be set, but only through a refusal to abdicate the prerogative of fiction which provides access to resistance, to alterity, to singularity, to all that is precious in human lives.

But *Nostromo* is not only a perfect fictional historiography—perfect in that it thematizes and enacts the failure of historiography. It is also an auto-biographical novel, not in any historical or factual sense—facts, as we know, are thoroughly discredited in this text—but in the resonance of anxiety which underlies the economy of writing. In this sense, Conrad's engagement with the writing of history is not only artistic or conceptual also deeply and painfully personal.

One possible answer to the troubling suicide of Martin Decoud—potential protagonist, narrator, and authorial counterpart—may suggest itself if we look once again at Conrad's description of his parting with the original Antonia, just before he left his father's land: "She was softened at the last as though she had suddenly perceived . . . that I was really going away for good, going very far away—even as far as Sulaco, lying unknown, hidden from our eyes in the dark-ness of the Placid Gulf" (xlvii). What we have here seems to be identical but is, in fact, diametrically opposite to Decoud's farewell scene—Decoud goes away when he has finally been assimilated into the patriotic narrative, and taken on the role of the national hero, the "young apostle of the separation." Conrad's decision to leave Poland was, at least in retrospect, a movement in the oppo-site direction, a leaving behind of his father's language and patriotic legacy. Decoud—whose skepticism is only skin-deep, caught between the inexorable movement of history and the indifferent silence of nature, cannot, after all, retain his own voice. But Conrad could, and did. Like other exilic writers, he was trying to awake from the nightmare of history. This, I believe, is why he had to let Decoud go.

If we need some consolation at the end of this magnificent novel which moves so uneasily between greatness and failure, we may find it in the thought that. Decoud's "double suicide" does not, after all, make him more dead. How-ever we formalize this odd strategy on Conrad's part, it does, in a way, decon-struct the finality of the end. Decoud drowns, but his voice goes on to tell the tale in the words of his author who will transmute the silver back into a living waterfall, the deadly matter of his own history into the telling of fictional tales.

Works Cited

Barthes, Roland. "The Discourse of History" (1967) and "The Reality Effect" (1968). Rpt. in *The Rustle of Language,* translated by Richard Howard. Berkeley: University of California Press, 1989. 127–40, 141–48.

Berthoud, Jacques. *Joseph Conrad: The Major Phase.* Cambridge: Cambridge University Press, 1978.

Carabine, Keith, ed. *Nostromo* (1904). Oxford World Classics Edition. Oxford University Press, 1984.

Carr, David. *Time, Narrative, and History.* Bloomington: Indiana University Press, 1986.

Certeau, Michel de. *The Writing of History* (1975). Translated by by Tom Conley. New York: Columbia University Press, 1988.

———. "History: Science and Fiction." In *Social Science and Moral Inquiry.* Edited by R. Bellah et al. New York: Columbia University Press, 1983, 125–52; rpt. in *Heterologies: Discourse on the Other* translated by Brian Massumi, foreword by Wlad Godzich. Minneapolis: University of Minnesota Press, 1986. 199–221.

Conrad, Joseph. *Nostromo* (1904). Edited by Keith Carabine. Oxford World Classics Edition. Oxford: Oxford University Press, 1984.

Culler, Jonathan. "Omniscience." *Narrative* 12.1 (January 2004): 22–34.

Demory, Pamela. "*Nostromo:* Making History." *Texas Studies in Literature and Language* 35.3 (1993): 316–46.

Erdinast-Vulcan, Daphna. *Joseph Conrad and the Modern Temper.* Oxford: Oxford University Press, 1991.

Jameson, Frederic. *The Political Unconscious: Narrative as a Socially Symbolic Act.* London: Methuen, 1981.

MacIntyre, Alasdair. *After Virtue.* London: Duckworth, 1984.

Mallios, Peter L. "Undiscovering the Country: Conrad, Fitzgerald, and Meta-National Form." *Modern Fiction Studies* 47.2 (Summer 2001): 356–90.

Miller, J. Hillis. "Narrative and History." *English Literary History* 41.3 (Fall 1974): 455–72.

Mink, Louis O. "Narrative Form as a Cognitive Instrument." In *The Writing of History.* Edited by Robert H. Canary and Henry Kozicki. Madison: University of Wisconsin Press, 1978. 129–49.

Robin, Christophe. "De l'histoire a la fiction: Temps et contre-temps dans *Nostromo.*" *L'Epoque Conradienne* 28 (2002): 9–26.

Said, Edward. *Beginnings.* New York: Basic Books, 1975.

Simmons, Allan, and J. H. Stape. "Preface" to *The Conradian: Centenary Essays on Nostromo* 29.2 (2004).

Watts. Cedric T. *A Preface to Conrad.* London: Longman, 1982.

White, Hayden. "The Fictions of Factual Representation." In *The Literature of Fact.* Edited by Angus Fletcher. Selected papers from the English Institute. New York: Columbia University Press, 1976. 21–44.

———. "The Historical Text as Literary Artifact." In *The Writing of History.* Edited by Robert H. Canary and Henry Kozicki. Madison: University of Wisconsin Press, 1978. 41–62.

———. "The Value of Narrativity in the Representation of Reality." *Critical Inquiry* 7 (1980): 5–27.

10

Time, History, Narrative in *Nostromo*

CHRISTOPHE ROBIN

Nostromo is a highly complex and innovative novel which questions the concepts of mimesis, representation, and narrative. One of the major innovations made by Conrad in the novel concerns the treatment of time and temporality. By using our experience as readers of a confusing and at times confused narrative temporality, Conrad is able to question our own relation to time. This experience is narratological but also, and more deeply, existential and ontological. For as Paul Ricoeur puts it in *Time and Narrative:* "Time becomes human to the extent that it is articulated through a narrative mode" (1990, 52). *Nostromo* explores and questions the limits of representation: in Derridean fashion, it deconstructs time and temporality and seems to disrupt narrative frames and identities. This "eclipse of narrative," however, does not lead to the "death of narrative": in *Nostromo* the narrative retrieves the "trace" of an unsaid to bring it back to language, inscribing it within new narrative structures which reshape and renew our vision of the world. Thus, *Nostromo*, by opening new narrative potentialities, reaffirms the power of narrative and ultimately remains committed to the vision of a humanized temporality.

Fiction and History

Nostromo is characterized by a strong referential anchorage, an inscription into real history, by the historicization of fiction through multiple historical references which intertwine the imaginary history of Sulaco and the real history of Latin America. The diegesis is replete with historically accurate references to the historical figures who shaped this continent, such as Charles IV, whose statue is in Sulaco, Napoleon III, and Sir Francis Drake. It also evokes the successive colonizations of Latin America by means of references to the Conquistadors, and the novel closely integrates the fictional characters with this historical background by comparing them to modern conquistadors. This intertwining of history and fiction is so tight that actual historical events have an impact on the course of fictional history as some fictional characters pattern their behavior on historical figures. For example, one of the actors of the Sulaco revolution, Pedrito Montero, a fictional character, has read some historical books on the French Second Empire and wants to reproduce the splendor of life at the court of Napoleon III. According to Roland Barthes, this intertwining of fiction and history serves to strengthen the anchorage of the literary text into reality since when historical characters are "mixed in with their fictional neighbors, mentioned as having simply been present at some social gathering, their modesty, like a lock between two levels of water, equalizes novel and history: they reinstate the novel as a family, and like ancestors who are contradictorily famous and absurd, they give the novel the glow of reality, not of glory: they are superlative effects of the real" (*S/Z*, 102).

Similarly, in the "Author's Note," the narrator playfully uses a metalepsis[1] and poses as a historian to claim (in a tongue-in-cheek manner) that he went to Sulaco in order to gather information which enabled him to write the novel *Nostromo*: "as I've said before, my sojourn on the Continent of Latin America, famed for its hospitality, lasted for about two years" (xliii). He also pretends to have based his narrative on a historical book that Don José Avellanos, one of the figures of the novel, himself a historian, is supposed to have written: "My principal authority for the history of Costaguana is, of course, my venerated friend, the late Don José Avellanos, Minister to the Courts of England and Spain, etc., etc., in his impartial and eloquent 'History of Fifty Years of Misrule'" (xliii). This is asserted in the "Author's Note," a textual space assumed to be outside the field of fiction, and the author thereby takes advantage of this position of authority to legitimize the historic validity of his claims.

---

1. We shall see further down that this metalepsis has deeper and more disquieting implications.

This historical anchorage, however, is played with in such a way that it ruins these "reality effects." History is in turn subsumed within fiction, thus creating a tension between historical time and narrative temporality. This questions both the ability of history to be homogeneous, synthetic, and teleological, and of the plot to create concordance, which is, according to Ricoeur, the very function of the plot. A plot, Ricoeur explains, is based on a tension between concordance and discordance, a concordance that synthesizes the events into a meaningful plot and a discordance represented by the peripetia that threaten the principle of concordance and dismember the story line. *Nostromo,* with its emphasis on temporal and structural discordance, could thus be said to partake of the logic of the antinarrative.

From the point of view of time and temporality, a tension between history and fiction arises because even though there exist strong historical references which localize the narrative within human history, the story paradoxically erases many chronological markers. Chronology seems to become mad and is replaced by a spiraling structure as the same events recur several times in the course of the narrative. The present repeats the historical past as the Sulaco revolution is revealed as just one more crisis in the cycles of bloody revolutions that punctuate the history of Costaguana, while the conquest of the Anglo-Saxons repeats Caesar's or the Conquistador's own conquests. Likewise the present of the story is carried away by a narrative flux which seems to dissolve it, thus abolishing the linkage between past and future, a linkage that would create both temporal and causal continuity. Ribiera's escape, for example, is treated both in the form of a prolepsis (chapter 2) and of an analepsis (chapter 20), and thus takes place outside the present of the story and thereby evades representation. Analyzing the treatment of Ribiera's flight, Jameson comments: "[I]t would be more adequate to suggest that in that sense it never really happens at all, for the initial discursive reference to it—not as scene but as fact or background—dispenses Conrad from having to 'render' it in all its lived presence later on. This central event is therefore present/absent in the most classic Derridean fashion, present only in its initial absence, absent when it is supposed to be most intensely present" (272). Realism is destroyed by an irresistible process of derealization of historical reality. Comparing *Lord Jim* and *Nostromo,* Jameson adds:

> the associational, aleatory movement of the text [of *Nostromo*] from detail to detail is no less intricate than in *Lord Jim,* and obeys, as we promised, the same fundamental principle of the slow analytic rotation around that central act about which we may fear that interrogated too closely, like the onion that was the symbol of being in the Upanishads, from which layer

upon layer was carefully removed, it will prove to bear nothingness at its heart. (271)

The reader is in turn caught in a narrative whirl and, like Decoud who "beheld the universe as a succession of incomprehensible images" (498), he or she is made to confront the unreadable. The text thus plays on the time of reading and blurs the psychological categories intuitively used by the reader to construct cross-references, textual cohesion, and meaning. Hence there is a tension between suggestion and erosion: the suggestion of a reality, chronologically and causally organized and safely situated in the History of the world, and the erosion of this very chronology which resists monolithic coherence, and, ultimately, remains undecidable as illustrated by the competing chronologies of *Nostromo* drawn up by various critics.

Conrad deepens this confusion between history and reality by blurring the epistemological frontier between fictional and historical narratives, thus implicitly casting doubt on the validity of historical discourse: "In *Nostromo*, Conrad comments on the problem of the relationship between history and the past, between the historical narrative and history, between, in effect, historiography as signifier and event as signified and, in doing so, critiques both the traditional nineteenth-century notion of history and the nineteenth-century realistic novel" (Demory, 317).

History as a discourse, as historiography, is also challenged by the device of metalepsis which is characterized by the shift between two levels of discourse, for example, the diegetic and extradiegetic levels. In his Author's Note, Conrad gives an account of the genesis of his novel and then subverts his status of author by pretending that the various characters of the diegesis are flesh-and-blood characters he met in real life and whose testimony he gathered to document his narrative: "If anything could induce me to revisit Sulaco (I should hate to see all these changes), it would be Antonia. [. . .] That afternoon, when I came in, a shrinking yet defiant sinner, to say the final good-bye I received a hand-squeeze that made my heart leap and saw a tear that took my breath away" (xlvi–xlvii). Fictional characters are promoted to the rank of coauthor, as in the case of Captain Mitchell, a notoriously unreliable character, to whom is delegated the task of recounting the concluding events of the Sulaco revolution.

The effect of metalepses is, according to Genette, to blur the ontological distinction "between two worlds, the world in which one tells, the world of which one tells," a transgression which has an uncanny effect: "The most troubling thing about metalepsis indeed lies in this unacceptable and insistent hypothesis, that the extradiegetic is perhaps always diegetic, and that the

narrator and his narratees—you and I—perhaps belong to some narrative"
(236). In *Nostromo*, this blurring specifically concerns the borderline between
historical and fictional discourses: this can be read as an early anticipation
of modernist or even postmodernist suspicion of historical discourse, as the
realization that history is, like fiction, a discourse, an ideological reorganiza-
tion of events to make sense of the past. Hence the novel suggests that history
is to some extent a linguistic construct that imposes a meaningful pattern
on a succession of events. The characters' historical discourses are revealed
to be ideological structures that confer meaning, a meaning relative to the
very interpretative criteria applied by the characters, to their conceptions and
misconceptions.

Conrad's awareness of literary codes, of the artificiality of art, of the
literariness of literature is typical of literary modernism.[2] *Nostromo* has an
undeniable intertextual dimension; it refers, through this dialectic between
fiction and reality, to the origin of the novel, in particular of the English novel.
According to Ricoeur the English novel is originally realist as it presumes a
congruence between words and world, fiction and reality. The novel appears
as "a new genre, defined by the proposal to establish the most exact correspondence possible between the literary work and the reality it imitates" (1985, 12).
This aesthetic is based on "the conviction [. . .] that language could be purged
of every figurative and decorative element and returned to its original vocation—the vocation, according to Locke, 'to convey the knowledge of things'"
(1985, 11). This was bound to have a deep impact on the underlying vision
of art which was then supposed to reflect reality, to be an accurate copy of its
model. From this perspective art had an undeniable ontological dimension
inasmuch as it was laden with reality. What was true of the eighteenth century
was also true of the nineteenth, which marked the culmination of the realist
novel. Thus, when Conrad questions historical discourse through its fictionalization, he simultaneously reassesses the ontological criteria that underlie the
historical narrative. He thereby lays the foundation of a narrative reflexivity
that will soon be a defining criterion of modernism and postmodernism and
that will contaminate all discourses, including historical discourses: "Instead
of mimetically authoring a new world, *Nostromo* turns back to its beginning
as a novel, to the fictional, illusory assumption of reality: in thus overturning
the confident edifice that novels normally construct, *Nostromo* reveals itself to
be no more than a *record* of novelistic self-reflection" (Said, 137).

2. Modernism is defined by Jeremy Hawthorn as "that art (not just literature) which sought
to break with what had become the dominant and dominating conventions of nineteenth-century
art and culture." Rejecting the realist convention of verisimilitude, modernism is characterized
by its metafictionality: "the modernist art-work is possessed, typically, of a *self-reflexive* element"
(Hawthorn 1990, 212–13).

The Monument and the Trace[3]

The tension between time and the untimely, between the historical and onto-logical reference on the one hand and the disruption caused by dechronolo-gization and fictionalization on the other, is replicated on a diegetic level. *Nostromo* is to a large extent devoted to the description of a social and political revolution which ushers in the revolution of "material interests" while simul-taneously inaugurating the time of chaos. Two temporalities stand thus in contrast: the time of the arche and the untimeliness of an-archy.

Although the beginning of *Nostromo* is organized around a shift from the mythical time of the incipit to the historical temporality of the following chapters, the historical discourses of the characters aim at turning history into a myth, at building an ideal temporality based on a master principle, silver, which also plays the role of a master signifier whose function is to engender master narratives. This is exemplified by Mitchell's relation of the concluding events of the Sulaco revolution in chapter 13. The fact that it is only through his narration that we have access to these events emphasizes the narrative dimension of historical discourse and the constructedness of history. Mitch-ellian historiography organizes the events into an identifiable ideological structure by inscribing the temporality of the revolution within what Ricoeur calls monumental time.

Monumental time is the time of metadiscourses, a time of synthesis, the time of generation, the time of the Same.[4] Modern times, the times of the Sulaco revolution, of the revolution of material interests, are character-ized by a desire to erase the tragic past of tyranny and unrest. The statue of Charles IV, which is described by Mitchell as an "anachronism" and which is therefore untimely, must be replaced by another monument: "a marble shaft

---

3. Our distinction between the monument and the trace indirectly refers to Nietzsche's monumental, antiquarian, and critical views of History defined in his essay entitled "Untimely Meditation: On the Use and Disadvantage of History for Life." For Nietzsche, monumental history lies in the belief "in the solidarity and continuity of the greatness of all ages and a protest against the passing away of generations and the transitoriness of things" (1997, 69). On the contrary, the critical method, to which the concept of trace is not unconnected, is a force of disruption of monumental history: "If he is to live, man must possess and from time to time employ the strength to break up and dissolve a part of the past" (75).

4. We allude here to Lévinas's philosophy in which the central notion of the Same refers to a totalizing system/ideology/philosophy, which is also totalitarian inasmuch as it is based on the negation of all form of otherness. Gould's ideology of "material interests," beyond its idealistic façade, is in fact an ideology of the Same, an imperial totalizing ideology which aims to resorb the alterity of Costaguana: "Everything is here, everything belongs to me; everything is caught up in advance with the primordial occupying of a site, everything is comprehended. The possibility of possessing, that is, of suspending the very alterity of what is only at first other, and other relative to me, is the way of the same" (2001, 37–38).

commemorative of Separation, with angels of peace at the four corners, and bronze Justice holding an even balance, all gilt, on the top" (482). This statue, ornamented with angels of peace and a representation of justice, reconstructs history to posit it within a clear teleological, eschatological perspective. It also serves to turn history into a myth whose role is to obliterate the contingency of history in order to naturalize and legitimize it: "What the world supplies to myth is an historical reality . . . and what the myth gives in return is a *natural* image of this reality. . . . The world enters language as a dialectical relationship between activities, between human actions; it comes out of myth as a harmonious display of essences" (Barthes 1972, 142; emphasis in original). It is such a "harmonious display of essences" that Mitchell's speech aims to construct as he shows his auditor round the Sulaco cathedral where the various icons commemorating the history of the Occidental Republic are visible:

> "Here," he would say, pointing to a niche in the wall of the dusky aisle, "you see the bust of Don Jose Avellanos, 'Patriot and Statesman,' as the inscription says, 'Minister to Courts of England and Spain, etc., etc., died in the woods of Los Hatos worn out with his lifelong struggle for Right and Justice at the dawn of the New Era.' . . . The marble medallion in the wall, in the antique style, representing a veiled woman seated with her hands clasped loosely over her knees, commemorates that unfortunate young gentleman who sailed out with Nostromo on that fatal night, sir." (477–78)

Mitchell's speech glorifies the major actors of the Sulaco revolution and inscribes history within a heroic, epic temporality. Through this cathedral, human history becomes monumental, it is sacralized and posited within a divine project, memory is turned into stone, marble, it is inscribed within the minerality of nature and resists the erosion of time, it unfolds in the shadow of religious metanarratives.

This monumental time coincides with the advent of a subject who emerges in a temporality that is understood and mastered: "Continuous history is the indispensable correlative of the founding function of the subject: the guarantee that everything that has eluded him may be restored to him, the certainty that time will disperse nothing without restoring it in a reconstituted unity; the promise that one day the subject—in the form of historical consciousness—will once again be able to appropriate, to bring back under his sway, all those things that are kept at a distance by difference, and find them in what might be called his abode" (Foucault 1982, 12). Constructing a temporality that is the abode of the subject, in which the subject can abide and beget himself beyond finitude, such is the desire of the characters: "It concerns me to keep on being what I am: every day alike" (253), Nostromo declares. He wants to keep on being what he is, to persevere in his being, to perpetuate the heroic image of himself.

This monumental time embodied by the cathedral gives way to the temporality of the trace. The trace marks the emergence of an untimely time, "this instant that is not docile to time" (Derrida, 1994, xx). In *Nostromo*, the logic of history and of fiction comes up against an alogical time, a time "out of joint" which dismembers both history and narrative. It is the time of historical anarchy and of narrative hiatuses, ellipses, anachronies. What emerges from this time "out of joint" is a ghost: *Nostromo* is the story of a man turned ghost, specter, haunting, like the two sailors of the incipit, the Azuera, chained to the treasure of being. To take up Derrida's pun in *Specters of Marx*, with *Nostromo*, the history of ontology turns into the story of hauntology.

The work of the trace can be observed when Nostromo comes back to the island where he had hidden the treasure:

> The Capataz picked up the spade, and with the feel of the handle in his palm the desire of having a look at the horse-hide boxes of treasure came upon him suddenly. In a very few strokes he uncovered the edges and corners of several ; then, clearing away more earth, became aware that one of them had been slashed with a knife.
>
> He exclaimed at that discovery in a stifled voice, and dropped on his knees with a look of irrational apprehension over one shoulder, then over the other. The stiff hide had closed, and he hesitated before he pushed his hand through the long slit and felt the ingots inside. There they were. One, two, three. Yes, four gone. Taken away. Four ingots. But who? Decoud? Nobody else. And why? For what purpose? For what cursed fancy? Let him explain. Four ingots carried off in a boat, and—blood! (494–95)

The very moment Nostromo is going to lay hands on the treasure, he is caught up by a past which comes back and suspends his movement. For the hide-box that contained the treasure bears the mark of slashes, it has been slashed in its middle. This opening is the trace of the absent Other whose presence persists in the trace of his passage: the having-been emerges in the present in the form of a disruptive, asystemic principle: "a trace is distinguished from all the signs that get organized into systems, because it disarranges some 'order.' The trace is 'this disarrangement expressing itself'" (Ricoeur 1988, 125).

One of the classical functions of narrative is to articulate a narrative identity, for, as Ricoeur puts it, our identities are "entangled in stories"(1984, 75).

Isn't, then, the function of an antinarrative to question the concept of identity and to define an anti-identity, to think another self, or, as Ricoeur puts it
"oneself as another"? Nostromo's entanglement in stories is evidenced by the
fact that in the first part of the novel, he is presented indirectly, through discursive references made by the characters, especially Mitchell who describes
Nostromo as being "'invaluable for our work—a perfectly incorruptible fellow'" (127). Nostromo's identity partakes of the same qualities as those of the
treasure: like it, he is invaluable and incorruptible. The treasure is described
by Nostromo as "an incorruptible metal that can be trusted to keep its value
for ever" (300). It is the treasure of identity, of a stable, incorruptible identity
based on the adequacy between being and language that Nostromo inherits
from the discourse of the other.

But the island/I-land of the Isabels turns out to be the land of the fading
of the subject to become the land of the specter. The ontological plenitude
symbolized by the treasure is reversed as Nostromo experiences a radical loss
and as presence suddenly turns into absence: "There they were. One, two,
three. Yes, four gone. Taken away" (495). "There they were," the ingots are there
and we believe that Nostromo is counting them. But in fact he is counting the
missing ingots: the treasure of being suddenly vanishes, the time of presence
gives way to the untimely, the time of absence, of dispossession, of the Other
who is always experienced as a thief.

On this island emerges a new consciousness, a modern consciousness:
"The necessity of living concealed somehow, for God knows how long, which
assailed him on his return to consciousness, made everything that had gone
before for years appear vain and foolish, like a flattering dream come suddenly
to an end" (414). Nostromo wakes up on "another stage," the stage of the fading of being, where the "I think" is irremediably disconnected from the "I am,"
sounding the death knell of the Cartesian subject. The experience of modernism is characterized, in Ricoeur's words, by the birth of the "wounded *cogito,*
a *cogito* which posits but does not possess itself, a *cogito* which understands its
primordial truth only in and through the avowal of the inadequation, the illusion, the fakery of immediate consciousness" (2004, 238). It is such a wounded
cogito that, with *Nostromo,* comes to language.

In this new consciousness is reflected the crisis of language that corrodes
metanarratives, the metanarrative of the material interests: "Theft is always
the theft of speech or text, of a trace" (Derrida 2001, 220). Nostromo experiences this ontological vacuity in and through language, a vacuity typical of the
modernist crisis of language which Foucault described in these terms: "From
within language experienced and traversed as language, in the play of its possibilities extended to their furthest point, what emerges is that man has 'come

to an end,' and that by reaching the summit of all possible speech, he arrives not at the very heart of himself but at the brink of that which limits him; in that region where death prowls, where thought is extinguished, where the promise of the origin interminably recedes" (Foucault 1994, 383). Nostromo's crisis coincides with the experience of suspicion toward language, the awareness of the duplicity of words, for it is language itself that becomes the site of alterity: "Language always seems to be inhabited by the other, the elsewhere, the distant; it is hollowed by absence" (Foucault 1982, 111). The text weaves a tight metaphoric network which intertwines money and language: "Always thinking of yourself and taking your pay out in fine words from those who care nothing for you" (253), Teresa says to Nostromo. But fine words, and words in general are not to be trusted for the treasure of language is fake: the treasure becomes a malediction, a curse, as Nostromo puts it, it is "accursed." The meaning of words cannot be taken for granted: language is ambivalent, it is a *pharmakon,* a remedy that turns to poison. Nostromo discovers that the discourse of the masters, the metadiscourse of the "material interests" is a discourse of forgers who put into circulation counterfeit money, fraudulent words and concepts whose value fluctuates unpredictably. "What's in a name?" Nostromo may have asked as he discovers that words have as little value as the name he has been given, a name that is "no name either for man or beast" (232). Like Jim in *Lord Jim,* Nostromo is the victim of a joke, of an equivocal, plurivocal language which plays upon and bluffs him.

Nostromo's suspicion towards language is the symptom of a wider suspicion towards all metanarratives and is a trace of what Daphna Erdinast-Vulcan calls the "anxiety of modernism" (185). *Nostromo* is deeply iconoclastic, in its form as well as its content, as it disarranges both the literary and ideological stage on which it emerged.

Inchoate Narrative and the Human Experience of Time

After this tragic discovery, Nostromo returns to society with regained lucidity, "as if sobered after a long bout of intoxication" (417). He has crossed his shadow-line, a crossing which is achieved in and through language. It is a similar shadow-line that Ricoeur invites us to cross:

> The situation in which language today finds itself comprises this double possibility, this double solicitation and urgency: on the one hand, purify discourse of its excrescences, liquidate the idols, go from drunkenness to sobriety, realize our state of poverty once and for all; on the other hand,

use the most 'nihilistic,' destructive, iconoclastic movement so as to *let speak* what once, what each time, was *said,* when meaning appeared anew, when meaning was at its fullest. . . . In our time we have not finished doing away with idols and we have barely begun to listen to symbols. It may be that this situation, in its apparent distress, is instructive: it may be that extreme iconoclasm belongs to the restoration of meaning. (1970, 27; emphasis in original)

Likewise, Ricoeur explains that suspicion is a mode of attestation: "Suspicion is also the path *toward* and the crossing *within* attestation. It haunts testimony, as false testimony haunts true testimony" (1992, 302). Does this mean that *Nostromo*'s antinarrativity can lead to a regained confidence in the power of narrative? For the very existence of antinarratives still testifies to the importance of narrative power in human culture: "[W]e have no idea of what a culture would be where no one any longer knew what it meant to narrate things," Ricoeur says (1985, 28).

The anarchy of *Nostromo,* in terms of structure, language, meaning, and temporality, can be interpreted positively. The unsaying which is at work in *Nostromo,* which "unworks" the literary work, the silence of a novel that expresses itself in the mode of reticence and of restraint, the narrative gaps and structural discordances that undermine the narrative dynamics, may be interpreted as traces of what Ricoeur calls "an inchoate narrativity that constitutes a genuine demand for narrative." Ricoeur exemplifies this notion of inchoate narrativity through psychoanalysis, which he defines as a "system of rules for retelling our life stories." He adds that our personal life story proceeds "from untold and repressed stories in the direction of actual stories that the subject can take up and hold as constitutive of his personal identity" (1984, 74). In *Nostromo,* the narrative discordances are an inchoate narration, traces of an unsaid story waiting to be phrased/narrativized. These narrative and structural hiatuses are the originary site of a new voice about to tell an as yet untold story. For the disjunction/différance between the "I think" and the "I am" which is at the heart of Nostromo's experience signals the time of loss, of dereliction, but simultaneously inaugurates the time of quest and inquest, of hermeneutics. Derrida's différance can henceforth be thought of in the light of Lyotard's definition of the différend: "The différend is the unstable state and instant of language wherein something which must be able to be put into phrases cannot yet be. This state includes silence, which is a negative phrase, but it also calls upon phrases which are in principle possible" (13). The différend according to Lyotard is a paradoxical linguistic state between saying and unsaying, a silence which is a potentiality of sentences, a reservoir of phrases, a negative sentence that invites further sentences. The inchoate narrativity of *Nostromo* is an attempt to probe beyond the phantasm of immediate consciousness, of the imperial subject, to give voice to the voiceless, to what is alogos, to what is denied the status of logos. The work of the novel *Nostromo* is precisely to listen to what "unworks" it and to bring Nostromo the ghost, the alogos back to language, in order to turn it into a story, to reinvent a new narrativity. Thus *Nostromo* is an apt illustration of the power of narrative, which is, according to Ricoeur, to confer meaning on what is apparently meaningless: "By saving or sparing and compression, the narrator brings what is foreign to meaning (*sinnfremd*) into the sphere of meaning. Even when the narrative intends to render what is senseless (*sinnlos*), it places this in relation to the sphere of making sense (*Sinndeuteung*)" (Ricoeur 1985, 80; emphasis in original). The trace of Nostromo's crisis has been submerged, engulfed in the secrecy of the Gulf which retains its secret, the secret adventure of Nostromo and Decoud, the secret story of a ghost haunting the world of ontology. But this secret is disclosed by the authorial voice, by the work of writing which brings to language the traumatic experience of this ontological crisis erased by official historiography, by monumental time. This trace is at the heart of the story of Nostromo the ghost and is represented in the scarifications/slashings/breachings of the narrative texture. Such is the process of unconcealment achieved by *Nostromo*.

Mitchell's memorial founds a forgetful memory, it is an archive which relegates the anarchy of thought to oblivion. Referring to Mitchell's speech in the Sulaco cathedral, Edward Said comments: "[T]he point is that propagandistic descriptions of monuments, as Nietzsche once observed, provide one with the most insufficient and inaccurate sort of history. And so goes the chronicle of Sulaco. It flourishes in its monumental prosperity, with its silver exports reaching every corner of the world, and excludes, in the manner described by Foucault, everything inimical to it. In Foucault's terminology one can also say that Sulaco's archives contain rarefied versions of its history"[5] (1982, 120). The story of Nostromo the ghost exists only under erasure, "*sous rature*," as a palimpsest, an erased trace which disarranges the discourse of the masters.

These blank pages of Sulaco's archives are a symptom of fear, of the fact

---

5. In a perceptive analysis, Jeremy Hawthorn has shown how the subtle use of the pseudo-iterative in *Nostromo*, whose function is to impart a sense of repetition and historicity to events, is used in a subversive way that serves to deconstruct history and the novel's historiographical discourses. A case in point is Mitchell's narrative of the 'historical events' pertaining to the Sulaco revolution: "[W]hat Mitchell represents is a travesty or parody of history, a travesty that reduces history to something mechanical and sterotyped, something unavailable to active human participation" (1998, 141).

that, in Foucault's words, we are afraid "to conceive of the Other in the time of our own thought" (1982, 12). This Other is typified in the novel by Nostromo, who, after the loss of the treasure, is marked by alterity: "I could see he was another man," Mitchell remarks. But this alterity is rejected at once and Nostromo's failure is relegated to oblivion: "I begged him not to think any more about the silver" (488). The failure of Decoud and Nostromo's plan is reintegrated within a meaningful structure by Mitchell's narration and resorbed within a final victory: "Miss Avellanos burst into tears only when he told her how Decoud had happened to say that his plan would be a glorious success. . . . And there's no doubt, sir, that it is. It is a success" (489). This success is built on an ellipsis, on a hiatus in a discourse which passes over the tragic moment. But simultaneously, this failure persists in Mitchell's discourse in the form of a trace, of an unsaid which undermines his narration. In Mitchell's naive account of the Sulaco revolution, the word "history" is a fetishistic symbol of a historiography which does not so much reveal as conceal: "Almost every event out of the usual daily course 'marked an epoch' for him [Mitchell] or else was 'history,'" the narrator comments (112–13). This history, however, is but an expression of blindness, of someone "utterly in the dark, and imagining himself to be in the thick of things." Confronted with the untimely, Mitchell's discourse collapses: "[H]e would mutter—'Ah, that! That, sir was a mistake'" (113). This mistake, this tragic event is phrased in an abortive narrative, it is not so much said as unsaid, muttered in a language in default, a language muted by the traumatic encounter with a ghost. The story of Nostromo the ghost, the story of an ontology turned hauntology is repressed by the ideology of material interests, a teleology incapable of thinking the trace of absence, of the absent ideal.

But the novel's re-enunciation of this initial discourse, of the grandiose revolution, takes us beyond the curse that plagues Nostromo. This re-enunciation, this narrative repetition, opens new virtualities: "Repetition thus opens potentialities that went unnoticed, were aborted, or were repressed in the past. It opens up the past again in the direction of coming-towards" (Ricoeur 1988, 76). Storytelling is indeed a means of making history, of creating a new history. This idea is articulated, among others, by Fredric Jameson who argues that the only way to escape Historical Determinism is to narrativize history. Drawing on Jameson's analysis, Hayden White explains that the power to narrate can have an impact on the course of history and can be interpreted as a historical causality called "narratological causality":

This would be a mode of causality that consists in a seizing of a past by consciousness in such a way as to make of the present a fulfillment of the former's promise rather than merely an effect of some prior (mechanistic, expressive, or structural) cause. The seizure by consciousness of a past in such a way as to define the present as a fulfillment rather than as an effect is precisely what is represented in a narrativization of a sequence of historical events so as to reveal everything early in it as a prefiguration of a project to be realized in some future. Considered as a basis for a specific kind of human agency, narrativization sublimates necessity into a symbol of possible freedom. (149)

Hayden White points here to the praxic function of fiction, as the respective horizons of fiction and history fuse. For Ricoeur, language, though marked by closure and self-reflexivity, is ultimately "oriented beyond itself," toward the world: "Language is for itself the order of the Same. The world is its Other. The attestation of this otherness arises from language's reflexivity with regard to itself, whereby it knows itself as being *in* being in order to bear *on* being" (*Time* 1984, 78). In the world of the novel, language is made to "bear on being" when Montero's historical readings influence the course of the history of Sulaco. In like manner, the fictional narrative *Nostromo* inserts itself within a historical reality and bears on the course of true history by unveiling the fundamental duplicity of colonial rhetoric and imperial discourses, and, more widely, of all ideologies that promise a brighter future and that lead, at best, to disenchantment and, at worst, to some of the most horrendous holocausts the history of the world has known. It is such disenchantment that Mrs. Gould foreshadows when, in a visionary, almost prophetic scene, the mine is compared to an atrocious god demanding human holocausts: "[S]he saw clearly the San Tome mine possessing, consuming, burning up the life of the last of the Costaguana Goulds; mastering the energetic spirit of the son as it had mastered the lamentable weakness of the father" (522). This anticipates Hannah Arendt's own vision of imperialism as being one of the "three pillars of hell," one of the origins of the totalitarianism that was to plague the twentieth century. The narrative *Nostromo* is an invitation to the reader to "see clearly," in the manner of Mrs. Gould, for one of the functions of narrative is "to replace perplexity with lucidity" (Ricoeur 1984, 19). This redescription of the world through fiction produces what Ricoeur calls "an iconic augmentation," leads to the apperception of meanings and realities as yet unrevealed: "[L]iterary works depict reality by *augmenting* it with meanings that themselves depend upon the virtues of abbreviation, saturation, and culmination, so strikingly illustrated by emplotment" (1984, 80). In this sense, fiction augments our understanding of history: "Fiction gives eyes to the horrified narrator. Eyes to see and to weep. The present state of literature on the Holocaust provides ample proof of this" (1988, 188). In this respect, it is striking to note how much Conrad himself believed in fiction's ability to convey historical truths, as if the ontological power of fiction exceeded that of historical discourse. In his famous essay "Henry James: An Appreciation," he writes: "Fiction is history, human history, or it is nothing. But it is also more than that; it stands on firmer ground, being based on the reality of forms and the observation of social phenomena, whereas history is based on documents, and the reading of print and handwriting—on second-hand impression. Thus fiction is nearer truth" (1921, 20).

In like manner, Ricoeur explains that the very experience of anarchic temporality is a means of deepening our experience of time: "If it is true that the major tendency of modern theory of narrative—in historiography and the philosophy of history as well as in narratology—is to 'dechronologize' narrative, the struggle against the linear representation of time does not necessarily have as its sole outcome the turning of narrative into 'logic,' but rather may deepen its temporality. Chronology—or chronography—does not have just one contrary, the a-chronology of laws and models. Its true contrary is temporality itself" (1984, 30).

The play with time in *Nostromo* leads to the experience of an existential temporality, the temporality of the unforgetful. This unforgetful is commemorated as a time of mourning, for mourning is a matter of time and memory. Mourning is the conservation of the trace of absence, of the Absent. Such a mourning and commemoration is dramatized by Linda's final words at the end of the novel, following Nostromo's death: "'It is I who loved you,' she whispered, with a face as set and white as marble in the moonlight. 'I! Only I! She will forget thee, killed miserably for her pretty face. I cannot understand. I cannot understand. But I shall never forget thee. Never!'" (566). Linda does not understand but refuses to forget: as such she inaugurates a new fidelity beyond the betrayal experienced by Nostromo, a fidelity to the event, to Nostromo's heritage, and to his testimony. She resists the oblivious logic of the archive to transmit the trace of an unforgettable past. Through this commemoration she reappropriates what cannot be understood in order to phrase the unsayable. She brings back to language Nostromo the ghost, the alogos who died carrying with him the secret of his unlawful wealth. She invents a new mode of memory which resists the forgetfulness of the other characters, the memory of trauma. She retrieves the trace repressed by historiography, thus opening up a new space of memory. To the work of history, which is essentially "cannibalistic," de Certeau opposes the work of "the mnemic trace." He claims that "any autonomous order"—and in his view historiography which is based "on a clean break between past and present" does create such an order—"is founded upon what it eliminates; it produces a residue condemned to be forgotten." But this "residue" comes back as otherness, as a trace that disrupts the present and the presence, it "resurfaces, it troubles, it turns the present's feeling of being 'at home' into an illusion, it lurks—this 'wild,' this 'ob-scene,' this 'filth,' this 'resistance' of 'superstition'—within the walls of the residence, and behind, the back of the owner (the *ego*), or over its objections, it inscribes there the law of the other" (3–4). It is this otherness that Linda harbors and transmits in her cry that rings aloud over the Gulf. It is this temporality of alterity that the narrator reconstructs and brings to being through narrative structures. Like *Gulliver's Travels,* which is mentioned in the Author's Preface, *Nostromo* debunks the naïve belief in a realism that could double and copy reality, and which is at the basis of a fetishistic vision of reality, of narrative and history. In *Nostromo,* Conrad reinstates through narrativity a truly human and humanized temporality that harbors the other, an other which ultimately resists the totalizing pretension of imperial time to open onto ethical time.

Works Cited

Barthes, Roland. *Mythologies*. Translated by Annette Lavers. New York: Hill & Wang, 1972.

———. *S/Z*. Translated by Richard Miller. New York: Hill & Wang, 1974.

Certeau, Michel de. *Heterologies: Discourse on the Other*. Translated by Brian Massumi. Minneapolis: University of Minnesota Press, 1986.

Conrad, Joseph. *Nostromo*. Edited by Keith Carabine, World's Classics, Oxford: Oxford University Press, 1966.

———. *Notes on Life & Letters*. London: J. M. Dent & Sons Ltd, 1921.

Cooper, John X. "Nostromo (1904)." *A Joseph Conrad Companion*. Edited by Leonard Orr and Ted Billy. Westport, CT: Greenwood Press, 1999.

Demory, Pamela H. "Nostromo: Making History." *Texas Studies in Literature and Language* 35.3 (1993): 315–46.

Derrida, Jacques. *Specters of Marx: The State of the Debt, the Work of Mourning, & the New International*. Translated by Peggy Kamuf. New York: Routledge, 1994.

———. *Writing and Différence*. Translated by Alan Bass. London: Routledge, 2001.

Erdinast-Vulcan, Daphna. "'Signifying Nothing': Conrad's Idiots and the Anxiety of Modernism." *Studies in Short Fiction* 33.2 (1996): 185–96.

Foucault, Michel. *The Archeology of Knowledge & The Discourse on Language*. New York: Pantheon, 1982.

———. *The Order of Things: An Archeology of Human Sciences*. New York: Vintage, 1994.

Genette, Gerard. *Narrative Discourse: An Essay in Method*. Translated by Jane E. Lewin. Ithaca, NY: Cornell University Press, 1980.

Hawthorn, Jeremy. *A Glossary of Contemporary Literary Theory*. 4th ed. New York: Oxford University Press, 2000.

———. "Repetitions and Revolutions: Conrad's Use of the Pseudo-iterative in *Nostromo*." In *Joseph Conrad 1: La fiction et l'autre*, edited by Josiane Paccaud-Huguet. Paris-Caen: Lettres modernes Minard, 1998.

Jameson, Fredric. *The Political Unconscious: Narrative as a Socially Symbolic Act*. Ithaca, NY: Cornell University Press, 1981.

Lévinas, Emmanuel. *Totality and Infinity: An Essay on Exteriority*. Translated by Alphonso Lingis. Pittsburgh: Duquesne University Press, 2001.

Lyotard, Jean-François. *The Differend: Phrases in Dispute*. Translated by George Van Den Abbeele. Minneapolis: University of Minnesota Press, 1988.

Nietzsche, Friedrich Wilhem. *Untimely Meditations*. Edited by Daniel Beazle, translated by R. J. Hollindale. Cambridge: Cambridge University Press, 1997.

Ricoeur, Paul. *Freud and Philosophy: An Essay on Interpretation*. Translated by Denis Savage. New Haven: Yale University Press, 1970.

———. *Oneself as Another*. Translated by Kathleen Blamey. Chicago: University of Chicago Press, 1992.

———. *The Conflict of Interpretations: Essays in Hermeneutics*. London: Continuum, 2004.

———. *Time and Narrative: Volume 1*. Translated by Kathleen Mc Laughlin and David Pellauer. Chicago: University of Chicago Press, 1984.

————. *Time and Narrative: Volume 2*. Translated by Kathleen Mc Laughlin and David Pellauer. Chicago: University of Chicago Press, 1985.

————. *Time and Narrative: Volume 3*. Translated by Kathleen Mc Laughlin and David Pellauer. Chicago: University of Chicago Press, 1988.

Said, Edward. *Beginnings: Intention & Method*. New York: Columbia University Press, 1985.

White, Hayden. *The Content of the Form: Narrative Discourse and Historical Representation*. Baltimore: Johns Hopkins University Press, 1987.

IV
Genre

11

Narrating Identity in
A Personal Record

J. H. STAPE

Conrad's *A Personal Record* has a peculiar status among the volumes of his nonfiction prose and, indeed, in his canon. After its contemporary reception, mainly favorable even if critics were somewhat bemused by its elusiveness and structure, there have been three broad trends of approach: psychoanalytic, aesthetic and formalist,[1] and documentary. Another, more recent and novel approach, has been to treat the text as a "highly ambivalent political document" deploying certain features of mock-autobiography.[2]

Assayed first by Gustav Morf in 1930, the psychoanalytic approach has considered *A Personal Record* a psychological document in which various underlying complexes are revealed. For Morf, Conrad discloses a "guilt complex" over his "abandonment" of Poland. (GoGwilt's [1995] considerably more sophisticated theoretical work about "the unconscious of the text" expands on this.) Frederick R. Karl, who also sees the text in psychoanalytical terms

1. See Kertzer 1975; Najder 1988 (rpt. Najder 1997); Abbot 1992; DeVinne 2002; and Kalnins 1998. Although of broad aim, Busza 2000 suggestively discusses the text's design and ideological underpinnings, also historicizing the biographical impulse.

2. See GoGwilt 1995, which discusses extensively Conrad's treatment of his Polish past in *A Personal Record* and places the work in the context of nationalist and racialist discourse reshaping the map of Europe at the time of its writing.

and emphasizes how facts yield to "myth-making," conflates Conrad's father Apollo in his pyjamas with Olmeijer similarly dressed (both failures, both men at the end of their tether) and relates this to a mode of observation that he calls a "burrowing method of narrative" (135, 245). The aesthetic and formalist approach, responding to the text's generic diversity, has focused on the several traditions it alludes to and borrows from—the confession and *apologia* in the tradition of St. Augustine, autobiographical experiment (influenced by the narrative strategies of Laurence Sterne's fiction), and Modernist "autography" (self-writing). It has also analyzed some of its aesthetic facets as, for instance, the ways in which Conrad applies fictional techniques to the story of his life. Lastly, the volume's status as a "record" of fact has been vigorously interrogated. Hans van Marle (1976 and 1988) and Zdzisław Najder (1983) meticulously compared its statements to the surviving documentary evidence and have shown how Conrad's reliance on the presentational techniques of fiction—rhythm and narrative shaping, Impressionist poetics—determined certain suppressions and omissions, most notably, the elision of Conrad's failed Merchant Service examinations to suit narrative shaping.

This essay takes the aesthetic and formalist approach in new directions. Although *A Personal Record* comprises seven separately written autobiographical essays, Conrad sought to give them coherence by flexibly adapting the conventions of both autobiography and epic and by two additional acts of bookmaking: the addition in the late summer of 1911 of "A Familiar Preface" to introduce the collection and partly to give it bulk, and in 1919 the addition of an "Author's Note" for a new edition.[3] Conrad's focus is on the development of his identities, first as seaman and then as English writer, not on the discreet facts and events of his life. Such a focus influences his choices about the beginning, middle, and end of his narrative. To demonstrate these claims, this essay will focus extensively on the beginning and then more briefly on the Furka Pass episode and the closing segment in Marseilles.

The alteration of the volume's original title ("Some Reminiscences") and the supplementary paratext attempt to mitigate internal tensions and strains deriving from haphazard composition. The volume, in short, lacks unity of impulse and a closely focused theme, cohering mostly by recurrent motifs, a circle of repeated and interlocking allusions, and associative strategies, although, as Andrzej Busza usefully summarizes: "The two lives mirror and throw light upon each other" (2000, 143). As much as unity, loosely defined, may have been an aim at the outset, Conrad's intentions shifted considerably

---

3. For a full discussion of the volume's textual history, see "The Texts: An Essay" in Conrad 2008. For a stimulating analysis of paratextual elements, including prefaces, see Genette 1997.

during actual composition. His initial idea that the work would be "concerned with Polish life and life at sea" (to J. B. Pinker, 18 September [1908], *Letters* 4: 125), was rapidly abandoned. Rather than topics in themselves, Poland and the sea serve as backdrops for meditations on the shape, activities, and motives of his life. The Polish material, in fact, plays only a minor role in the final text, being altogether absent from the last four sections, as the theme of his two vocations as seaman and as writer became his principal subjects. Urged by Ford Madox Ford to compose memoirs somewhat in the vein of *The Mirror of the Sea* but more coherently organized, Conrad was moved to explore selected facets of his past despite his antipathy, temperamental and professional, to self-display. To reveal intensely personal concerns in a public venue mainly to make money was to fail in simple good manners and to abandon an imperative of self-restraint: to recall Conrad's own phrase in the "Author's Note" to *Notes on Life and Letters,* he expressed his horror of appearing publicly *en pantoufles* (3). Part of this is a reaction to "mediatization" of the author, in its first flush in the opening decade of the twentieth century when journalists saw opportunities in fomenting and then pandering to public curiosity about a writer's personal life. For Conrad, to indulge such a vein was to abandon Parnassian concerns for what might be considered self-indulgent gossip. He largely opts, then, for a highly selective exploration of the origins of his two vocations: his maritime experience, already long behind him and viewed from retrospect, and the career of authorship, likewise once an adventurous turn in the path but, with time, a daily necessity urged on by the simple need to earn a living.

Not surprisingly, a work hedged in by such fundamentally self-protective attitudes sometimes quarrels with its generic predecessors and is also on occasion anxiously self-conflicted. In this light, Conrad's hostility to Rousseau's confessional mode, as the tendency to exaggeration reveals, is, in part at least, self-defensive posturing. Conrad disdains to "confess" but must do so or appear to do so, having chosen to write about "himself." This tension between inner priority and exterior necessity accounts for the text's unorthodox, apparently casual structure. The reader is shown selected fragments of the seaman's life and the writer's life, being granted what purport to be privileged glimpses of both, whilst the subject often engages in a sophisticated game of hide-and-seek, at moments teasingly present and frustratingly absent.

There is here as well the influence of Impressionist poetics, which may also help to explain Conrad's resort to outright padding: paraphrase and word-for-word translations from Bobrowski's memoirs function as a convenient subterfuge to meet deadlines and to fill a quota of words, but borrowing implicitly released him from total commitment and responsibility, and digression serves as a mask behind which he could disappear. However much Sterne or the Polish writer Aleksander Fredro might be invoked as structural precedents for the sense of randomness and the deftly interwoven presentation of personality, incident, and atmosphere, complex psychological factors also determine the work's contours. No less does Conrad's impatience with established generic categories. Evident in his experiments with the realist novel (in texts such as *Lord Jim* and *Nostromo,* for instance), this manifests itself structurally. Non-linked episodes and the reliance on the fragment suggest a heightened reality, conveying more effectively and efficiently than linearity the inner meaning of his life.

J. M. Kertzer, writing toward the end of New Criticism's hegemony, seeks a thematic unity throughout, justifying the inclusion of the Nicholas B. sections as motivated by the charge of "betrayal": "the patriotic example of Nicholas B. suggests to Conrad, by way of contrast, his own irresponsible self-indulgence" (1975, 297). Why a desire to go to sea should, *prima facie,* appear self-indulgent and irresponsible suggests the tenacity of Eliza Orzeszkowa's hysterical charges, first made in 1899.[4] Looked at differently, the episode exposes Kertzer's viewpoint as decontextualized and ahistorical. Nicholas B.'s ardent Napoleonism, the basis for his "patriotic example," was founded upon an illusion. As Conrad's treatment of the celebrated Lithuanian dog episode shows, Napoleon cynically and systematically exploited the promise of national restoration for his personal political ends. Conrad's attitude toward "the great liberator," here and in "Autocracy and War" and in "The Duel" (in which the fanatical Feraud seems partly based on Mikołaj Bobrowski), suggests the degree to which he distances himself from his great-uncle's perspective. Indeed, Nicholas B.'s boundless admiration for Napoleon, whose project was to subjugate all Europe yet reward Poland with nationhood for participating in his depredations, is no less "Quixotic" or imaginative than Conrad's desire to go to sea, except that his grand-uncle's grand illusion was a communally shared one.

The work's loosely woven plot is that of all stories of the archetypal hero who discovers and forges his identity in the crucible of experience: following abandonment by (or departure from) the original parents comes adoption by the cultural parent(s), the fraught discovery and realization of a unique personal destiny through strife and travail, and, finally, the fulfillment of a fate or destiny through achievement in the world.[5] Conrad's manipulation of his

---

4. Speaking of Conrad, she writes: "[T]his gentleman, who writes popular and very lucrative novels in English has almost caused me a nervous breakdown" (Najder 1983, 1987). At the time, Conrad was selling in a few thousand copies and in serious financial difficulties.

5. For a classic study of the hero and the mythological stages marking his birth and development, see Campbell 1949.

autobiographical materials affords him the hero's typical double birth: first, into "the world as it is" (his birth in the Polish Ukraine to political idealists of Romantic inclination) and, later, into "the world as he wishes it to be" (rebirth as a French and then as an English sailor, and, finally, as an English writer).

On offering these reminiscences in book form, Conrad expressed the hope that readers would, on completing it, have a sense of "a coherent, justifiable personality both in its origin and in its action" (*A Personal Record*, xxi). This retrospectively reveals the aim of the work written during 1908–1909. It also betrays a gnawing anxiety that the enterprise required explanation, and it suggests awareness that the methods Conrad had used to present aspects of himself and experience might have proved overly subtle. Even more, the statement places Conrad's chosen methods under self-interrogation: in autobiography, the boundaries between the art brought to bear on the narrating subject and the subject itself shift fluidly, with, in short, an argument made for the work's "coherence" and "necessity" as well as for the public self presented in it.

As it turns out, these keywords are related to one of the text's projects of understanding, on the one hand, how the personality and activities of Conrad's parents, those of his "personal" father (to use a Jungian term), Apollo Korzeniowski, poet, translator, and nationalist, affected his life, and, on the other, a self-aware appreciation of the nexus of paternal and maternal relationships alluded to (and in some sections more elaborately developed) that contributed to shape and influence his personality and values. The concept of parentage necessarily opens out to embrace not only the motherland/fatherland of "Poland" (to use that shorthand for a cultural condition not then expressed in a nation-state) but also England and the tongue that "adopted" him. Commonplace in themselves, the metaphors have far-reaching psychological implications and emerge more strongly in the text published in 1919, since Conrad, contrary to his usual procedures in his prefatory statements, which chattily concentrate on a given work's "real-life" origins, focuses on a defense of his father's politics and on his "adoption" of English as the language for his creative endeavor. Indeed, only in the "Author's Note" of 1919 does Conrad deal extensively with his father, defending him from the charge of being a "Revolutionist."

Orphaned at the age of eleven, Conrad experienced a conflictual relationship with his actual parents who, in psychological terms, had "abandoned" him by their premature deaths,[6] and not incidentally *A Personal Record* deals

---

6. Drawing on a number of contemporary psychoanalytic and critical technologies, Ash (1999) builds a case for seeing Conrad's unfinished mourning for Apollo Korzeniowski as a significant motivating force in his writings. For a broad, if high speculative, psychoanalytic analysis of the father image in Conrad's work, see also Dobrinsky 1989.

with themes more fully and fretfully explored in the work Conrad was stalled with, *Under Western Eyes,* where orphanhood, abandonment, and betrayal figure as key motifs. Tellingly, a passage cut from *A Personal Record* in the transition from its serial to book text uses the metaphor of inadequate husband and father to portray Rousseau's impact on France's political life: "The writer hailed as the Father of the French Revolution (the husband of the meek Thérèse was obviously predestined to know nothing of his various children) was not in general an abundantly blessed person, and in that respect he was not blessed at all" (1909, 62–63). The deletion of this slighting accusation, an irrelevant diversion from the main discussion, is justified on artistic grounds, but its presence in the serial version indicates the degree to which the theme of the father who abandoned and neglected his offspring is woven throughout the work.

This discussion now turns to three narrative and rhetorical highpoints that structure the themes mentioned: the opening in the Seine at Rouen and concluded at Tadeusz Bobrowski's estate Kazimierówka in the Ukraine, the Furka Pass episode, and the closing segment in Marseilles.

Rouen: Aboard the *Adowa*

In "A Familiar Preface," Conrad replied to criticisms of the method he had adopted to narrate his life story, offering a spirited defense: "Could I begin with the sacramental words 'I was born on such a date and in such a place?' The very remoteness of the locality would have robbed the statement of all interest" (xx). From the outset, then, he rejected, even disdained biography's and autobiography's most conventional organizational patterns—time and place—for a narrative truer to his sense of himself.[7] As in his fiction, he elects to hammer out formal structures appropriate to his material. Not time but fragments of experience and significant emotional moments structure his narrative in an attempt to mirror the essential discontinuity of his experience.[8] Such a narrative method, in the fashion of a kaleidoscope, offers patterns that articulate and insist on an inner cohesiveness and patterns of meaning not present in the mere recitation of events in the order in which they occurred. The problem of beginnings is actualized here, not just signaling Conrad's distance from the popular biographer, whose life narrative broadly conforms to conventional chronological and thematic expectations. His rhetorical question

7. "Autobiography" is convenient shorthand for a genre with multiple formal manifestations. Smith and Watson identify no less than fifty-two "genres of life narrative" (2001, 183–207).

8. For a discussion of moments of time in Conrad's fiction, see Paccaud-Huguet 2006.

reveals how the problem of beginnings blends into and significantly colors the presentation of narrative overall. As Edward Said has usefully observed in *Beginnings,* "Conrad's radical uncertainty about himself" derives from two modes of experience: one that frames reality as "an unfolding process, as action being-made, as always becoming," the other involving a sense of reality "as a hard quantity, very much 'there' and definable" (1975, 106). The interplay of these contradictory modes of experience is fully evident in the multiple identities Conrad puts on display in the opening "chapter" of *A Personal Record.*

The chronological displacement and the absence of traditional time-markers (the opening chapter mentions not one date), engender a similarly fluid spatial flexibility: the Seine at Rouen flows, as it were, into the River Pantai of a remote corner of Borneo, past Bessborough Gardens in Pimlico, to a ship off the Cape Colony, to a remote corner of the Ukraine. Further memories are staged on the Congo River, at Friedrichstrasse Bahnhof in Berlin, and in Warsaw. Indeed, it is as if the ship's stasis, the enforced wait to depart from Rouen, engendered a flow of memory of almost unceasing movement—in ships, trains, boats, in a sledge through the snowbound countryside—across large swathes of time. Just as Conrad rejects limiting time to forward (or backward) movement by privileging flux and randomness, he refuses definition by spatial limits. The strategy, which emphasizes a sense of becoming and the accumulation of experience, thus gradually helps to define a layered, multiple self. Conrad famously confessed to being a "*homo duplex,*" but the phrase *homo multiplex* more aptly describes the individual he puts on display.

What is absent at this beginning is a conventional discussion of origins, given almost unique explanatory power in much biographical writing: "I am this *because* I was that," or perhaps, "I am this because my parents were that." Instead, Conrad opens with a general philosophical statement about the writing of books: "Books may be written in all sorts of places." This "personal record" begins, then, in impersonality: not "My books" but "Books" in general. He then goes on to describe what, in view of his life experience, is a seemingly inconsequential moment: the interruption of his writing by a coworker. This insistence on "nowness" on the part of the man in the middle of life's way is, however, purposeful: the focus on engagement in social activity, both self-imposed and imposed by the economic order, argues that presenting the facts of his genesis would render an inadequate and ultimately misleading account of him. Conrad disdains the formulaic "I was born in such and such a place" precisely because, in his case, it lacks explanatory power: to invoke this worn-out cliché would, moreover, be surrendering to narrative passivity. The announcement of birth and parentage is not simply deferred: only part of it is made at all, the "where" of his birth is more or less revealed but not the "when." His narrative gambit thus replaces "This happened to me" ("I was born," an action over which one exercises no choice or control) with deliberate, elected activity: "I am engaged in doing this," or more specifically, "I am writing," or even "I was busy writing *Almayer's Folly* until Young Cole interrupted me." Morf finds a sinister procedure in this: Conrad "hides much more than he reveals" about his family, childhood, and coming of age (1930, 190), but to say this is to misunderstand his purpose, for Conrad is intent less on the biography of a man than on that of an artist and, thus, of a sensibility, a project more akin to Wordsworth's in *The Prelude* (1805) than, for example, to *The Autobiography of Benjamin Franklin* (1793). He is not, then, "hiding" details about his background and past, but choosing to emphasize only those that suit his manifest intentions. Proust in *À la recherche* (an autobiographical fiction) uses his childhood experience as a crucial element in the genesis of artistic sensibility. Conrad's tack to play these down is an artistic gambit of equal validity.

Rejecting or modifying the time-honored generic announcement of the subject's birth in a specific social and cultural milieu, he begins instead in "the berth of a mariner on board a ship" (3) with the "birth" of a book, and by extension of its writer. The pun "birth/berth" dominates the narrative's opening and replaces Victorian autobiographical convention—"I am born," as Dickens's *The Personal History and Experience of David Copperfield the Younger* (1849–50) famously begins—with a Modernist gesture, situating the seemingly self-generated writer in the act of creating meaning and perpetuating himself through language. By a series of allusions and by employing various narrative techniques, the heritage Conrad lays claim to is literary. Borrowing the *in medias res* convention of epic, with the hero embroiled in vicissitude and confronting his destiny, he stakes claims on narrative "paternity" in a genre associated with national identity and nation-founding projects. Traditionally, epic situates the individual and heroic identity within a large cultural and historical framework: either the birth of a society, as in Virgil, or cultural survival against an antagonist, as in Homer or Spenser. The generic claim is particularly bold, as the artist-hero stakes out his individual destiny and argues that writing is fundamentally an activist, even heroic, engagement, deeply social however solitary.

Conrad completes his gesture toward epic by, in effect, the traditional invocation to the Muse, in this case Flaubert, "in his unworldly, almost ascetic, devotion to his art a sort of literary, saint-like hermit" (3). The trope established with the words "devotion" and "saint" is further developed, Conrad noting of his shipboard activity that "we were leading then a contemplative life" (5), and thus evoking secluded monastic orders, and, by extension, the dedication of one's life to witnessing a revealed word. The trope's main thrust, however, moves, contrariwise, to formulate the writer as a bard and visionary, and thus giving him an explicitly social function. Through the mythification of Flaubert (a secular saint devoted to his "work"), Conrad gestures to the long tradition of writing as a sacral act. Writing involves not only the transformation of the writer, the vehicle, but also the eventual transformation of society through the transformative power of language. The artist, then, figures as an epic hero, leading his society to a new destiny or a new revelation.

Significantly, in declining to reply to Young Cole's naïvely put question "What are you always scribbling there, if it's fair to ask?" (4) Conrad withholds precisely this transformation. Alienated from both his intruder and the activity he was engaged in, Conrad, by way of answer, casts his eyes from his interrupted work to the quay outside, and, highly self-conscious about the act of writing, deflects the readers' attention to two fragments of transitory reality: first, to "[a] red-nosed carter in a blouse and a woollen nightcap" leaning against a wheel and to an equally "idle, strolling custom-house guard" depressed by "the weather and the monotony of official existence" (that is, to two individuals engaged in the workaday world), and, then, to a literary event. His sight of the Café Thillard on the Quai de la Bourse (neither named) recalls Emma Bovary's going to the opera at the nearby Théâtre des Arts. Conrad declines to answer Young Cole's query, excusing himself by an appeal to temperament, both his and his interlocutor's: "I could not have told him that Nina had said: 'It has set at last.' He would have been extremely surprised and perhaps have dropped his precious banjo" (4). The elements of rhetorical exaggeration ("extremely," "precious") and deprecatory humor express slight resentment toward Cole's ordinary destiny and sensibility. The retreat from response is strategic: on the one hand, the focus on visual details affirms the novelist's craft (the incorporation of selected elements from the external world into his constructed one) and, on the other, it announces a method of indirection and association that will allow Conrad, more fully and honestly, to explain "what" he is "always scribbling."

This deferral has other parallels in the narrative: the self-imposed task of talking about himself is at times deflected by talking about others. The Mikołaj Bobrowski episodes are tangentially and associatively linked to Conrad's experience but not his own life. Conrad elects Flaubert as a model artist, an observer of "hermetic" disposition, disengaged and distanced from the subject of observation. In short, this scene, which relies on several fictional strategies (dialogue, chronological and perspectival mobility, literary allusion) proposes an aesthetic of activist engagement at the same time it posits aestheticist withdrawal. The narrative, thus, both announces and enacts an artistic stance and program.

Aboard ship in Rouen and engaged in writing, Conrad the narrated subject thus positions himself as simultaneously doing "the work," the *real* work, of writer *and* seaman, laboring at the two tasks that constitute his subject matter and that, at this stage of his experience, formed his personal and social identities. This focus insists, then, on deferring information about his ancestry and parents and serves instead to convey what was, arguably, the more important *public* fact about himself: his self-elected maritime and artistic callings. By sleight-of-hand, the narrative lights precisely on public identity, the text's allusions self-consciously placing the writer *and* the seaman, or the writer-seaman, in specific historical contexts and in heredity lines stretching back in time. No less significantly, Conrad presents himself as enmeshed in action, impelled to respond, on the one hand, to the demands of his imagination, and, on the other, to his mundane but life-supporting duties as a ship's officer that require artistic endeavor to be laid aside. However viewed from the outside—and Conrad carefully sets up the banjoist third officer in the role of a counterbalancing normative figure[9]—both demands were for Conrad himself insistent and ineluctable: quotidian reality might at times prevent him from writing, but it also makes up the essential parts of a reality he looks back on and complexly meditates and develops.

Musing retrospectively about the influence of Flaubert on *Almayer's Folly,* Conrad casually introduces material that again seems incidental or even irrelevant, recalling Flaubert's "fancy" about his possible Viking origins.[10] This "fancy" (a deliberate use of a word popular in Romantic literature), unrelated to Flaubert's immediate family history, evokes Viking sovereignty over Normandy in the ninth century. The reference thus meaningfully emphasizes how "the kind Norman giant" (3) was, at least imaginatively, engaged in the same quest for origins as Conrad, finding himself indebted to and explained by remote historical and political events that shaped a specific regional identity and, by implication, his imposing physical presence. Conrad's reference to Flaubert not as a Frenchman but as a "Norman" stresses a cultural identity grounded in a clearly delineated ancient territory over a secondary, if more embracing, national and linguistic identity arrived at through strife and political compromise. Flaubert's layered and multiple identities—Norman, Frenchman, artist-writer, saint, hermit—presage the sense of a *multiplex* self that Conrad proceeds to develop.

Literary, not personal, paternity is the issue here, the adoptive son following in the footsteps of the adoptive father, "Joseph Conrad" following Flaubert, the

9. Young Cole's banjo playing none the less hints at another seaman engaged in artistic pursuits.

10. Kertzer (1975, 294) emphasizes the Vikings as seafarers, and thus as a link to the sea.

champion of impersonality in art, not Józef Konrad Korzeniowski following or diverging from the path traced by poet and dramatist Apollo Korzeniowski, who is effectively erased. The descendant of the creator of *Madame Bovary* (a work mentioned a few paragraphs later), Conrad posits filial homage and allegiance to the father of his choice, substituting Flaubert for the father given him by fate. By this gesture, the narrative simultaneously abandons and redefines the narrowly conceived nationalist aspirations traditional of epic. The nation, the tribe, to which Conrad traces his origins is that in which Flaubert had gained his place: the "tribe" of literary men, whose progeny are the books of other literary men.

The narrative then carefully sets up of a series of allusions to paternity more fully to work out this theme. The next topic, again seemingly casual, is the vexed father-daughter relationship depicted in *Almayer's Folly*. Conrad's quotation from his own text is a meaningful gesture (whether he was actually working on this part of the novel is, of course, undiscoverable). The long-awaited sunset will free Nina Almayer from her failed father into the larger world represented by her lover, Dain Maroola: "'It has set at last,' said Nina to her mother, pointing to the hills behind which the sun had sunk" (3). What awaits Nina, the result of her efforts, is maturity, womanhood, and liberation from paternal authority, indeed, paternal tyranny. Sanctioned by her mother, her actions present the whole (dysfunctional) family nexus: scheming daughter and mother and dream-besotted father, the latter introduced only by the periphrasis, mentioned in the phrase "Almayer's romantic daughter" (3). The time chosen for Nina's liberation draws on archetype: sunset, the moment of symbolic death into Mother Ocean, presages renewal and rebirth even as it enacts extinction.[11]

That Nina's words are borrowed from Adam Mickiewicz's poem *Konrad Wallenrod* (1828) complicates the psychological and literary issues at hand. Her rejection of her father's self-serving dreams for her future and her comprehensive repudiation of his cultural identity and attachments become entangled with Conrad's assessment of his past at the very moment when he publicly begins to record it. Jean M. Szczypien, reading this echo in Morfian fashion, argues that "the exiled Pole residing in England, by echoing *Konrad Wallenrod* . . . is stating resolutely if indirectly that he too is serving his fatherland, even though he is writing in English" (1998, 98). Leaving aside the assertion that Conrad is in "exile"—a word normally suggesting involuntary

---

11. Those inclined to discern the unconscious of text might see "son-set" in the unpronounced word "sunset," with Nina, in the role of Conrad's self-projection, poised to leave her dream-besotted father in his enclosed, decaying world for a new, self-made destiny.

expatriation (not Conrad's case)[12]—and that he could have expected none of his contemporary English and American audience for which *A Personal Record* was written to recognize the quotation from Mickiewicz, this is, at most, private shorthand. It is not an "allusion," which, by definition, relies on an audience's (potential) recognition of the source recalled. More importantly, Szczypien's sentimental assumption is insouciant to context: Nina not only desires to escape from inherited emotional ties (Almayer, his dreams, and plight) and a stultifying death-in-life sociocultural environment, but she also *acts* to effect her escape. For her, the sunset she looks upon is the very last of the old dispensation as Almayer drifts into the past and Dain becomes her future. Her ardent desire for individual identity, shaped by her own actions, and her flight from paternal oppression represent Conrad's situation. Rather than "majestically" affirming "service" to the fatherland, the private appeal to a canonical Polish literary model acknowledges a desire, even an eagerness, to flee entanglements forged during a severely traumatic childhood. Conrad's expatriation, a complex act, ended in his liberation from family pressures and cultural constraint. He thus opens his reminiscences, that part of his life he wished to make public, by an appeal to cosmopolitan literary traditions, incarnated by Flaubert and through epic including the whole Western European tradition. In developing these claims, he situates himself in the literary culture of France and, by the mere fact of writing in English, of England.[13]

The dramatic present in which Conrad situates his opening scene of multiple reminiscence—of reading (Flaubert's *Madame Bovary*) at a time and place unspecified, of writing (chapter X of *Almayer's Folly*), and of the humid and sun-drenched tropics—is a delayed ship (unnamed) in Rouen (unnamed) awaiting release. The ship "frozen fast in the river" and "gripped by the inclement weather" acts as a metaphor for his condition at a transitional moment with, as he states, his experience at sea mainly over and his writing life in its fledgling state. Although based on the *Adowa's* real-life circumstances in December 1893 (again the temporal frame is unmentioned), Conrad's

---

12. The term's meaning has apparently become unsettled: Brooke-Rose (1996, 294) characterizes Conrad as a "voluntary exile," while Suleiman in the same special issue of *Poetics Today* appears to rely on the word's more conventional meaning: "expatriates can go home any time they like, while exiles cannot" (1996, 283).

13. See Knowles 1996, for a nuanced and contextualized discussion of Conrad's departure from Poland for Marseilles. The charge made as early as Orzeszkowa's "Emigration of Talent" of 1899 (see Najder 1983, 182–91) is partly based on the assumption that Conrad would have become a writer had he never left Poland. The still odder assumption is that he ought to have written in Polish while the life-experience he mined for his creative work was experienced largely in English. Tarnawski (1964, 109) follows this line of thinking: "If disloyalty came into it at all, it lay in handing over his creative talent—his soul, as it were—to a foreign literature."

presentation gains symbolic force, emphasizing and underlining references to oppression, entrapment, and immobility—with the contraries of flight, progress, and motion—the unspoken keywords that will permit the ship to enter into its function and the writer to assume and then fully inhabit his chosen identity.

The reference to *Madame Bovary* further elaborates and reinforces the pattern of oppressive familial relationships, patriarchal and cultural authority, and flight. Seeking to escape her marriage, Emma Bovary flees into a substitute reality so "romantic" that it renders her existence in the world impossible. In a tripartite reference, the scene in which Charles and Emma Bovary attend *Lucia di Lammermoor,* Donizetti's 1835 operatic adaptation of Sir Walter Scott's 1819 novel *Bride of Lammermoor,* Conrad recalls another flight: that of Lucy Ashton fleeing her situation. She does so in three stages: by murdering the husband whom her brother (the representative of paternal and cultural authority) has forced her to marry, by sinking into insanity, and, in ultimate flight from a world hostile to her feelings and sensibility, simply by dying. Extending the theme of escape from psychological oppression, this contrapuntal reference also emphasizes ways in which literary works have antecedents and progeny: Lucia, the creation of Scott, migrates first into Salvatore Cammaranno's libretto for Donizetti, and then into Flaubert's writing, and then into Conrad's. To explore the full context of these allusions is not to suggest that Conrad was consciously working out patterns that cumulatively amount to an open quarrel with his "personal" father or the larger more encompassing archetypal "father" constituted by culture and heritage, but to argue that threaded throughout the text are accusations of constraint that, for psychological and artistic reasons, are made indirectly.

By way of compensation, the chapter alludes to several positive fathers and father figures: the retired colonel, the father of "Young Cole"; the father of Flaubert's Emma Bovary, Père Roualt (misremembered as Père Renault); and "Dear Captain Froude," the first of several father surrogates; and, centrally, Tadeusz Bobrowski, guardian of "many orphans of land-owning families" (23) and of Conrad himself. The chapter's culminating reference to paternity is to Conrad's own, as a father wishing to leave for his sons in addition to his artistic legacy, "the colours and figures of his hard-won creation" (24), the memory of his early impressions, although, indeed, this is a wish that the text leaves mainly unfulfilled. In a chapter with several references to (surrogate) fathers and (adoptive) sons, Apollo Korzeniowski is present only passingly, as Conrad mentions that his mother, Ewa Korzeniowska, had "followed my father" into exile (23), a fact research has revealed as untrue: condemned to exile, she was an actor in her own right, not simply playing the role of the faithful wife.

From the Furka Pass to the Vieux-Port and England

Conrad's liberation from paternal and cultural constraint at the end of section 2 is seemingly tagged onto the story of Nicholas B. and his (in)famous dinner of Lithuanian dog. Remembering his "childish horror" of his uncle's act, he shifts the narrative focus from the participants back to himself and then expands on his own exotic fare—trepang, *la vache enragée* (misery)—partaken of during his voyages and travels to move to the more serious issues of self-sacrifice and the motivations for action. Structured associatively and by a series of contrasts, the narrative maintains a surface casualness belied by the general reflections about the irresolvable "contradictions of human nature" and the essential inexplicability of the self. Literary allusion, a particularly appropriate means to explore the topic of the writing self, further develops the biographical material: Don Quixote, motivated by dreams and misunderstood by a community in which he is an outsider, is a trope for the imaginative man, the Other within the social framework and, specifically, for Conrad himself. Don Quixote, reading about chivalry, fashions himself a knight; Conrad, reading about the sea, fancies himself a mariner. The hinted-at parallel composes part of an argument whereby Conrad states that inner vision must contend with and finally trump outer constraint. The Barber and The Priest, the normative figures of Don Quixote's story hostile to his imagination, fade before the image of the *ingenioso hidalgo*, "his head encircled by a halo—the patron saint of all lives spoiled or saved by the irresistible grace of imagination" (37). (Again, the religious imagery heightens the sense of vocation, with its attendant notions of dedication, service, and self-sacrifice.)

In figuring his embattled younger self in literary terms, Conrad is again claiming membership in a community of dreamers, and thus also embracing the ill-fated Nicholas B. who dreamed, vainly, of a country of his own. From these general associations, Conrad then turns to a specific memory, and for once to a date, to 1873 and the emotional climax: of his last schoolboy holiday, that moment when his tutor (who is unnamed in the text), the delegate of avuncular (patriarchal) and cultural authority, at the top of the Furka Pass in the Swiss Alps, yielded to Conrad's desire to go to sea.

The episode introduces yet another surrogate father, who is replaced by yet another: vanquished by his concession, Pulman yields place to the "unforgettable Englishman" (40), the harbinger of Conrad's future. Self-consciously dramatic, the moment is also self-conscious mythmaking as Conrad embraces his dreamt-of future. The climax is staged on a mountaintop, the intersection-point between the upper world and the world of day-to-day experience and thus the traditional locus of visions and of transformation.[14] Behind this scene lies a range of romantic illuminations (Wordsworth, in particular, both in *The Prelude* and in *Sketches from the Alps* and Caspar David Friedrich) and the charting of destiny. The Conrad who goes down the mountain is no longer the one who has gone up it: not a boy in his tutor's charge, he is a man ready to give actuality to his vision.

At this point the narrative moves from retrospect to look forward to the future (now the past): with his master's certificate gained, Conrad remembers Pulman's death, singling out his former tutor's professional achievement as a healing physician. He pays filial homage to the man who facilitated his discovery of his own first calling, also an opportunity to develop aspects of his personality and to widen his knowledge of the world. The intensely rhetorical conclusion to the section, by subtle understatement, pays tribute to his own persistence and achievement: "What greater reward in ambition, honour and conscience," Conrad writes of Pulman, "could he have hoped to win for himself when, on the top of the Furca [*sic*] Pass, he bade me look well to the end of my opening life" (45). Pulman, then, his function fulfilled, leads Conrad to an imaginative act of self-definition. The boy setting out is counseled to consider the man he will become, regarding "the end" (both as conclusion and purpose) of his chosen life path. At this moment, Pulman, too, is transformed, dropping his role as Barber and Priest, and becomes, if only momentarily, a visionary himself, seeing how accepting Conrad's viewpoint was right: "How short his years and how clear his vision!" (45).

With a long by-excursion to speak generally of writing fiction and of the labored composition of *Nostromo*, Conrad emphasizes his achievement as a writer and thus the fulfillment of his second vocation. The narrative then recounts his Board of Trade examinations and picks up the thread dropped at the close of the Furka Pass scene in that staged in Marseilles's Vieux Port, in which Conrad reinvented himself. The method is again reminiscent of fictional procedures, in particular the interpolated narrative (of Fielding or Dickens, for instance) whereby the main plot is developed and expanded by thematically germane side incidents. Continuous in a way that no other chapters are, chapters 6 and 7 follow upon one another as if Conrad were belatedly conceding to generic expectations and the demands of serialization. Chapter 6, with Conrad now ensconced in Marseilles receiving *la belle* Madame Delestang's warning that he should be wary of "spoiling his life" (127), not on its surface

14. Moses on Mount Sinai, Christ at the Transfiguration, Francis of Assisi on Mount Alverno, and other figures poised to communicate with the upper world on mountains form the episode's literary and cultural background.

an especially dramatic moment, is rhetorically worked up to become another turning point and perhaps the major statement of Conrad's attempt to give his life story coherence: by recalling it.

He proves that he had followed the dictates of this woman, the incarnation of conscience at a moment in his feckless youth, and hereby too he replies to the groundless charges of desertion and dereliction of duty. He did not, indeed, "spoil his life," giving both a private and public significance to the vision that motivated it and to which he had as much right to individual claim as his ancestors who chose to devote themselves to a political cause. Made "thoughtful" by this announcement of destiny, Conrad states himself ready for action: "haunted by no ghosts of the past and by no visions of the future, I walked down the quay of the Vieux Port to join the pilot-boat of my friends" (127). Again the call is to action within a specific communal context and developed into an initiation into the craft of the sea under the tutelage, *in loco parentis,* of "l'Ancien," the *patron* of the Third Company, and, collectively, of the Syndicate of Marseilles Pilots. Conrad thus establishes a maritime parentage no less thoroughly as his invocation of Flaubert sets out his literary one. And he does so at another transitional moment: his hand reaches out to touch an English ship on his "last outing with the pilots" (134) of Marseilles. Not wholly complete for some years, the transition is from French to English seaman: the "*Larguez*" of the *patron* of the Third Company is replaced by the "Look out there" from the deck of the *James Westoll.* This is an economy of substitution in several ways. The command to "cast off," made in French, and the English injunction relate not only to the boat and the steamer but also symbolically frame Conrad's youthful experience: he is to let go and to do so with caution. As if by compensation for the boldness of setting out, the Red Ensign unfurls on the English ship offering, as Conrad points out, protection to the ship and, as his rhetoric establishes, to himself—"the protecting warm bit of bunting." "Symbolic" in its function, it also offers a new national identity and evokes a tradition of seamanship, Conrad almost literally wrapping himself in the flag of the British Merchant Service.

Unsurprisingly, he argued that this ending was "a perfect terminal" to his reminiscences and that any addition would be damaging. Cut short because of his quarrel with Ford, the text was to have had other installments, but the "personal record" closes with Conrad paying filial homage to the safe lodging, "the roof," provided by the Red Ensign. The conclusion plays off the time-honored return of the wandering sailor, who, having braved the terrors of the deep, (re)finds his permanent shelter on the land, by extension, his family, nation, and culture. In Conrad's case the "roof" claimed replaces the psychic territory lost through his parents' deaths and to the traumas of bereavement and orphanhood. The note is genuinely celebratory and grateful, not defensively embattled or apologetic, and to speak of this work as one written to settle "an outstanding debt"[15] is to be deaf to its tonal registers of celebration and achievement. Edward W. Said has rightly noted how both *The Mirror of the Sea* and *A Personal Record* close "with rapt invocations to symbols of national sentiment" (1966, 156), this sense of rapture celebrating nationality as a conscious and deliberate choice rather than mere accident. The synecdoche of "the roof" is singularly revealing, for though Conrad makes no explicit call on the Ulysses story (as he does in *The Mirror of the Sea*), the sailor-king's homecoming to Penelope with its affirmation of familial ties and national identity, lies in the background and influences the triumphalist close of *A Personal Record*. The twist, however, is that the returning adventurer-hero discovers "home" in an English and maritime identity. To reaffirm the sense of continuity the narrative closes with a circular structure of departure and return, ending where it opened, at sea, with the tidal Seine standing in for mighty ocean and the link between seaman and writer complete.

15. The words are those of Wit Tarnawski, who goes so far as to claim that Conrad wrote *A Personal Record* to compensate for what he calls his "abandonment" of Poland (1984, 106–7).

Works Cited

Abbot, H. Porter. "Writing and Conversion: Conrad's Modernist Autography." *Yale Journal of Criticism* 5.3 (1992): 135–63.

Ash, Beth Sharon. *Writing in Between: Modernity and Psychosocial Dilemma in the Novels of Joseph Conrad.* New York: St. Martin's Press, 1999.

Brooke-Rose, Christina. "Exsul." *Poetics Today* 17.3 (1996): 289–303.

Busza, Andrzej. "Conrad's Rhetoric of Affirmation and the Moderns." *Stanford Humanities Review* 8.1 (2000): 142–65.

Campbell, Joseph. *The Hero with a Thousand Faces.* Bollingen Series. Princeton, NJ: Princeton University Press, 1949.

Conrad, Joseph. "Some Reminiscences." *English Review,* April 1909, 59–69.

———. *A Personal Record.* In The Mirror of the Sea *and* A Personal Record. Edited by Zdzisław Najder. Oxford World's Classics. Oxford: Oxford University Press, 1988.

———. "Author's Note." In *Notes on Life and Letters,* edited by J. H. Stape. The Cambridge Edition of the Works of Joseph Conrad. Cambridge: Cambridge University Press, 2004, 3–5.

———. *The Collected Letters of Joseph Conrad.* 9 vols. Edited by Frederick R. Karl et al. Cambridge: Cambridge University Press, 1983–2007.

———. *A Personal Record.* Edited by Zdzisław Najder and J. H. Stape. Cambridge: Cambridge University Press, 2007.

DeVinne, Christine. "Begging the Question of Confession: Joseph Conrad's *A Personal Record.*" *Prose Studies* 25.3 (2002): 82–99.

Dobrinsky, Joseph. *The Artist in Conrad's Fiction: A Psychocritical Study.* Ann Arbor: UMI Research Press, 1989.

Genette, Gérard. *Paratexts: Thresholds of Interpretation.* Translated by Jane E. Lewin. Cambridge: Cambridge University Press, 1997.

GoGwilt, Christopher. *The Invention of the West: Joseph Conrad and the Double-Mapping of Europe and Empire.* Stanford, CA: Stanford University Press, 1995.

Kalnins, Mara. "Introduction." In Joseph Conrad, A Personal Record *and* The Mirror of the Sea, edited by Mara Kalnins. Penguin Twentieth-Century Classics. Harmondsworth: Penguin Books, 1998.

Karl, Frederick R. *Joseph Conrad: The Three Lives—A Biography.* New York: Farrar, Straus and Giroux, 1979.

Kertzer, J. M. "Conrad's *Personal Record.*" *University of Toronto Quarterly* 44.3 (Summer 1975): 290–303.

Knowles, Owen. "The Life." In *The Cambridge Companion to Joseph Conrad,* edited by J. H. Stape. Cambridge: Cambridge University Press, 1996. 1–24.

Knowles, Owen, and Gene M. Moore. *Oxford Reader's Companion to Joseph Conrad.* Oxford: Oxford University Press, 2000.

Marle, Hans van. "Plucked and Passed on Tower Hill: Conrad's Examination Ordeals." *Conradiana* 8 (1976): 99–109.

———. "An Ambassador of Conrad's Future: The *James Mason* in Marseilles, 1874." *L'epoque Conradienne* 14 (1988): 63–67.

McLauchlan, Juliet. "'Piety' in Joseph Conrad's *A Personal Record.*'" *Polish Review* 19.3 (1984): 11–23.

Monod, Sylvère. "*Souvenirs personnel:* Notice et notes." *Conrad: Œuvres.* 5 vols. Bibliothèque de la Pléiade. 3:1408–47. Paris: NRF–Gallimard, 1987.

Morf, Gustav. *The Polish Heritage of Joseph Conrad.* London: Sampson Low, Marston, 1930.

Najder, Zdzisław. *Joseph Conrad: A Chronicle.* Translated by Halina Carroll-Najder. Cambridge: Cambridge University Press, 1983.

———. Introduction. In The Mirror of the Sea *and* A Personal Record, edited by Zdzisław Najder. Oxford World's Classics. Oxford: Oxford University Press, 1988. vii–xxi.

———. "Joseph Conrad and Thadeusz Bobrowski." In *Conrad in Perspective: Essays on Art and Fidelity.* Cambridge: Cambridge University Press, 1997. 44–67.

Orzeszkowa, Eliza. "The Emigration of Talent." In *Conrad under Familial Eyes,* edited by Zdzislaw Najder and translated by Halina Carroll-Najder. Cambridge: Cambridge University Press, 1983. 182–92.

Paccaud-Huguet, Josiane. "Those trifles that awaken ideas": The Conradian Moment." *Conradian* 31.1 (2006): 72–85.

Said, Edward W. *Joseph Conrad and the Fiction of Autobiography.* Cambridge, MA: Harvard University Press, 1966.

———. *Beginnings: Intention and Method.* New York: Basic Books, 1975.

Smith, Sidonie, and Julia Watson. *Reading Autobiography: A Guide for Interpreting Life Narratives.* Minneapolis: University of Minnesota Press, 2001.

Suleiman, Susan Rubin. "On Signposts, Travelers, Outsiders, and Backward Glances." *Poetics Today* 17.3 (1996): 283–88.

Szczyzpien, Jean M. "Conrad's *A Personal Record:* Composition, Intention, Design: Polonism." *Journal of Modern Literature* 16.1 (1989): 3–30.

———. "The Historical Background for Joseph Conrad's *A Personal Record.*" *Conradian* 15.2 (1991): 12–32.

———. "Echoes from Konrad Wallenrod in *Almayer's Folly* and *A Personal Record.*" *Nineteenth-Century Literature* 53.1 (1998): 91–110.

Tarnawski, Wit. *Conrad the Man, the Writer, the Pole: An Essay in Psychological Biography,* translated by Rosamond Batchelor. London: Polish Cultural Foundation, 1984.

12

Conrad's *Lord Jim*

Narrative and Genre

JAKOB LOTHE

Two valuable manuscripts in the possession of the Houghton Library at Harvard University are the "sketch" of Joseph Conrad's novel *Lord Jim* and a letter he wrote to John Livingstone Lowes on 29 November 1921. Taking my cue from these two manuscripts, I want to explore how Conrad, in *Lord Jim,* activates the distinctive features of a number of subgenres in order to create one of the most original and influential novels of European modernism. Providing an illustrative example of Mikhail M. Bakhtin's notion of the novel as "the most fluid of genres" and "a genre-in-the-making" (1982, 11), Conrad's *Lord Jim* appropriates and cumulatively combines aspects of other subgenres of fiction, including the sketch, the tale, the fragment, the episode, the legend, the letter, the romance, and the parable. Moreover, although a work of prose fiction, *Lord Jim* activates elements of the lyric and of drama, especially tragedy.

Identifying and commenting on all of these genres, this essay aims to show how they are linked to each other in the discourse of *Lord Jim,* and how the generic characteristics of each are evoked, molded, and shaped by the narrative strategies which Conrad employs. *Lord Jim* is, I posit, possessed of a remarkable generic instability. The main reason why this kind of instability is different from the generic combination of earlier novels is that, given what Conrad is trying to do with Jim and his story, he needs the combination of genres—or at least he makes that combination serve the larger goals he sets himself with

Jim and his story. The novel's modernist identity follows from the working out of the more specific narrative problems, including that of presenting textual segments or parts possessed of different generic markers, which Conrad took on in trying to make Jim's story as effective and engrossing as possible. My argument, then, is not only that the combination of genres makes *Lord Jim* a modernist novel but also that its generic combination is a crucial element of this particular novelistic project (regardless of its period classification). One significant feature of this project is the fictional exploration of Jim. The narrative presentation of Jim deals with various aspects of his qualities as a main character, including ambition, fear, pride, and honor. What the novelistic project of *Lord Jim* also highlights, however, is the multifaceted interplay of Jim's life and character qualities on the one hand, and the range of narrative devices and techniques serving to present them on the other. Moreover, these elements are linked to each other through the interests and characteristics of the novel's narrators, especially Marlow, who thus function as character narrators. The elements of genre become constituent parts of the novel's sustained attempt to understand the enigma of Jim.

By "genre" I mean a category or class of literature. Literary works have been grouped into different genres at different times. That the criteria on which the classifications have been made are variable is evident already in Aristotle's *Poetics*. Aristotle's distinction between epic, lyric, and drama draws on the formal features and conventional usage of each generic category. And yet, as Dan Clinton (2007) notes, "Aristotle's genre binary of Tragedy and Comedy rests on some observation of the objects of imitation themselves."[1] In this essay, I will use commonly accepted understandings of the relevant genres. However, since the criteria on which generic classifications are based still tend to vary, I will specify these understandings as I take up each one.

To consider the generic multiplicity of *Lord Jim* as original and thematically productive is not to claim that no earlier novel draws on and combines different genres. Several do, and the most important example is *Don Quixote,* written nearly three hundred years earlier, in which Cervantes's ingenious blend of the chivalric romance, the pastoral novel, and the picaresque novel plays a major role in forming what is, in most critics' judgment, the first modern novel.

Even though Cervantes uses different variants of narrative fiction from Conrad in *Lord Jim,* there is a notable affinity between the two sets of variants. In his still valuable study of the self-conscious novel, Robert Alter finds

---

1. "[Comedy] tends to represent people inferior, [tragedy] superior, to existing humans" (Aristotle 1995, 35).

that one measure of Cervantes's genius is "the fact that he is the initiator of both traditions of the novel; his juxtaposition of high-flown literary fantasies with grubby actuality pointing the way to the realists, his zestfully ostentatious manipulation of the artifice he constructs setting a precedent for all the self-conscious novelists to come" (Alter 1975, 3–4). This is a valid observation, but what is distinctive about Conrad is that he *combines* both traditions of the novel initiated by Cervantes; and this is why, as Thomas Moser puts it in his succinct introduction to the Norton Critical edition, "*Lord Jim* has the rare distinction of being a masterpiece in two separate and apparently conflicting genres. It is at once an exotic adventure story of the Eastern sea in the popular tradition of Kipling and Stevenson and a complexly wrought 'art novel' in the tradition of Flaubert and James" (Conrad 1996, ix).[2] The different subgenres of fiction under consideration in this essay can all be subsumed under the two broader generic categories which Moser extrapolates from *Lord Jim;* and his apposite phrase "conflicting genres" can equally be applied to the variants of genre which I discuss. Thus, one essential reason why Conrad's novel combines both traditions initiated by Cervantes is suggested by the way in which, like its predecessor *Don Quixote, Lord Jim* exploits and combines various established genres in order to create a new kind of novel.

The occasion of Conrad's letter to John Livingstone Lowes becomes clear in its opening: "You ask whether the tale the summary of which you sent me is one of the usual sailors' yarns. That it certainly is not" (Conrad 2005, 385). Unsurprisingly, this letter of 29 November 1921 contains no reference to *Lord Jim.* Yet the terms which Conrad employs in his reply to Lowes are linked to the range of epic subgenres observable in the novel published twenty-one years earlier. Whether this is coincidental or not is not my concern here; what is remarkable about this letter is Conrad's awareness of different—related yet also conflicting—generic variants of short fiction. The most significant of the terms he uses in the course of the letter are "tale," "sailors' yarns," "legend," "sailors' talk," and "narrative." To these generic designations I add that of the text in which they occur, that is, the genre of the letter. Interestingly, *Lord Jim*'s narrative discourse draws on all of these. Moreover, a sentence toward the end of the letter signals, albeit obliquely, how these genres are used and combined in *Lord Jim.* Commenting on "the narrative of the Norwegian sailor," Conrad claims that "the manner of telling alone would reveal whether the tale had the nature of a legend or was merely a patchwork" (386). In *Lord Jim,* it is exactly

2. Although the adventure story needs to be distinguished from the literary realism of novelists such as Balzac, Stendhal, Tolstoy, and Dickens, it is certainly closer to this kind of writing than to the "art novels" of Flaubert and James. This said, what Moser calls "an exotic adventure story" may seem to fit more closely with the romance, as I suggest later in the essay.

Conrad's "manner of telling" which enables him to introduce, use, and combine the various subgenres I now proceed to identify and discuss. I start with the genre of the sketch.

Can the conception and writing process of *Lord Jim* tell us something important about his attitude to, and use of, genre? "Tuan Jim: A Sketch" suggests it can. Looking at the original manuscript in the Houghton Library at Harvard reveals that Conrad wrote this sketch on the blank pages of a leather album of Polish poems from the 1820s. All the poems in the album were copied by the same hand, that of Teofila Bobrowska, Conrad's grandmother. Subtle forms of textual continuation, elaboration, and repetition are involved here. Seen thus, this sketch is a textual intersection—a place where artistic creativity and creative repetition meet.

.p1
Tuan *Jim: A sketch*
All the white men by the waterside and
the captains of the ships in the roadsteads
called him Jim. He
was over six feet and stared
downwards at one with an
air of overbearing
watchfulness. You felt sometimes that
were You to say something,
the one special thing which he
did not want to hear, he
would knock you down
without more ado. But as a
water-clark of a leading ship chandler
in a certain Eastern port, he
was popular

.p2
Afterwards when his
perception of the intolerable
drove him away from the
haunts of white men, the
Malays of the village where he
without exercising
his perceptive faculty called
him Tuan Jim—or one might

Lord Jim.
He had never to any one's
knowledge been guilty
of an assault, this provoking
and brutal stare being only the result
of an exquisite sensibility[3]

I make three comments on the beginning of this sketch. First, we note that even at this early stage of the story's conception, Conrad's focus is very much on Jim and his link to Patusan. This strong character focus bears an indirect yet significant relation to the novel's medley of epic subgenres: Conrad needs to access and appropriate the resources of different genres in order to present satisfactorily his enigmatic main character. This point is central to my argument because it suggests that the modernist facet of the novel's generic combination is closely linked to, and in large part motivated by, Conrad's portrayal of his main character through the use of narrators who (affiliated as they are with various genres) understand Jim only partly and imperfectly. Second, "Afterwards" is a key word in this passage. It is not just that it contains an oblique reference to the *Patna* incident. Activating and even highlighting the beginning's narrative dimension, it also draws attention to Jim's "exquisite sensibility," including his "perception of the intolerable." Third, the beginning of the sketch reveals to what extent it is an *impression*—the narrator's impression of a character rendered irresistibly intriguing because he is tantalizingly elusive. We get the sense of a personified, human narrator, because a third-person, omniscient narrator does not typically get an impression of character in this way. Since the published version of this part is indeed narrated by a third-person narrator, the sketch's impressionist qualities may provide an early signal of Conrad's need for different kinds of narrators in *Lord Jim*. Impressionism, as *Brewer's Dictionary of Phrase and Fable* puts it, "broke down the distinction between a sketch and a finished painting" (549). Although we should not minimize the difference between the sketch "Tuan Jim" and the novel, it is remarkable how strongly the former text reflects the latter's impressionist qualities.

Turning to the novel itself, we note how closely the title of the sketch, "Tuan Jim," is related to the novel's title, *Lord Jim*. This link between the two textual versions becomes particularly striking in a key sentence in the third paragraph of chapter 1: "They called him Tuan Jim: as one might say—Lord

---

3. I am grateful to J. H. Stape for enabling me to use this accurate transcription, done by Ernest Sullivan and Robert Trogdon for the forthcoming Cambridge Edition of *Lord Jim*.

Jim" (8). Since this sentence is told by the third-person narrator, what we have here is not just a tentative translation but a complex form of appropriation: it is as though the narrator is attempting to negotiate the temporal, spatial, and cultural distance between his own perspective and that of the inhabitants of Patusan. One indication of the difficulties involved in this negotiation is that at the same time he appears to be insisting on that difference: "as one might say" suggests a European highlighting that in Europe one would *not* say this. Seeing this sentence in *Lord Jim* in the light of "Tuan Jim," it becomes an early signal of the difficulty of locating Jim, of the problem of understanding him, and of the challenge of rendering an adequate account of his life. Remaining and eventually "pass[ing] away under a cloud" (246), Jim's features are peculiarly sketchlike.[4]

If there is a significant link between "Tuan Jim" and *Lord Jim*, there is also an important connection between "sketch" and "tale." A sketch (from Italian *schizzo,* and Greek *skhedios,* which both mean "done rapidly") is a constellation of notes not necessarily planned or governed by a preconceived idea, often taken with a view to later elaboration and expansion. In the case of *Lord Jim,* this textual expansion assumes the form of a narrative reflecting two characteristic features of the tale. First, the tale of *Lord Jim* has a distinctly oral dimension. It is related to another term used by Conrad in his letter to Lowes, "the so-called sailors's yarn." The yarn is an oral form: it is spoken, and it tends to be repeated. The principal narrative agent is of course Marlow, yet his yarn about Jim is supplemented by the accounts and impressions of other narrators and characters. Second, this kind of combination of narratives highlights the significance of repetition in the novel. As in Faulkner's *The Sound and the Fury* (1929) and *Absalom, Absalom!* (1936), two key modernist novels strongly inspired by Conrad's, repetition assumes a variety of forms in *Lord Jim*—constituting, as Hillis Miller has shown in *Fiction and Repetition* (1982), an intricate interplay of narrative structure, relations between narrators and characters, and an existential thematics raising questions rather than providing answers.

Considering possible alternatives to the term "novel," Conrad may have been attracted by the relative vagueness of the word "tale." As his letter to Lowes shows, Conrad's use of "tale" is rather imprecise, approximating to both "legend" and "sailors's yarn." And yet his emphasis on "the manner of telling"

4. See Jeremy Hawthorn's contribution to this volume, especially his discussion of Rebecca Stott's comments about the way in which the text of *An Outcast of the Islands* offers the reader glimpses of his/her destination and of a tantalizing object toward which the text moves, while simultaneously dissolving that object. Clearly this comment could also be applied to both *Lord Jim* and Lord Jim.

suggests that Conrad regards the tale's narrative dimension as crucially important, and in *Lord Jim* it certainly is. In the novel's narrative situations in particular, constituent elements of the tale are combined with one another. That they are also linked to aspects of other genres such as the fragment enhances, rather than reduces, the significance of the novel's subtitle.

There is a strong sense in which the overall discourse of *Lord Jim* is fragmentary, and the novel's fragmentation is generated not least by the way in which its incorporated subgenres retain, and thus display, many of their defining generic features within the overall narrative discourse. What I want to stress is how early this process of fragmentation commences, and how closely it is related to the combination of tension and connection observable in the textual interplay of "Tuan Jim: A Sketch," *Lord Jim: A Tale,* and the fragment from Novalis which Conrad chose as the epigraph to the novel: "*It is certain my Conviction gains infinitely, the moment another soul will believe in it*" (1996, 3; emphasis in original). This is one of Novalis's fragments; and the fragment is a subgenre in its own right. A possible first comment on this evocative epigraph is that, considered as a speech act within the framework of Conrad's novel, it is not wholly clear who the speaker is. Since the epigraph is from fragment 153 of Novalis's *Das allgemeine Brouillon* (1798–99)—"Es ist gewiss, dass eine Meynung sehr viel gevinnt, so bald ich weiss, dass irgend jemand davon *überzeugt ist—sie wahrhaft annimmt*" (29; emphasis in original)—in one obvious sense the speaker is Novalis (the poet Friedrich von Hardenberg [1772–1801], a prominent representative of German Romanticism). Yet since an epigraph immediately raises the issue of its relevance, function, and thematic effect, the reader is invited to relate the epigraph to the agents involved in the production and narrative presentation of the text we are reading. As the statement is part of a fictional text, it does not unproblematically represent Conrad. It does, though, indicate that Conrad knew Novalis's work; and on a second reading it suggests a significant connection with Stein's description of Jim as "romantic—romantic" (131) later on in the narrative. The epigraph's origin seems to be not just one identifiable speaker but rather a blend of voices and perspectives. This kind of indeterminacy furthers its interpretive suggestiveness, which would have been reduced had it been unambiguously connected with, or anchored in, an identifiable comment made by the third-person narrator, Marlow, Jim, or Stein. In extremely condensed form, the epigraph illustrates one of Bakhtin's main points about the novel as a genre: that it speaks with several voices, and that no single voice is possessed of absolute authority. Nor is there one single genre possessed of such authority in the multifaceted narrative discourse of *Lord Jim.*

From a narrative perspective, the epigraph may at first sight seem to be divorced from the mechanics of the novel's plot and narrative intricacies. And yet the epigraph is part of the narrative in the sense of providing an oblique comment on it: its meaning is considerably reduced if it is not, as it asks to be, related to the following story. One way of doing so is to link the epigraph to Jim's attempt to make Marlow believe his version of the story. The epigraph is not just a prologue to the plot of *Lord Jim,* it is also a kind of epilogue because an adequate understanding of the epigraph presupposes a response to the whole novel—a multilayered narrative produced by a series of narrators of whom Marlow is clearly the most important.

As in *Heart of Darkness,* however, Marlow is not the first narrator the reader encounters as he or she proceeds from the elements of text just considered to the opening of chapter 1. Providing an important link to "Tuan Jim: A Sketch," the first four chapters of the novel are told by a third-person narrator. Then, again in a manner comparable to the introduction of Marlow in *Heart of Darkness,* Marlow takes over. Commenting on this narrative transition, Michael Greaney finds that "Marlow's appearance . . . could scarcely have been more timely; as he assumes the position of narrator, he transforms what might have been a painfully systematic study in the psychology of cowardice into something far more subtle, open-minded, and open-ended" (2002, 78). Most readers of *Lord Jim* probably agree, and yet a statement of this kind tends not only to reduce the narrative and thematic importance of the opening chapters but also, perhaps inadvertently, to minimize the significance of the narrative transition at the end of chapter 4.

The "conflicting genres" identified by Moser clash here: in a manner which calls the second paragraph of Knut Hamsun's *Hunger* (1890) strikingly to mind,[5] Conrad dispenses with the kind of traditional, knowledgeable, and unidentified third-person narrator he has been using so far, turning instead to a narrative agent whose attitude to Jim is far more "open-minded" (Greaney) and exploratory, even including, as a potentially decisive factor for the narrative undertaking, an "unhealthy curiosity" (34) on Marlow's part. Thus not only Jim, but narrative motivation and narrative practice are questioned—the narrative endeavor directed at and prompted by Jim becomes at once suspect and irresistible. The main point in the context of my argument is to underline the extent to which one of the novel's most important narrative transitions is

---

5. While the first paragraph of *Hunger* seems to conform to the conventions of nineteenth-century realist fiction by presenting a first-person narrator who looks back at, and begins to tell about, his past experiences, the second paragraph, preceded by an ellipsis, opens thus: "Lying awake in my attic room, I hear a clock strike six downstairs" (3). For Dorrit Cohn, *Hunger* is "one of the earliest and most sustained examples of consonant first-person narration. . . . Not once in this entire novel does its narrator draw attention to his present, narrating self" (1983, 155).

correlated with, in part forged through, the juxtaposition of different genres. It is not just the genre of the adventure story that gives way to what Moser calls "a complexly wrought 'art novel,'" however. Equally important is the juxtaposition of various subgenres associated with both of these broad generic categories.

Although critics have noted that the first significant narrative transitions of both *Lord Jim* and *Heart of Darkness* are closely affiliated with modulations of narrative perspective, insufficient attention has been paid to Conrad's dissatisfaction, and impatience, with the parameters of the realist novel which they reveal. The ending of chapter 4 is instrumental in demonstrating a kind of narrative change or rift which signals one beginning of modernist fiction. On the level of narrative, this rift curiously parallels the structural and thematic one between the novel's first and second parts, that is, the part dealing with and revolving round Jim's jump from the *Patna* (chapters 1–20) and the Patusan section (chapters 21–45). Chapter 4 ends thus:

> And later on, many times, in distant parts of the world, Marlow showed himself willing to remember Jim, to remember him at length, in detail and audibly.
>
> Perhaps it would be after dinner, on a verandah draped in motionless foliage and crowned with flowers, in the deep dusk speckled by fiery cigar-ends. The elongated bulk of each cane-chair harboured a silent listener. Now and then a small red glow would move abruptly, and expanding light up the fingers of a languid hand, part of a face in profound repose, or flash a crimson gleam into a pair of pensive eyes overshadowed by a fragment of an unruffled forehead: and with the very first word uttered Marlow's body, extended at rest in the seat, would become very still, as though his spirit had winged its way into way back into the lapse of time and were speaking through his lips from the past. (24)

In apparent contradiction to what I have suggested, the narrative thrust of this semantically dense and evocative passage seems to be away from modernist fiction rather than toward it. Constituting a narrative situation reminiscent of, to use the German sociologist Ferdinand Tönnies's terms (2001), a *Gemeinschaft* (community) rather than *Gesellschaft* (civil society),[6] Marlow here seems effortlessly to assume the role of the traditional storyteller, imparting the story

---

6. Even though Tönnies's distinction is broadly typological, it is imbued with a historical dimension. While a *Gemeinschaft* is relatively traditional (in one sense premodern), *Gesellschaft* is associated with modern societies in which secondary relationships have become more important than familial or community ties.

of Jim to his audience on the verandah. Although on closer inspection we can see that this *Gemeinschaft* is presented as vulnerable, curiously fractured, I want to stress its forceful presence in the narrative situations, and thus also in the narrative discourse, of *Lord Jim*. Though fragile and anachronistic—or perhaps rather, to extend my allusion to Walter Benjamin's classic essay "The Storyteller," belated—this narrative situation and storytelling community on the verandah provide an oblique, fictionalized illustration of one of the main points argued by Alasdair MacIntyre in *After Virtue*—that man is "essentially a story-telling animal" (1997, 216). The narrative situation also illustrates a perceptive point made by Daphna Erdinast-Vulcan in her discussion of *Lord Jim* in *Joseph Conrad and the Modern Temper*, "We all construe our sense of identity in terms of our role in the narrative we are part of, and this fictional identity is not necessarily fictitious as long as one can maintain some measure of congruence between the fictional ego-ideal and one's actual conduct" (1991, 38). An essential part of the suspense of *Lord Jim* turns on this "measure of congruence": presenting a problem and (after the jump) prompting an identity crisis for Jim, it attracts the attention and continuing interest of Marlow and his narratees—and indeed the reader.

This passage is indebted to, and promises to contribute to, the genre of the traditional tale by telling the story of somebody whose actions, though dubious, are exceptional and even in part heroic. The element of *Gemeinschaft* highlights the unusual link between the traditional mode of telling and the modernist narrative: the former is incorporated into the latter, but at the same time the latter (i.e., the modernist aspect of the narrative of *Lord Jim*) is anchored in, and indebted to, the long tradition of storytelling. This paradox serves Conrad's novelistic purpose in a number of ways. For example, it enables him to combine elements of various kinds and techniques of narrative fiction from different periods. It also makes it easier to integrate elements of genres which may add to his exploration—and, as a corollary, the narratees' and the reader's understanding—of Jim. Marlow's role here is crucially important. In one sense, Marlow is the typical narrator of a *Gemeinschaft*. In a different yet related sense, the aspect of *Gemeinschaft* which he represents is vulnerable as well. Suspecting that his interest in Jim may approximate to an "unhealthy curiosity" (34), he has serious doubts about his own narrative venture; and surely it remains incomplete and fragmented in ways most contributions to narratives of a premodern community do not. Moreover, Marlow's telling is also his remembering. Remembering Jim "at length, in detail and audibly," he does not just narrate to his narratees on the verandah but also to himself.

The phrase "one of us," which Marlow repeatedly uses when talking about Jim, exemplifies another facet of *Gemeinschaft* and its vulnerability. By referring to Jim as "one of us" (50, 214, 246), Marlow not only includes him in the community of sailors but also links him more closely to the group of people constituting the narrative situation on the verandah. "One of us" signals two constituent elements of this community: a sense of duty and honor closely connected with the responsibility of being one of the "officers of the mercantile marine" (8), and a more indirect but equally strong sense of Jim as fallen—as someone who, after having failed his test, "is become as one of us" (Genesis 3:22). Even though this kind of maritime *Gemeinschaft* appears to be relatively stable, Marlow's narration presents it as fragile, even threatened. If Marlow and his narratees want to include Jim in their *Gemeinschaft*, they also feel a strong need to distance themselves from him. What is at stake for Marlow—as it is, albeit in varying ways and to a higher or lesser degree, for Brierly and the other characters and narrators—is a problem which assumes the form of a question: what does it mean for me, for all of "us," if one of us could act as Jim has acted on the *Patna*?

Drawing on and combining various narrative strategies and elements of different genres, the narrative discourse of *Lord Jim* provides rich and varied response to this difficult question. The elements of legend in Marlow's tale about Jim are detectable in the protagonist's dream of great deeds, and in the terse connection between these imagined feats and the course of action he actually pursues (in spite of the ironic manner in which the imagined deeds are presented). Thus the elements of legend make Jim into a figure of fascination for the subculture of sailors. One definition of legend (from Latin *legenda*, meaning "things to be read") is "a story or narrative which lies somewhere between myth and historical fact and which, as a rule, is about a particular figure or person" (Cuddon 1999, 452). That the story of Jim grows longer, and perhaps also taller, as it is told and retold is another indication of its legendary qualities, which are further strengthened in the Patusan section. Yet the textual positioning of the passage also complicates elements of the traditional tale and legend. While in the traditional tale the introduction typically marks the beginning of the narrator's story, here we have a break, a kind of new start which signals both a growing dissatisfaction with the narrative strategy first embarked on and a readiness to distort, or even invert, the characteristic features of the genres by which the narrative is inspired. Jim is worthy of narrative attention not because he is a hero (as he would have been in the traditional legend) but because he has shown himself to be a problem, and because his action and their consequences highlight a kind of problem we may all potentially confront. Thus, the point of Marlow's story is not just a legendlike tale involving some kind of moral or illustration; it is also the presentation, or gradual unfolding, of an enigma that calls attention to the value structure of the subculture of those who dedicate themselves to the sea.

The elements of legend blend into those of the episode, another subgenre which Conrad uses in order to present the story of Jim. An episode (from Greek *epeisodion,* meaning addition or insertion) is an event or action relatively independent of what precedes and succeeds it. The episodes of *Lord Jim* are typically told by different narrators, and they focus on different aspects of Jim as a character.[7] The character portrayal which the episodes present, however, is confusing rather than clarifying. As the French lieutenant puts it: "[T]here are many things in this incident of my life (*dans cet épisode de ma vie*) which have remained obscure" (87).

This combination of the illustrative and the enigmatic, forged through the novel's narrative and observable in embryo in the passage briefly considered here, is distinctly parabolic, pointing in the direction of Kafka's fiction and even a more recent novel such as J. M. Coetzee's *Waiting for the Barbarians* (1980). A parable (from Greek *parabole,* meaning "side throwing" or "comparison") is commonly understood as the illustration of a spiritual truth through a story from the earthly world. However, the parable can also have a meaning corresponding to the Hebrew word *mashal,* which means riddle or enigmatic narrative. Although illustrative, the parable can be difficult in a way that requires interpretation on the part of the narratee and the reader. Aspects of this dual, complicating meaning of the parable are reflected in *Lord Jim.* Jim seems to illustrate a problem, but it turns out to be very difficult to ascertain what this problem is. The character Jim remains tantalizingly elusive, enigmatic, passing "away under a cloud" (246). As in the parable, this kind of difficulty requires interpretive activity: it is as if Marlow's, the other narrators', the narratees', and the reader's interpretations complete or add an end to the incomplete, puzzling story of Jim. Perhaps this is why Marlow, as the quoted passage indicates, keeps retelling the story of Jim, adding fragment to fragment in repeated attempts to understand him. One reason why Marlow goes on telling his listeners and us about Jim is suggested by the latter's stubbornness. In his essay on *Lord Jim* in this volume, James Phelan defines "the stubborn" as "textual recalcitrance that will not yield to our efforts at interpretive mastery but that nevertheless functions intelligibly within a larger artistic design." One of the points Phelan makes about Jim's stubbornness is that the repetitions which further the novel's narrative progression "add to rather than remove the recalcitrance of Jim's experience to our full understanding." I would suggest that the combination, and repetitive layering, of genres has a comparable

---

7. J. Hillis Miller notes that "*Lord Jim* is made up of episodes similar in design" (33). Signaling that this activity as a narrator involves a process of evaluative selection, Marlow at the beginning of chapter 19 remarks to his listeners that "I have told you these two episodes at length to show his manner of dealing with himself under the new conditions of his life. There were many others of the sort, more than I could count on the fingers of my two hands" (118).

effect. Regardless of what genre Conrad, using the elastic narrative instrument of the novel, draws on and incorporates into his narrative, Jim, and the problem he represents, stubbornly and successfully resist the attempts at interpretation which he invites and which we—narrators, narratees, and the reader—repeatedly make.

The passage which marks the end of Marlow's oral narrative and the transition to the written one highlights the importance of the genre of the letter in Conrad's novel:

> With these words Marlow had ended his narrative, and his audience had broken up forthwith, under his abstract, pensive gaze. Men drifted off the verandah in pairs or alone without loss of time, without offering a remark, as if the last image of that incomplete story, its incompleteness itself, and the very tone of the speaker, had made discussion vain and comment impossible. Each of them seemed to carry away his own impression, to carry it away with him like a secret; but there was only one man of all these listeners who was ever to hear the last word of the story. It came to him at home, more than two years later, and it came contained in a thick packet addressed in Marlow's upright and angular handwriting.
>
> The privileged man opened the packet, looked in, then, laying it down, went to the window. His rooms were in the highest flat of a lofty building, and his glance could travel afar beyond the clear panes of glass, as though he were looking out of the lantern of a lighthouse. (200)

As with the passage that introduces Marlow's oral telling, the features of the narrative situation are significant. Comparing these two passages, we note a striking combination of affinity and difference. On the one hand, both are told by a third-person narrator, and the atmosphere of this situation too is evocative, almost magic. This effect is achieved through a combination of syntax, punctuation, and key words such as "seemed" and "impression." Conrad establishes a significant link between the man's presence as a narratee on the verandah and the "flat of a lofty building" in the unidentified city, possibly London, where he now lives. Moreover, the time of day is the same, as the second paragraph informs us that "the driving rain mingled with the falling dusk of a winter's evening." On the other hand, "the privileged man" is alone. It is as though Conrad moves from the narrative situation of teller and listeners on the verandah, from a pre-Lapsarian narrative community of *Gemeinschaft*, to a different kind of narrative situation reflecting the isolation of the modern reader in an urban setting. In contrast to the traditional narrator, writes Benjamin, the novelist is isolated, alone, and—by logical extension—so is the reader.

This kind of isolation, which, for Benjamin, is a distinctly modern phenomenon, is here illustrated both by the character's isolation in his flat and by the fact that he alone receives the packet from Marlow.

Seen in this light, the genre of the letter plays a key role in the second part of *Lord Jim*. Conrad's letter to Lowes at a late stage of his career can serve as a token of the importance he attached to this genre. As Owen Knowles and Gene Moore note, many of Conrad's letters have a distinctly literary dimension (2000, 204). Moreover, letters serve as integral parts of Conrad's fiction. Illustrative examples include Decoud's long letter to his sister in *Nostromo* and the letters incorporated into *Lord Jim*. The packet received by the privileged reader actually contains three letters: an explanatory letter by Marlow, Marlow's written account of Jim's Patusan adventures, and "a very old letter" (202) to Jim from his father.

These letters, and their positioning within the novel's overall structure, are a significant addition to the subgenres activated and combined in *Lord Jim*. First, continuing the tale about Jim, the letter to the privileged man is at once a variant on and an extension of the fragmented oral narratives about him presented earlier on in the discourse. The teller of this tale is still Marlow, whose written narrative resembles his oral one. There are two important differences, though. Since Marlow is now telling the story of Jim's life in Patusan, a region unknown to most white men, he can no longer enrich his own account by incorporating the accounts of other narrators, with the important exception of Brown. One effect of this narrative modulation is to strengthen the aspects of legend associated with Jim's life and death in Patusan. Furthermore, since the "privileged man . . . in the highest flat of a lofty building" has been substituted for the group of narratees on the verandah, and since the act of writing a letter cannot be repeated the way an oral narrative can, this last part of the "incomplete story" is more determinate, and in one sense more disillusioned, than the first. Second, there is a link between the incomplete story of Jim and Marlow's explanatory letter, which accompanies the main one. Although Marlow claims to have "fitted the pieces together," he admits that the "information was fragmentary" (203). Thus the genre of the fragment is actualized once again, establishing an important connection between this concession on Marlow's part and his concluding observation that "that's the end. He passes away under a cloud, inscrutable at heart, forgotten, unforgiven, and excessively romantic" (246). Finally, the packet contains "a very old letter" (202) to Jim from his father. The fact that this letter, which Marlow thinks is the last "he ever had from home," is from the time before Jim joined the *Patna* strengthens the structural and thematic links between the *Patna* and Patusan. Since this letter is not given in full, and since Marlow's summary of it is preceded by his mention of Jim's attempt at a letter to somebody—headed "The Fort, Patusan" (202) but possessed of neither content nor addressee—the fragmentary nature of his life, and of information and communication about his life, are further accentuated.

Referring to the novel's Patusan section, I have used the word "romance." For J. A. Cuddon, the genre of the romance is "a form of entertainment" (1999, 758) whose constituent elements include fantasy, improbability, love, adventure, extravagance, and naivety. All of these aspects are present in *Lord Jim;* and as an adventure story this text is related to, and inspired by, the long tradition of the romance in European literature. Marlow seems to be aware of this feature of his narrative: "Romance," he notes at the beginning of chapter 29, "had singled Jim for its own" (168). However, the novel not only incorporates elements of romance, it also displays the incongruities of romance by contrasting them with the realities of Jim's ordinary life. Conrad achieves this kind of generic destabilization not least by relating aspects of romance to the characteristic, in part conflicting, features of the fragment, the sketch and the parable.

Although there is a very considerable difference between, say, the romance and the fragment, most of the genres discussed so far are variants of narrative fiction. It is a token of the generic hybridity of *Lord Jim,* however, that the novel also incorporates aspects of tragedy and of lyric poetry. Even though Conrad's understanding of tragedy derived in large part from his reading of Shakespearean tragedy, it was colored by notions about the genre prevalent in his own time. Characteristically, however, the Victorians—who held tragedy to be a reflector of essential qualities of their culture—understood the genre inclusively, relating it not just to drama but also to the novel. Tragedy "was frequently used, as it is today, to mean an extremely sad and unexpected event" (King 1978, 2). Jim's jump is surely both "extremely sad" and, at least for himself, "unexpected." His losing his life in Patusan is similarly sad and unexpected. This sense of tragedy illustrates a key point argued by Jeannette King in *Tragedy in the Victorian Novel:* "Tragedy arises out of the gap between what the character is—his true self—and what he does—the identity he presents to the outside world" (99). Such a gap is observable in *Lord Jim* too. Indeed, Jim's problem after the *Patna* episode is, in one sense, to come to terms with the gap between his behaviour and his conception of his true self. Furthermore, his initial success in Patusan leads him to believe that he has closed that gap. Jim proves himself to be a good and responsible leader for the group of people who trust him. But then Brown arrives, and Jim's fatal error in judging Brown has tragic consequences for the *Gemeinschaft* of Patusan. Jim's decision to accept his fate at Doramin's hands is also a decision, from his perspective, to keep the gap between his behavior and his conception of his character closed. Conrad, however, ingeniously uses Jewel and Marlow to cast doubt on whether we should view Jim's decision that way. When Jim approaches Doramin in order to pay for his mistake, this act makes Jewel scream that "You are false!" (245). And Marlow, as I have noted already, is unable to render any definitive judgment on Jim.

Let me now turn to the novel's lyric qualities. These are apparent in the following example:

> Every morning the sun, as if keeping pace in his revolutions with the prog-ress of the pilgrimage, emerged with a silent burst of light exactly at the same distance astern of the ship, caught up with her at noon, pouring the concentrated fire of his rays on the pious purposes of the men, glided past on his descent, and sank mysteriously into the sea evening after evening, preserving the same distance ahead of her advancing bows. . . . Such were the days, still, hot, heavy, disappearing one by one into the past, as if falling into an abyss for ever open in the wake of the ship; and the ship, lonely under a wisp of smoke, held on her steadfast way black and smouldering in a luminous immensity, as if scorched by a flame flicked at her from a heaven without pity.
>
> The nights descended on her like a benediction. (15)

The lyric effect of this evocative passage is obtained by repetition, by per-sonification of the sun and of the ship, by the light and dark imagery, and by a rhythmical syntax which seems to imitate the ship's slow movement across the Indian ocean. The scene's lyric qualities are also generated by the way in which repetition is linked both to beginning and to a possibly apocalyptic ending, and they are further enhanced by our sense of reading a description based on, and inspired by, an act of intensified memory. The speaker is the unidentified third-person narrator, but the attitudinal distance between this narrative agent and the implied author is reduced in this passage. In this scene the narrative register approximates to the lyric. Thus, as James Phelan notes in his discus-sion of lyricality in *Living to Tell about It,* "the authorial audience is less in the position of observer and judge and more in the position of participant" (2005, 162). The passage is an illustrative example of the "epistemology of tem-porality" (Peters 2001, 95) which can be extrapolated from Conrad's fiction, and which is here closely associated with his presentation of space.

Rather than making the subgenres we have noted less important, the nov-el's aspects of the tragic and the lyric actually increase their significance as integral parts of the novel's narrative discourse. For instance, the elements of legend draw on aspects of the tragic; and there is a connection between memory as a constituent element of the lyric and aspects of memory in Marlow's willingness "to remember Jim, to remember him at length, in detail and audibly" (24). Building on my discussion of these subgenres, genres which can be subsumed under the genre of the novel exemplified by *Lord Jim*, I conclude by briefly considering some important narrative and thematic effects of this particular combination of subgenres in the novel.

In a comprehensive study entitled *The Modern Movement*, Chris Baldick finds that Conrad was "not committed to radical disruptions of form" (2004, 399). Even though his observation may seem convincing enough with a view to some of Conrad's works, this discussion indicates that it is not an apt characterization of *Lord Jim*. Disrupting the form of the nineteenth-century realist novel and questioning its assumptions about reality, the combined characteristics, textual positioning, and thematic effects of the different genres discussed here are integral parts of the novel's narrative, thus contributing significantly to the formation of modernist fiction. *Lord Jim* is not only, as Moser suggested and numerous critics have seconded, a novel combining the generic features of the adventure story and the "art novel." Rather, exploiting features of the adventure story, *Lord Jim* becomes a modernist novel by combining, and contrasting, these features with constituent elements of several subgenres of narrative fiction. Significantly, the situations which provide the starting- and reference points for the novel's two parts are reversed, in that the "traditional" narrative situation introduces the "modernist" part and the "modern" one the more traditional Patusan part. One effect of this reversal is to destabilize the relationship between the two main parts of *Lord Jim;* a related effect is to bring them closer together. Although the elaborate interplay of parts one and two of *Lord Jim* is not a question of the combination of different epic subgenres only, it is furthered and shaped by the way in which Conrad activates and appropriates aspects of such genres. He does so both in the two narrative situations considered here and in the narratives for which they provide the basis. Conrad's employment of epic subgenres is not mechanical or repetitive in a manner the reader can preempt; rather, generic appropriation here involves forms of inversion. It is the combination, repetition, and original use of aspects of different genres that prove innovative: characteristic features of each subgenre become constituent aspects of a novelistic project at once motivated and informed by Conrad's literary ambition to render a nuanced account of an alluring but elusive protagonist.

In his study of early modernism, Christopher Butler draws attention to the close connection, at this point in the history of the novel, between changes of literary form and developments in the visual arts. *Lord Jim* provides a rich literary illustration of several of the points Butler makes. I have already mentioned the novel's impressionist qualities, relating them to the genre of the sketch. If the impressionist paintings of a visual artist such as Monet problematize the relationship between the sketch and the finished product, Marlow's sketchlike impressions of Jim further a new kind of fiction in which subjective, inevitably incomplete narratives attempt to render through language what cannot be clearly seen. "I am trying," notes Marlow, "to interpret for you [his narratees, and by implication the reader] into slow speech the instantaneous effect of visual impressions" (33). At once indicating and responding to the difficulties of telling the story of Jim, Conrad's use of different genres as integral parts of repetitive yet varying narratives (within the overall genre of what becomes a modernist novel) turns Marlow's narrative failure into a remarkable narrative success: putting the fragments together, he manages to simultaneously enrich and complicate the narrative portrayal of a character who remains enigmatic throughout.

Works Cited

Alter, Robert. *Partial Magic: The Novel as a Self-Conscious Genre.* Berkeley: University of California Press, 1975.

Aristotle. *Poetics.* Edited and translated by Stephen Halliwell. Cambridge, MA: Harvard University Press, 1995.

Bakthin, M. M. *The Dialogic Imagination: Four Essays.* Edited by Michael Holquist. Austin: University of Texas Press, 1982.

Baldick, Chris. *The Modern Movement.* Oxford: Oxford University Press, 2004.

Benjamin, Walter. "The Storyteller." In *Illuminations,* edited by Hannah Arendt. London: Fontana, 1979. 83–109.

Brewer's Dictionary of Phrase and Fable, 15th ed. New York: HarperCollins, 1995.

Butler, Christopher. *Early Modernism: Literature, Music, and Painting in Europe, 1900–1916.* Oxford: Oxford University Press, 1994.

Clinton, Dan. "Genre." http://humanities.uchicago.edu/faculty/mitchell/glossary2004/genre.htm. Accessed 12 February 2007.

Cohn, Dorrit. *Transparent Minds: Narrative Modes for Presenting Consciousness in Fiction.* Princeton, NJ: Princeton University Press, 1983.

Conrad, Joseph. *Lord Jim: A Tale.* Edited by Thomas Moser. 2nd ed. New York: Norton, 1996.

———. *The Collected Letters of Joseph Conrad,* vol. 7. Edited by Laurence Davies and J. H. Stape. Cambridge: Cambridge University Press, 2005.

———. "Tuan Jim: A Sketch." Ms. Houghton Library, Harvard University.

Cuddon, J. A. *The Penguin Dictionary of Literary Terms and Literary Theory.* 4th ed. London: Penguin, 1999.

Erdinast-Vulcan, Daphna. *Joseph Conrad and the Modern Temper.* Oxford: Oxford University Press, 1991.

Greaney, Michael. *Conrad, Language, and Narrative.* Cambridge: Cambridge University Press, 2002.

Hamsun, Knut. *Hunger.* Translated by Sverre Lyngstad. Edinburgh: Rebel, 1999.

Holy Bible. Authorized King James Version. Oxford: Oxford University Press.

King, Jeannette. *Tragedy in the Victorian Novel: Theory and Practice in the Novels of George Eliot, Thomas Hardy and Henry James.* Cambridge: Cambridge University Press, 1978.

Knowles, Owen, and Gene Moore. "Letters." In *Oxford Reader's Companion to Conrad.* Oxford: Oxford University Press, 2000. 201–4.

Lothe, Jakob. "Conrad's *Lord Jim* and the Fragment: Narrative, Genre, History." In *"Lord Jim" de Joseph Conrad,* edited by Nathalie Martinière. Nantes: Éditions du Temps, 2003. 15–24.

MacIntyre, Alasdair. *After Virtue: A Study in Moral Theory.* 2nd ed. London: Duckworth, 1997.

Miller, J. Hillis. *Fiction and Repetition: Seven English Novels.* Oxford: Blackwell, 1982.

Novalis. *Das Allgemeine Brouillon: Materialien zur Enzyklopädistik 1798/99.* Hamburg: Felix Meiner Verlag, 1993.

Peters, John G. *Conrad and Impressionism.* Cambridge: Cambridge University Press, 2001.

Phelan, James. *Living To Tell about It: A Rhetoric and Ethics of Character Narration.* Ithaca, NY: Cornell University Press, 2005.

Tönnies, Ferdinand. *Community and Civil Society.* Edited by José Harris. Cambridge: Cambridge University Press, 2001.

——. *Ferdinand Tönnies Gesamtausgabe.* Edited by Lars Clausen et al. Critical ed., 24 vols. Berlin: De Gruyter, 1998.

Wilpert, Gero von. *Sachwörterbuch der Literatur.* 8th ed. Stuttgart: Alfred Kröner Verlag, 2001.

afterword

JAKOB LOTHE,
JEREMY HAWTHORN,
and JAMES PHELAN

When we write critical essays our attention is primarily directed over our shoulder, back toward those critics who have produced studies of those texts with which we are now attempting to engage. But when we read a collection of critical essays on a common theme, sometimes we are prompted to look ahead, to recognize a temptingly unexplored territory the collection makes at least partially visible. In this Afterword, we would like to call attention to two salient features that we glimpse in the landscape of future studies of Conrad and narrative theory. Let us call them a thicket of narrative ethics and a meadow of narrative sequence. We choose these features because they emerge from an effort to look across the boundaries of our own categories of voice, sequence, history, and genre, and because we believe that they also display two different relations between narrative theory and Conrad's practice as a writer. We hasten to add that we do not want to claim that these two features of the landscape are the only ones the collection makes visible, and we especially do not want to have our focus on them restrict the vision of other readers. Instead, we offer our descriptions of these two features as both an illustration and an invitation: an illustration of how the collection as a whole helps identify new territory, and an invitation to other readers to use the collection to identify other salient features within it.

Narrative is, among other things, the means by which we organize the particulars of our experience into patterns that make sense for ourselves and for others. Narrative theory is, among other things, the means by which we account for the ways in which narrative makes sense of experience. Behind those two similar phrases "make sense" and "account for" are large issues. Classical narratology accounted for narrative's way of making sense by trying to write its grammar, or more particularly, by trying to identify its constituent elements, their individual natures, and their various modes of combination. Contemporary narrative theory, however, while still indebted to the work of Roland Barthes, Gérard Genette, Tzvetan Todorov, and other early narratologists, finds that their focus on grammar frequently fails adequately to capture narrative's explanatory power. There is too much missing from analysis in the classical mode: while it is helpful to identify differences between cardinal functions and catalysts or those between homodiegetic and heterodiegetic narration, such identification by itself cannot account for narrative's capacity to affect our emotions, our values, our politics, our sense of selfhood and so much else that we compose and consume narrative for. Consequently, as the essays in this volume indicate, contemporary narrative theory draws on a range of theoretical discourses in its various efforts to account for narrative's ways of making sense of experience. The many essays concerned directly or indirectly with narrative ethics—those by James Phelan, Gail Fincham, Jeremy Hawthorn, Christophe Robin, Daphna Erdinast-Vulcan, and J. Hillis Miller—provide an especially good example of this phenomenon.

In *Ethics and Narrative in the English Novel, 1880–1914* (2001), Jil Larson articulates a principle that surely all those writing about Conrad and ethics would accept. Arguing that "[o]f all the fiction writers I consider, Joseph Conrad is the most committed to the ideal of ethical principles," she explains:

> [H]is novels are full of identifiably good and evil characters, and his narrators and implied authors rarely shy away from moral judgments. Still, the radical ways in which Conrad departs from nineteenth-century narrative tradition complicate the principled, clearly defined morality that can be identified in his texts as a Victorian inheritance. (14–15)

This passage contains the crucial perception: change the narrative techniques and you alter the moral and ethical dimensions of the narrative itself. The perception itself is based on an underlying principle, derived from the Russian formalists and from later narrative theorists, that technique does not simply serve to transmit or convey an already formed content. Technique is both the means by which that content is shaped and communicated and an integral part of that content—including its moral and ideological dimensions. However, our contributors are far from producing a uniform delineation of how the ethics of Conrad's techniques is linked to, and blends with, the larger ethical force of his narratives. (It is for this reason that we have chosen to refer to the new territory of Conrad and narrative ethics as a thicket.) Phelan emphasizes the ethics of the telling in *Lord Jim,* while Miller analyzes *Nostromo* as a parable about the deficient ethics of Western capitalism. Robin draws on poststructuralist theory to explore, among other things, *Nostromo*'s concern with the relation between "imperial time" and "ethical time." Focusing on Conrad's use of the language teacher in *Under Western Eyes,* Fincham draws on both classical and contemporary narrative theory in order to discuss Conrad's exploration of the ethical relations within the "rationality-sympathy-vision" cluster. Hawthorn does something similar, though his theoretical sources are not exactly the same as Fincham's, in analyzing how Conrad in *An Outcast of the Islands* exposes the negative ethical consequences of reducing a life such as Willems's to linear metaphors of progress. Erdinast-Vulcan relies on yet another set of theorists—Hayden White, Alasdair MacIntyre, and others—to show how *Nostromo* exposes the nightmare of history.

Our contributors are not, of course, the first commentators on Conrad's fiction who have been struck by—and who have attempted to investigate—the way this body of work requires the reader to ponder over the ethical issues that it dramatizes. The English critic F. R. Leavis, for example, whose book *The Great Tradition* did more than any other critical work to establish Conrad's reputation in the mid-twentieth century, declared of *Nostromo* that its "rich and subtle but highly organized pattern . . . is one of moral significances," and he drew attention to "the question that we feel working in the matter of the novel as a kind of informing and organizing principle: what do men find to live *for*—what kinds of motive force or radical attitude can give life meaning, direction, coherence?" ([1948] 1962, 211; emphasis on original). This statement is strong on ethics but weak on narrative technique, which is buried in there, no doubt, as part of the novel's "highly organized pattern."

By 1995, however, the ethical turn in narrative studies was well underway, a phenomenon reflected in Adam Zachary Newton's chapter on *Lord Jim* in his *Narrative Ethics.* Newton linked Conrad's novel to Sherwood Anderson's *Winesburg, Ohio* and found both works "paradigms for narrative ethics." Discussing a passage from *Lord Jim,* Newton suggests that it shows "how complexly hermeneutic, representational, and narrational ethics intersect" (1995, 78), and his chapter offers a painstaking and sensitive investigation of this complexity.

The contributors to the present volume seek, in different ways, both to add some further revolutions to the ethical turn in narrative studies and to build on the specific work of critics such as Leavis, Newton, and Larson in ways that—taken together—illuminate not just single texts but the novelist's fictional *oeuvre* in its development and its variations. Looking forward, we are less interested in the particulars of their differences and disagreements than in their more general concern with narrative ethics in Conrad's fiction. Because our contributors both share this concern and take diverse approaches to it, they help open up the territory of Conrad studies for productive debates and new insights about the relations between technique and ethics, the ethics of the told and the ethics of the telling across the rich corpus of his work.

Furthermore, a look at this thicket shows one kind of relation between narrative theory and Conrad's narratives. Since these essays demonstrate that Conrad's narratives respond remarkably well to a variety of theoretical approaches, they collectively indicate that in this thicket theory operates as a powerful lens affecting our vision of those narratives. At the same time, Conrad's narratives retain the power to disconfirm what a given theory might predict we should see in them. Again this situation is one in which we neither move toward a single, grand vision of Conrad's narrative ethics nor conclude that it will always be impossible to adjudicate different visions. Instead, we immerse ourselves not in anything so grand as Stein's destructive element but rather in the thicket of critical views of Conrad's ethics.

The issue of narrative sequence is an even more pervasive concern in the collection. There are, of course, the three essays in this volume's section on Sequence: Hawthorn's essay on metaphors of life's progress in *An Outcast of the Islands;* Susan Jones's analysis of character movement in *Heart of Darkness;* and Josiane Paccaud-Huguet's discussion of flashes of insight across Conrad's work. But we can easily add to this group Phelan's effort to trace the progression of *Lord Jim;* Simmons's interest in following the voyage of the *Narcissus* across the expanse of Conrad's text; Erdinast-Vulcan's exploration of Conrad's challenge to linearity in *Nostromo;* Lothe's attention to the sequence of shifting genres in *Lord Jim;* and Stape's analysis of Conrad's experiment in autobiography. We believe that these essays collectively provide a good basis for new studies of Conrad's various and complex solutions to the problem of moving his narratives from beginning through middle to end. We also believe that, in this meadow of narrative sequence, it is Conrad's narratives that are the dominant partner in the relation between theory and object of study. While the diverse essays draw upon another eclectic body of theory, in each case, the critic is using the theory to try to catch up to—and do justice to—Conrad's varied, complex, and challenging practice.

There are no doubt multiple reasons for the differences between what we see in the thicket and in the meadow. Conrad's experiments with narrative sequence, despite their complexity, appear to be matters about which we are more likely to reach agreement. The diversity of ethical theory is arguably greater than the diversity of theory on narrative sequence. At the same time, we also need to notice that our meadow and our thicket are less distinct than our metaphors indicate. Going back to the principle that technique is inextricably related to ethics, we can recognize that in order to engage fully with the ethics of Conrad's novels and short stories we need to attend to the complexities of their sequences, particularly the ways in which they often challenge linear progression and put the chronological out of joint.

But again we are interested in taking an even broader view, one which focuses less on both the overlap between thicket and meadow and on the *reasons* for the differences between these features of the Conrad-and-narrative-theory landscape. We regard the situation as a healthy one: the push-and-pull between theory and narrative, with first one and then the other in the ascendancy but neither wholly dictating to the other, ensures the flourishing of that landscape. Theory provides a valuable influx of nutrients for the soil, its flora, indeed, for the whole ecosystem, but theory should never be mistaken for the landscape itself. At the same time, without those nutrients, the landscape will soon be used up. If *Joseph Conrad: Voice, Sequence, History, Genre* succeeds in persuading its readers of the mutual dependence of Conrad and narrative theory, we believe it will have itself made an important contribution to the flourishing of that landscape.

Works Cited

Larson, Jil. *Ethics and Narrative in the English Novel, 1880–1914.* Cambridge: Cambridge University Press, 2001.

Leavis, F. R. *The Great Tradition* (1948). Peregrine edition. Harmondsworth: Penguin Books, 1962.

Newton, Adam Zachary. *Narrative Ethics.* Cambridge, MA: Harvard University Press, 1995.

contributors

DAPHNA ERDINAST-VULCAN is professor of English language and literature at the University of Haifa, Israel. She is the author of *Joseph Conrad and the Modern Temper* (1991), and *The Strange Short Fiction of Joseph Conrad* (1999). She is currently working on a study of Bakhtin and the question of the subject.

GAIL FINCHAM, head of the English Department at the University of Cape Town, has edited, coedited, and contributed to three collections of essays on Conrad: *Under Postcolonial Eyes: Joseph Conrad After Empire* (1996); *Conrad at the Millennium: Modernism, Postmodernism, Postcolonialism* (2001); and *Conrad in Africa* (2002). She has published in South African and international journals, and is one of the editors and contributors to *Literary Landscapes from Modernism to Postcolonialism*.

JEREMY HAWTHORN is professor of modern British literature at the Norwegian University of Science and Technology, Trondheim. His book *Sexuality and the Erotic in the Fiction of Joseph Conrad*–his third monograph on the author–was published in 2007. He has edited Joseph Conrad's *Under Western Eyes* and *The Shadow-Line* for Oxford World's Classics (both 2003), and the fifth edition of his textbook *Studying the Novel* appeared in 2005.

JAKOB LOTHE is professor of English literature at the University of Oslo. His books include *Conrad's Narrative Method* (1989) and *Narrative in Fiction and Film* (2000). He has edited or coedited several volumes, including *Conrad in Scandinavia, European and Nordic Modernisms* and *The Art of Brevity*. In 2005–2006 he was the leader of the research project "Narrative Theory and Analysis" at the Centre for Advanced Study, Oslo.

J. HILLIS MILLER taught for many years at the Johns Hopkins University and then at Yale University before going to the University of California at Irvine in 1986, where is he now UCI Distinguished Research Professor. He is the author of many books and essays on nineteenth- and twentieth-century English, European, and American literature, and on literary theory. Among his most recent books are *Others, Speech Acts in Literature, On Literature, Zero Plus One,* and *Literature as Conduct: Speech Acts in Henry James.* A *J. Hillis Miller Reader* appeared in 2005 from Edinburgh University Press and Stanford University Press. He is at work on books about communities in literature and about Jacques Derrida's late work.

ZDZISŁAW NAJDER, professor of the Humanities, Tischner European University, Cracow, Poland, is a historian of literature and philosopher who is also a noted civic activist and political commentator. Educated at Warsaw and Oxford, he has taught at several American and Polish universities. His books include *Conrad's Polish Background* (1964), *Values and Evaluations* (1975), *Joseph Conrad: A Chronicle* (1983 and 2007), and *Conrad in Perspective* (1997).

JOSIANE PACCAUD-HUGUET is professor of modern British literature and literary theory at the University of Lyon 2 (France). She has just published two volumes of collected essays (*Joseph Conrad. L'écrivain et l'étrangeté de la langue*, 2006; *Conrad in France*, 2007) and is completing a book on the Modernist moment of vision revisited from a Lacanian perspective, with chapters on Conrad, Woolf, Mansfield, and Joyce.

JAMES PHELAN is Humanities Distinguished Professor of English at The Ohio State University. He is the editor of *Narrative;* the coeditor of The Ohio State University Press's series on the Theory and Interpretation of Narrative; and the author, editor, or coeditor of numerous books of narrative theory, the most recent of which are *Living to Tell about It* (winner of the Perkins Prize for the best book in Narrative Studies in 2005) and *Experiencing Fiction*, also published by The Ohio State University Press (2007).

CHRISTOPHE ROBIN teaches at the University of Lille 3 in France. His main area of study is modernism in English literature. He has published numerous articles on Joseph Conrad as well as D. H. Lawrence. He also works on Virginia Woolf.

ALLAN H. SIMMONS is reader in English literature at St. Mary's University College, Strawberry Hill. He is the general editor of *The Conradian*, the journal of the Joseph Conrad Society (UK), and an executive editor of *Conrad Studies*. His recent publications include *Joseph Conrad* (2006), *Conrad's "Heart of Darkness"* (2007), and an edition of *Lord Jim* for Penguin (2007).

J. H. STAPE, research fellow at St Mary's College at Strawberry Hill, Twickenham, has taught in universities in Canada, France, and the Far East, and has published extensively on Conrad's life and work. The editor of *The Cambridge Companion to Joseph Conrad* (1996), he has also edited Conrad's *A Personal Record* and *Notes on Life and Letters* and coedited volumes 7 and 9 of *The Collected Letters of Joseph Conrad*. General editor of seven Conrad volumes in Penguin Classics, he serves as contributing editor to *The Conradian*, the journal of the Joseph Conrad Society (UK).

index

Theory and Interpretation of Narrative

James Phelan and Peter J. Rabinowitz, Series Editors

Because the series editors believe that the most significant work in narrative studies today contributes both to our knowledge of specific narratives and to our understanding of narrative in general, studies in the series typically offer interpretations of individual narratives and address significant theoretical issues underlying those interpretations. The series does not privilege one critical perspective but is open to work from any strong theoretical position.